Truth versus Precision in Economics

ADVANCES IN ECONOMIC METHODOLOGY

General Editor: Warren J. Samuels
Michigan State University, US

This major new series presents original and innovative work in economic methodology, including all aspects of the philosophy, sociology and rhetoric of economics as well as the relationship of economics to other disciplines.

The series reflects the renewed interest in all aspects of economic methodology as well as the deepening sense both of conceptual and technical crisis plaguing the economics profession and that the crisis involves deep methodological considerations. It is also hoped that the series will contribute to the better understanding and solution of the economic problems of both mature and developing countries.

The series is open to all points of view and approaches.

Truth versus Precision in Economics

Thomas Mayer

Professor of Economics
University of California, Davis, US

Edward Elgar

Published by
Edward Elgar Publishing Limited
Gower House
Croft Road
Aldershot
Hants GU11 3HR
England

Edward Elgar Publishing Company
Old Post Road
Brookfield
Vermont 05036
USA

Reprinted 1994

A CIP catalogue record for this book is available from the British Library

Library of Congress Cataloguing-in-Publication Data
Mayer, Thomas, 1927–
    Truth versus precision in economics/Thomas Mayer.
      p. cm.
    Includes bibliographical references.
    1. Economics—Methodology. I. Title.
    HB131.M39   1992
    330—dc20   92–25821
                                                      CIP

ISBN 1 85278 546 2 (cased)
     1 85278 552 7 (paperback)

Printed in Great Britain by Ipswich Book Co. Ltd., Ipswich,
Suffolk

To Milton Friedman who has had an even
greater effect on the methodology of
economics than on its substance

Contents

Preface   ix

1. Introduction   1

2. Economists as Economic Agents: Towards a
    Positive Theory of Methodology   10

3. Two Types of Mainstream Economics   23

4. Honour them Both   41

5. Truth versus Precision   56

6. Other Types of Damage   68

7. New Classical Theory – General Characteristics   80

8. New Classical Theory – Specific Hypotheses   103

9. Model or Die   122

10. Empirical Testing: Driving a Mercedes down a
    Cow-track   132

11. Good Dentists or Bad Physicists?   152

References   165

Index   185

Preface

Economists do not lack for questions that need addressing. Some prefer one type of question, some another. Some want to work out precise solutions to problems that have been specifically set up to be tractable. Others want to explain, if necessary in a less rigorous manner, what we actually observe in the economy. The shining ideal is, of course, a rigorous analysis of the actual world. But that is often beyond us. So we have to compromise by choosing more of one, and less of the other. We would be the poorer if all economists chose the same point on the budget line.

It is hardly surprising that everyone thinks that his or her choice is the appropriate one, and superior to the choices of others. Such a tension might even be useful, if everyone realized that good work can be done at various levels of abstraction, and that a ranking of research by its degree of abstraction does not map into a ranking by merit. But such tolerance does not reign in economics. Rigour and precision, if needs be at the cost of having less to say about observable behaviour, have become the shining goals, if not to most economists, then at least to those who set the profession's tone.

It would be bizarre to deny that rigour, precision and elegance have great value, but they are not the only values that scientists should respect. They do not play a dominating role in the empirical sciences, and should not lay claim to that role in economics. I therefore distinguish between two types of economic theory. One is formal theory whose models are mathematics and logic. The other is empirical science theory that takes the empirical sciences as its models.

This book is a defence of empirical science economics against the intrusion of the criteria appropriate to formal economics. But it is not a criticism of formalist economics per se. It is merely the notion of an intellectual hierarchy with formal theory on top, and empirical science economics as its poor relation that I want to combat. This notion has done much damage by distracting the attention of economists away from those parts of a problem that cannot be treated rigorously. This would not matter so much if economists were aware of what they are doing as they brush aside part of the problem. But often they are not. As a result, they frequently act as though the strength of their whole argument is equal to the strength of its strongest link.

Many people have helped me to write this book. One group consists of those whose writings I am citing for support at various points even though many of them would surely disagree with other points I am making. Another group comprises various colleagues whose methodological statements set me thinking, often in the opposite direction. Since I do not remember them all, I cannot thank them all, but I do want to express my gratitude to Don McCloskey whose remark that economists have adopted the criteria of mathematicians was an eye-opener, and whose writings on rhetoric have made me much more aware of what I am doing. I am deeply indebted to those who have read the whole or parts of the manuscript and provided many helpful comments: Roger Backhouse, Mark Blaug, Thomas Cargill, David Colander, Daniel Hammond, James Hartley, Abraham Hirsch, Kevin Hoover, Arjo Klamer, William Milberg, Julie Nelson, Boris Pesek and Nancy Wulwick. I am also indebted to Erick Eschker for excellent research assistance and to Mary Jung for first-rate secretarial work. Elizabeth Teague provided deft copy-editing and Julie Leppard and Edward Elgar were most helpful. Their efforts are much appreciated.

Davis, California

1. Introduction

Economics in the United States is thriving. Enrolments in economics courses are high, and so are the salaries of economists relative to those of other scientists, physical as well as social. Newspapers report from time to time the views of noted economists, and economists can now attain Nobel prizes, alongside physicists and poets. A philosopher, Alexander Rosenberg, reports that his fellow philosophers hold economics in almost as great esteem as they do physics (Rosenberg in Caldwell, 1987, p. 233), though Kevin Hoover (1991b), an economist who hobnobs with philosophers, has not found this to be the case.

Not only does the market signal its approval, but this approval seems justified by the increasingly scientific nature of economics. No longer can economists be looked down on as would-be scientists, who cannot even speak what is widely regarded as the language of science, mathematics. Mathematical economists can now converse in that tongue as fluently as physicists. Powerful theorems are being discovered all the time. The extensive listing of newly completed working papers in the *Quarterly Report* of the National Bureau of Economic Research gives the impression of rapid advances. Economics no longer requires the unique insights of great thinkers to make any progress but can proceed step-by-step as a normal science, just like the natural sciences do.[1]

Such an optimistic view deserves to be taken seriously. But there is also a darker side. Granted that our understanding of the economy is improving every decade, is it improving at a much faster rate than it did in previous decades? Perhaps it is. But, even if so, is the rate of improvement commensurate with the vast increase in resources that have enriched economics in recent decades? It seems likely that we now devote more hours to academic economic research each year than we did over the whole century 1776–1876, and we possess vastly superior computational technology and data. Has our knowledge increased commensurably? Surely not. Moreover, although a vast number of working papers present impressive results, these results are often

1

conflicting. While basic disagreement among economists on strictly economic issues is less common than is widely believed, still there is much more disagreement than is the case in the natural sciences.[2]

Recently Arnold Harberger (1992, p. 1) spoke of 'the general malaise a number of us feel concerning the direction in which the profession is going. The malaise ... [arises] from a sense that the scientific material being produced is not doing the job that economics was traditionally assumed to do.'

It is not surprising, and should not be a matter of concern, that some economists do not like the direction economics is taking; every field has its stragglers. But when within three years the presidential addresses before the Econometric Society (Hahn, 1970), the American Economic Association (Leontief, 1971) and the Royal Economic Society (Phelps-Brown, 1972) all seriously criticized the way economics is going, can one say that all is well, particularly when the tendencies they complained about have become more pronounced since then? Wassily Leontief (1971, pp. 1–3) wrote:

> Uncritical enthusiasm for mathematical formulation tends often to conceal the ephemeral substantive content of the argument behind the formidable front of algebraic signs. ... In the presentation of a new model, attention nowadays is usually centered on a step-by-step derivation of its formal properties. ... By the time it comes to interpretation of the substantive *conclusions*, the assumptions on which the model has been based are easily forgotten. ... Continued preoccupation with the imagery, hypothetical, rather than with observable reality has gradually led to a distortion of the informal valuation scale used in our academic community to assess and to rank the scientific performance of its members.

The Econometric Society was told by its president, Frank Hahn (1970, p. 1):

> The achievements of economic theory in the last two decades are both impressive and in many ways beautiful. But it cannot be denied that there is something scandalous in the spectacle of so many people refining the analyses of economic states which they give no reason to suppose will ever, or have ever, come about.

Similarly, Sir E. H. Phelps-Brown (1972) in his presidential address to the Royal Economic Society castigated economists for emphasizing abstract models at the expense of realistic observation.

One might be tempted to dismiss such criticisms with the uncharitable comment that by the time someone attains the presidency of any of these organizations he or she is no longer able to appreciate the new and exciting work that the younger members of the profession are doing. But that argument is easily rejected by looking at the opinions of the young. When Arjo Klamer and David Colander (1990) interviewed graduate students in six top-ranking American economics departments (Chicago, Columbia, Harvard, MIT, Stanford and Yale) they found much dissatisfaction with economics, though some of that may be due to a self-selection bias in their sample (Siegfried, 1991). Klamer, in his interpretation of student responses speaks of 'an identity crisis – a conflict between ... [the students'] idea of what an economist is, and the identity that their graduate training imposes ... they are most uncomfortable about the career direction in which they are being pushed' (pp. 170, 179). He reports that among MIT students none 'seemed to care for the highly technical papers – and these are top-notch students at the point of joining the elite at the frontier of economic research' (p. 171). He was 'quite affected by the undertone of ambivalence and cynicism' of students at Harvard, MIT and Columbia, though not at Chicago (p. 175). Moreover, he argues, such a loss of faith is not confined to graduate students:

> Many members of the profession appear to lack faith in what they do. They will confess, usually at unguarded moments, that their highly sophisticated research produces ultimately meaningless results. ... 'Of course this assumption is absurd,' a well-known economist noted during a recent seminar, 'but hey, isn't all we do absurd and utterly unrealistic?' People laughed and he continued to solve the model. ... How long can irony and cynicism sustain the economics profession? (pp. 184–5)

Similarly, Klamer and McCloskey (1988, p. 8, italics in original) tell us that: 'An economist asked why he goes on writing such dubious stuff will say with lame cynicism, "I don't really *believe* it: I just do it for fun." ... Party loyalty provides a career. The young upwardly mobile economist always votes at his party's call. And never thinks of thinking for himself at all.'

Certainly not all economists feel that way. Most of the abstract theorists seem happy with the way economics is going. But many, perhaps the majority of economists, are not. Some continue playing the game because they believe that it is the only game in town, that there is no other way of doing research. Others play it cynically because

following certain procedures, such as 'sticking in the maths', is necessary to publish in good journals, and thus to earn tenure. Probably
quite a number of the already tenured have responded by, more or less,
giving up on research. Certainly not to all, perhaps not even to most,
but to many economists, the rules and conventions that currently determine what is considered good research have become a hollow ideology. Recent events suggest that a hollow ideology is not likely to
endure.

WHY BOTHER WITH METHODOLOGY?

Such a situation, when some economists feel exhilarated by what they
see as rapid progress, and others feel alienated and cynical, provides
an opening for what is often considered an anti-social act, the publication of yet another book on the methodology of economics. But rather
than mounting a full-scale justification of methodology, I will just
defend my particular incursion into methodology.[3]

At an American Economic Association meeting I overheard someone
castigate a methodologist in approximately the following words: 'Who
does he think he is, telling us how we should do research?' Such an
attitude is not surprising; it does take some arrogance to tell others
what they should think. But aren't we economists all in the business of
doing just that? When we publish a paper in a professional journal we
hope to change our colleagues' minds. So why single out
methodologists? I suspect that there are two reasons for this. One is a
denial that methodologists know something others do not. Here the
proof of the pudding is in the eating. The second reason is that
methodologists are, often with justice, looked upon like the château
generals of World War I; they sit back and send others to do the dirty
and dangerous work. To this argument I have a simple answer. I have
spent most of my professional life in the trenches of substantive research, and intend to return to them.

A more subtle objection to methodological discussion is that it is
unnecessary. Those doing substantive research are driven, as if by an
invisible hand, to do their work as well as it can be done.[4] But the invisible hand works its wonders only when there is a market in which
producers must sell their wares. If the standards that govern production are set, not by the consumers, but by the producers themselves,
the invisible hand is moribund. More specifically, as I will argue in the

next chapter, the self-interest of economists biases their methodological choices. Besides, if those who do the substantive work really know best, how is it that many economists disagree about methodology?

Another complaint about methodologists is that they are often authoritarians, laying down the law as if from on high, telling economists that they should cease doing this or that. But what I am trying to do is free economists from having to meet unrealistic criteria imposed on them by authoritarian colleagues.

Still another reason why many working economists have little use for books on methodology is that so many of these books consist of institutionalist and post-Keynesian attacks on classical theory couched in the language of Virtue Militant. Having been defeated on the battlefield of substantive research, they have retreated to the barren hills of methodology, from where they carry out guerrilla attacks on mainstream economics. This book is different. There are no laudatory references to Kenneth Galbraith, Thorstein Veblen, Joan Robinson or other heroes of the heterodox. I like neo-classical theory. To me the exemplar of good methodological practice is Milton Friedman.[5] The reason I criticize mainly formalists rather than institutionalists is that the former are in power, and hence able to do more damage.

Those books on methodology that are not institutionalist or post-Keynesian tracts are mostly applications of philosophy of science to economics. They classify economic theories into their proper philosophical pigeonholes, or apply to economics the ideas of some favoured philosopher of science. Such books can certainly be useful, but most economists consider them irrelevant to their everyday work.

This book, by contrast, contains almost no discussion of philosophy of science, and can therefore be read by someone who thinks the problem of induction has something to do with electric motors. This is not because I hold philosophy of science in low esteem. On the contrary, if I had my way every economics student would take a course in it. But my message is a simple one that does not relate to the subtle and complex issues that philosophers of science discuss. Hence, I do not wear the livery of any particular philosopher of science. What I am preaching against is the so common pretence at precision that glides over the weak parts of the argument, and such pretence is not justified by any philosophy of science. Thus, although this book makes occasional references to philosophical concepts, it can be read easily by those totally unfamiliar with philosophy. Except for the next paragraph, my few references in the text (though not in the notes) to philosophy of science are explained either in the text itself or in the notes. Rather than being philosophical this book is an exercise in what Hausman (1988, p. 105) has called, 'the unphilosophical but possibly valuable empirical task of investigating what techniques of economic knowledge acquisition might be efficacious.'

But for those who have some familiarity with more formal methodology here is a brief description of my underlying position. It is eclectic. From Popper I take the idea that theories in the empirical sciences should be falsifiable and should be ruthlessly tested. From Kuhn and McCloskey I have learned that one should look at what scientists actually do, though as discussed in the next chapter, I do not believe that the invisible hand always impels economists to do what is best. As mentioned in the preface, a remark of McCloskey has had much influence on me, and I hope that this book will be useful to those working on the rhetoric of economics. In one important respect my methodology is close to the pluralism and critical rationalism advocated by Bruce Caldwell (1988, 1991a), that tries to evaluate various research programmes in terms of their own goals. However, I am more judgemental than Caldwell since I insist on balance.

Those who wish to see the case against excessive formalism developed along deeper philosophical lines should read Henry Woo's (1986) *What's Wrong with Formalization in Economics?* I do not attempt to compete with Woo's scholarly philosophical discussion, but to complement it by conveying much the same message at a lower level of abstraction, and by giving numerous examples of how excessive formalism has led to questionable conclusions.[6] I stress examples because practice is the ultimate judge of methodology. Any methodology that does not lead to bad practices is not a bad methodology. My examples generally come from macroeconomics. This is not because I think that microeconomics is not worth bothering about, or that it is immune from the problems I discuss. It just reflects my own background in macroeconomics. Neva Goodwin (1991) provides examples from microeconomics. My examples come primarily in the later chapters. Indeed Chapters 7 and 8 treat new classical theory as an example of misapplied formalism.

WHAT IS TO COME

This book argues that we should draw a much sharper distinction than is usually done between two types of economic theory. One, formalist theory, is abstract theory that is concerned with high-level generalizations, and looks towards axiomization. The other, empirical science theory, focuses on explaining past observations and predicting future ones. While both are perfectly legitimate, applying the criteria appropriate to one to evaluate the other generates confusion and misunderstanding.[7] Such a confusion is common because the great prestige of formalist theory has allowed it to invade the territory that rightfully belongs to empirical science theory, and to impose on it unrealistic criteria of rigour and precision. In trying to meet these unrealistic criteria empirical science economists have been tempted either to dress up formalist theory as empirical science theory, or to focus attention on the strongest link in the chain of their argument, and to pretend that their whole argument is rigorous because this one link is. This I will refer to as 'the principle of the strongest link'. Stage magicians often produce their effects by distracting the audience's attention from what they are doing unobtrusively with one hand, by flamboyant activity with their other hand. Economists do the same. Not consciously, of course, but then it is not intentions, but 'as if' that matters.

Essentially, this book is a plea for a more modest economics, an economics that recognizes the inherent difficulty of making precise and indubitable statements about the actual world, and accepts that there is a trade-off between rigour and relevance. I certainly agree that one should be as rigorous as one can be; I just oppose trying to be as rigorous as one can *not* be. The book is also a plea for maintaining an appropriate role for empirical science economics. Not being an institutionalist, I do not disparage the great contribution that formalist theory makes. But formalist theory has been used where it should not have been. As a result, economists often draw policy conclusions from models that, for reasons of tractability, deal only with a part of the problem. That failing has a long tradition in economics. Schumpeter (1954, p. 473) called it the 'Ricardian Vice'. It is this Ricardian Vice, and not the use of abstract theory per se, that is my target.

The next chapter is a digression intended to dispose of the argument tnat, in methodology as elsewhere, the market knows best, so that methodology does not need discussing. Readers who do not accept that argument may want to skip Chapter 2, and go directly to Chapter

3, which describes the difference between formalist and empirical science economics. Chapter 4 argues that both types of economics are valuable. Chapters 5 and 6 discuss the damage done by confusing the two types and by evaluating either type by the criteria applicable only to the other type. Chapters 7 and 8 then take up in detail a single example, new classical theory. Chapter 9 is a short chapter on modelling, that questions the widespread notion that there can be no useful economic analysis without a formal model. Much of the justification for modelling is that models are validated by econometric testing. But Chapter 10 shows that our econometric tests are often not stringent enough to evaluate models reliably. The final chapter offers some suggestions for changing the pattern of research, publication procedures and graduate training. Although all of these chapters are components of a particular argument, any one of them can be read on its own. Thus, someone interested in new classical theory might only read Chapters 7 and 8, and someone interested in econometrics just Chapter 10, while those who simply want the gist of the book could read only Chapters 3–6.

NOTES

1. I see no purpose in discussing whether economics actually is a science. Philosophers have not succeeded in finding a criterion that distinguishes science from non-science (see Rosenberg, 1983), and the question whether a field is an empirical science may even lack clear meaning (see Putnam, 1990). Fortunately, nothing hinges on whether one calls economics a science or not, and the question can be left to lexicographers. Knowing whether economics is a science would not allow us to decide whether it should use the same methods as the natural sciences, since not all sciences necessarily use the same methods. What methods economics should use can be decided better by looking at specific methods and specific problems than by talking in general about 'scientific method'. Similarly, knowing whether economics is a science would not allow us to say whether it provides answers that deserve a high degree of credence. The science of weather forecasting does not, while the non-science of history does.

2. More precisely, the volume of disputation may not be greater in economics, but while just about all physical scientists agree about many propositions that are not obvious to a lay person, the volume of such undisputed propositions is less in economics. Much of the disagreement among economists is due to economists having a tradition of commenting on all economic issues that are important, even when they lack the tools to resolve them convincingly. Given the low quality of competing commentators that is by no means bad. Now that natural scientists feel impelled to answer pressing ecological questions that their sciences cannot answer convincingly, we also see much disagreement among them. Another important, but also much neglected reason for the divergence among economists' recom-

mendations is disagreement about the efficiency of the government, a topic at least partly outside economics.

3. For a more extended review of the objections to discussing methodology, and an excellent refutation, see Caldwell (1988) and Backhouse (1991).

4. Donald McCloskey (1992), himself a distinguished methodologist, suggests that if methodologists really knew better than other economists how to conduct substantive research, they would turn out better research. But that makes no allowance for the division of labour. Medicine is grounded in physiology, but physiologists are not better diagnosticians than are physicians.

5. For an excellent discussion of Friedman's methodology that brings out his empiricist emphasis see Hirsch and de Marchi (1990).

6. My use of examples should not be rejected as an application of verificationism since I am not trying to establish any general law with them. I am, of course, open to the criticism that my sample is too small and biased. My examples can convince only to the extent that they resonate in the reader's own experience in reading economics.

7. It is not only in economics that failure to appreciate differences in goals generates misunderstanding. Those who, like myself, listen to music for enjoyment tend to disparage composers like Schönberg whose music is not enjoyable. But Schönberg did not intend to offer enjoyment. He believed that 'music should not decorate. It should be true.' (Cited in Beller, 1989, p. 121.) A similar belief applies to much of modern art.

2. Economists as Economic Agents: Towards a Positive Theory of Methodology

It is a strange fact that social scientists ... are exceedingly naive when it comes to examining the social origins of their own theories and models. ... [R]arely do we examine the social determination of our own thought (Paul Streeten, 1972, p. 60).

The man who takes historic fact seriously must suspect that science does not tend towards the ideal that our image of its cumulativeness has suggested. Perhaps it is altogether another sort of enterprise (Thomas Kuhn, 1970, p. 96).

If I am going to claim that there is something seriously amiss in the way economics is done I have to explain why this occurs, why here the market does not work effectively. I am not asserting that too many resources are devoted to refining pure theory, and too few to solving practical problems. Both activities are worth pursuing, and it is hard to determine their optimal mix. Rather, the market is inefficient in the sense that, given the same output of pure theory, we could achieve a better output of applied work. We are not at the production frontier.

The reason for this market failure is that the market is dominated by the producers, predominantly academic economists, so that the usual market discipline does not exist. Unlike academic researchers in fields such as medicine or law who work for a large market of practitioners, academic economists, by and large, write for each other. Hence their tastes, not the consumers', determine what is produced. Such producer sovereignty is not confined to academic research. It is a well known problem in the organization of medical services. It may also play an important role in the arts, where consumers, afraid of being labelled philistines, defer to the tastes of producers (see Thomas Wolfe, 1981). Robert O'Connell (1989) has argued that military history provides many examples of a dysfunctional emphasis on the Homeric ideal of the combat of heroes.

10

In such a situation public choice theory may be more applicable than the theory of competitive markets.[1] As Charles Wolf (1979, pp. 121–2) points out, when there are no competing producers, 'non-market agencies often develop "internalities" that bear no very clear or reliable connection with the ostensible public purpose which the agencies were intended to serve.' One of the resulting distortions that Wolf (p. 124) cites is an overemphasis on sophisticated high-tech methods: 'Non-market agencies, ... may establish advanced technology or technical "quality" as an agency goal. In medicine, a bias towards "Cadillac" health care may result, and in the military a sometimes compulsive tendency towards development and procurement of the "next generation" of sophisticated equipment.'

LETTING PUBLIC CHOICE THEORY BITE THE HAND THAT FEEDS IT

The market for academic research in economics has much in common with the market for government services. Like the latter it deals in a public good, and the producers (universities) claim to work for the public welfare. Moreover, they cannot appropriate profits as efficiently as can those in the for-profit sector. In addition, as is true for many government services, the beneficiaries are not identical to those who pay for the service, and hence lack sufficient incentives to monitor the efficiency of the producers. Even if they did have sufficient incentives, they would still lack the requisite technical knowledge. One of the basic insights of public choice theory, that the producers of government services possess considerable leeway in deciding what type and how many services to provide, surely applies also to the providers of academic research.

Although the ultimate consumers of much academic research, the public, therefore do not play a great role in the market for academic research in economics (henceforth simply called 'research'), the individual researcher is not free to do as he or she pleases. To be successful he or she must meet the standards set by the editors and the other members of the 'invisible college' that referee papers and grant proposals and decide what papers to cite. What incentives, apart from encouraging the dispassionate search for the truth, do the members of the invisible college have?

Editors are concerned with both the prestige and the circulation of their journals. The prestige of a journal depends in large part on its evaluation by researchers, so that in this respect it is the preferences of researchers that drive the decisions of editors. But editors may also pay attention to their own tastes. These m*a*y differ from those of the majority of researchers, both because editors tend to be the more distinguished members of the profession, and because they are usually older than the average researcher. Moreover, since they are concerned with the circulation of their journals, it is possible that they take some account of the preferences of those readers who are not active researchers. An extremely technical and esoteric journal may have high prestige, but may not survive. Concern about the size of the market, and hence publishability, may be an even larger factor for editors of books. But all in all, it seems plausible that editors more or less share the methodological predilections of researchers.

Beyond their obvious roles as producers of research and as referees of papers and grant proposals, researchers play three other roles in the market for academic research. One is to act as consumers of research by using and citing papers, thus enhancing a researcher's reputation and salary. Second, researchers subscribe to journals, and very occasionally might even buy a book. Third, each individual researcher is to some extent his or her own market. Few economists write papers that they themselves think are trivial or wrong. Surely, one motive for doing research is interest in the problem, and the satisfaction that results from solving it.

The market for economic research is therefore self-referential; we write papers to please ourselves and each other. This would be consistent with maximizing the public's welfare if we evaluated papers entirely objectively by their social utility, without being biased by our self-interest. But the assumption that producers disregard their self-interest is one that we would be loath to make about others.

The existence of biases due to self-interest does not mean that economics is somehow inferior to the 'real' sciences. They have the same problem. Thus David Bloor (1981 p. 203), a leading sociologist of science, writes:

[T]he literature that deals with professional vested interest in science ... describes the concern shown by scientists in expanding the areas to which their competences apply. Much that goes on in science can be plausibly seen as a result of the desire to maintain or increase the importance, status and scope of the methods and techniques which are the special property of a group.

But let us constrain our professional cynicism. To show that certain biases infest research does not amount to showing that they dominate and leave little room for objective analysis. Those who evaluate research are, of course, likely to prefer research that makes their own work look valuable. Yet I doubt that many referees would accept a paper they consider seriously flawed, merely because it cites one of their own papers. Hence, the biases discussed below suggest that there is some divergence from optimality, but not that economic research is largely self-serving. If forced to choose between the two polar hypotheses: (a) academic research in economics is entirely objective, or (b) it is totally self-serving, I would choose the former. But it is not necessary to choose between the two; a middle ground exists.

What evidence is there that economic research is not largely self-serving? Not much. But one fairly strong piece of evidence is the relatively fast rise of mathematical economics in the postwar period. In 1938, when Paul Samuelson was just a promising graduate student, most economists knew almost no maths; to be a mathematical economist required no more than a year of calculus and perhaps a course in differential equations. Most economists, including senior members of the profession and many editors of leading journals, had an incentive to protect their human capital by keeping it that way. They could have done so for some time by rejecting mathematical papers, and by re-serving the more desirable academic jobs for 'literary economists'.[2] But they did not. They accepted the great contribution that mathematics can make to economics. This shows a willingness of leaders of the profession to subjugate their self-interest to the search for truth, and makes me proud to be an economist.

All the same, self-serving biases may well play more than a trivial role in determining the standards that the profession adheres to. The utility function an economist brings to bear in evaluating a piece of research contains two arguments: the validity of the research when considered objectively; and the extent to which, in ways discussed below, it makes him feel good about his own status as a scientist.

The latter may play a much larger role than is apparent at first glance, even if 'objective validity' dominates self-interest in the economist's utility function, because the objective validity of a paper is often far from obvious. Hence, we form our ideas about what is valid in part by what we read. But what we read depends on what referees approve of. Hence, if referees are at all swayed by self-interest, this has an indirect effect, as well as a direct effect. One can easily model a situation in which the effect of what one reads on what one considers good work is so strong that even a slight initial bias in what reaches print results in a cumulative move of the literature away from what is valid to a corner solution where validity is zero. But I do not think that such a model is plausible because I believe that the function relating what we believe to what we read is convex, that at some point, well short of the corner solution, good sense asserts itself to constrain even appealing nonsense. All the same, indirectly even a small bias could distort research substantially.

Whether the resulting distortions are large or small is an empirical issue that can only be settled by looking for specific instances where the profession has been misled by its self-interest. Much of this book is an exhibition of the trophies from such a hunt for distortions. But first, let us look at the biases that are likely to distort research.

SOME OF OUR BIASES

Academic economists, like other professionals, derive feelings of self-worth from attributing a high value to their profession, and hence they have an incentive to exaggerate the intellectual stature of economics. A leading historian of science, Derek de Solla Price (1986 p. 98) wrote: 'Many of the personality traits found ... seem to be consistent with the hypothesis that many scientists turned to their profession for an emotional gratification that was otherwise lacking.'

Economists are primarily recruited from among those who have a high opinion of economics to start with. And graduate and professional training socializes economists, like other professionals, into accepting the value system of their profession. Few would want to think that they have undergone their initiation rites for nothing! Hence, one would expect economists to attribute a higher worth to economics than is justified. The benefits that they thus obtain from holding an exaggerated view of economics are matched, at the margin, by the resulting costs: the discomfort they feel if observable facts clash with their views, the danger of appearing mistaken, or even ridiculous to others, and the failures in research that can result when one overvalues some theory or technique. But, all in all, it seems plausible that the marginal benefit and the marginal cost of exaggerating the efficacy of economics intersect at a positive level of exaggeration.

If economists want to enhance their own and other people's good opinion of economics, what should they do? The most important step is to protect the status of economics, and thus their intellectual capital, by showing that professional economists know something that others don't. Surely, one of the most annoying aspects of being an economist is having to put up with the chatter of those who lack both training in, and any intuitive grasp of economics, but feel called upon to set you right on various economic issues. Moreover, it is hardly pleasant for economists to see their well established theories brushed aside in public debates and in the media.

Beyond claiming superior knowledge for themselves economists also need to claim objectivity.[3] They need to demonstrate that economic analysis is not just a public relations tool used by various pressure groups, or that it is just a cloak to hide the intellectual nakedness of mere ideological preference.

METHODOLOGY IN THE SERVICE OF PRESTIGE

The best way for economists to lay title to the possession of specialized and objective knowledge is to assert scientific status for economics.[4] As Philip Mirowski (1989, pp. 356–7), a scathing critic of what he calls 'physics-mongering', has pointed out, 'Economic research has always met with the greatest difficulties in establishing the credibility of its results and in fending off charges of charlatanism and quackery. Consequently to usurp the legitimacy of science has always weighed down economic research. ...'

Not only is science the paradigm of specialized and objective knowledge, but scientists are also accorded high status because of the material achievements that science has fostered. But not all sciences. The social sciences, particularly sociology, have low status. Hence, while economists can hardly deny that economics is a social science, they have a strong incentive to differentiate economics from other social sciences, and to claim a kinship to the hard sciences, in spirit, in mental toughness, in techniques, and even in achievement.[5] Generally conceded to be the most advanced of the social sciences, economics would love to drop the bar sinister of a social science and take its rightful place as a member of the true scientific aristocracy. Most economists, though certainly not all (see Solow, 1985, pp. 328–9), would be pleased if a leading sociologist were to state that economics and sociology differ sharply, and would surely be thrilled if a leading physicist were to declare that economics is very much like physics. It need not be a coincidence that one of our journals, *Economics Letters*, has a name and mission similar to those of a leading physics journal.

If for these reasons economists want to appear like physicists what should they do? The ideal solution, turning out work that rivals physics in quality, is limited by familiar constraints, but another possibility is to use one or more of the tools that physicists use. One basic tool of physics, laboratory experiments, is employed to some extent in economics (see Smith, 1989), but obviously much less than in physics. That leaves the other great tool of physics, mathematics. Using mathematics is not the same as doing science. Indeed, a philosopher of science, Alexander Rosenberg (1983), argues that economics is not a science because, 'like geometry, economics is best viewed as a branch of mathematics' (p. 311).[6] All the same, since the general public tends to confuse science and mathematics, economists have an incentive to demonstrate the mathematization of economics. As Mirowski (1989, p. 393) notes:

> Neoclassical economics has successfully arrogated the aura and trapping of science, if only because a greater part of the populace excluded by the rigors of mathematics in science are convinced by the superficial resemblances, whereas many others of modest technical skills are convinced because they recognize the physics of Engineering 101 as of the same character as that found in economics.

This tendency to enhance scientific status by decorative devices is not confined to economics. Thus Michael Ghiselin (1989, p. 170), a marine biologist, writes, 'Science is supposed to be quantitative. Therefore, one bends over backward to appear more quantitative than the competition. Put numbers on everything.'

Moreover, since many people have school-day memories of mathematics as a difficult subject, they consider those who use advanced mathematics to be extraordinarily gifted. In addition, some people probably assume, quite erroneously, that it is not possible to make ideologically charged or silly statements in the form of equations. Furthermore, mathematics can readily be used to silence most non-economists who pontificate on the subject.[7] Economics is not the only field that uses mathematics as a barrier against criticism by the unwashed (see Whitley, 1977, pp. 145–6).

Using mathematics impresses not only others, but also oneself. Mathematics is one of the great achievements of mankind, and hence using it makes one feel good. Besides, there is beauty in a neat mathematical proof, and it appears eternal.

None of this implies that economists, consciously or unconsciously, use mathematics primarily to lay claim to the prestige and awe accorded to physical scientists and to mathematicians, or to make themselves feel good. And it surely does not deny that mathematical techniques have an important, and indeed a central place in economics. All it means is that, beyond the obviously great aid that mathematics offers in solving problems, its use also helps to raise the status and self-respect of economists. Hence, there is an incentive to over-use it.[8] Such an over-use probably shows up more in the papers of those who know little mathematics than in the papers of those blessed with genuine mathematical talent. The former often just repeat in mathematical symbols something they have already said in words and sometimes do not even use any mathematical operations.

The use of mathematics is not the only way economists assert similarity to the physical sciences. They also claim, rather questionably (Mayer, 1980), to adhere to the positivistic methodology of evaluating hypotheses by their predictive success, which they identify with 'scientific method'.

Another way economists strive for status and self-respect is by using complicated theory even when discussing straightforward problems that could be resolved without it. It is something that only those with training in economics can do and, besides, it seems to justify the effort made in acquiring the theoretical tools of economics. Beyond this, it distinguishes economics from the other social sciences that do not possess such a powerful theoretical core. Thus, Arnold Zellner (1987, p. 7) refers to 'many economists' "religious" belief in complexity in spite of the fact that the evidence on the performance of complex theories and models is mainly negative.'

Working with complex theories also has another advantage. While much of the criticism that economists cannot forecast exaggerates the errors in our GDP forecasts (McNees, 1990), and also ignores the fact that GDP forecasting is only a small part of economics, it is true that we have only limited success in dealing with many practical problems. But if anyone tries to attribute this to economists having second-rate minds, we can refer with pride to the imposing intellectual structure that we call economic theory. Put somewhat differently, working with abstract theory allows us to feel that we are clever, much more so than dealing with practical problems does.

Economists can also gain prestige and public approval by tackling pressing social problems. Certainly someone writing sweeping sentences on how to combat inflation or unemployment is more likely to be quoted in newspapers than someone writing on proofs of existence and uniqueness. However, within academia it is rigorous solutions to narrow problems that carry prestige. The problems for which economists can provide such rigorous solutions are usually not only narrow ones, but consist primarily of working out the formal implications of certain assumptions. It seems hardly possible to satisfy at the same time the pressure for rigorous solutions and the pressure to deal with important practical problems. But economists have worked out a way of seeming to do both. This is to take an important practical problem, and to work primarily on those aspects of it that can be formalized, and hence treated rigorously. The other aspects of the problem are then handled by arm-waving. The following chapters provide many examples of this practice.

Still another, rather obvious way to enhance our status and feelings of self-esteem is to praise the power of our standard maximizing paradigm. It has certainly proved its worth and deserves praise, but we have an incentive to praise it beyond its deserts. Few of us can fail to be thrilled by Gary Becker's demonstration that our basic paradigm can be made to explain much behaviour otherwise explicable only by sociological factors, and it is tempting to brush aside the question whether our explanations are actually better than the sociological ones. Just like journalists who, having a comparative advantage in investigating fraud, attribute the Savings and Loan débâcle primarily to fraud, economists, who have a comparative advantage in uncovering deeper and more complex causes, blame such factors as maturity mismatch and the moral hazard generated by deposit insurance and de-emphasize fraud.[9]

Economists also have an incentive to use the latest and most complex techniques. Such techniques enhance an economist's self-respect, both because it is satisfying to demonstrate one's ability, and because it provides a feeling that one has not wasted one's time in learning these techniques. Moreover, the use of sophisticated techniques impresses referees and editors, as well as readers. Such a reaction is not entirely unwarranted, but is justified by asymmetric information. Ability to use difficult techniques is correlated with intelligence, and hence suggests that a paper that uses them is of high quality. Hence researchers have an incentive to participate in an intellectual arms race. An additional motive for using complex techniques is that the researcher does not know the referee's tastes. And it seems more likely that a referee with a taste for high-tech will reject a paper because it uses only simple methods, than that a referee with low-tech tastes will reject a paper because it employs high-tech methods. Better play it safe. This exacerbates the intellectual arms race since, the higher the average technical level of published papers, the greater is the incentive for low-tech referees to learn and to value complex techniques, and the greater is also the technical level that high-tech referees believe that they should enforce.

Self-interest also induces us to de-emphasize the weaknesses of our empirical tools and data, to criticize our tools only when we have good replacements and not before. Hence we tend to ignore errors that are endemic to economics rather than specific to a particular paper. Chapter 10 provides several examples. Similarly, we have an incentive to ignore the weaknesses of our data, and more generally, to focus on those facts that are available to us, and to de-emphasize the importance of those on which we lack information (see Hayek, 1989).

Like other producers we have an incentive to disparage the tools of our competitors, such as survey methods. The issue is not whether questionnaire evidence is absolutely reliable – obviously it is not – but whether it can be a useful supplement to or check on the econometric evidence, which is also not without its problems. Economists' sneering references to evidence from questionnaires surely has something in common with the way that a president of a steel company might talk about aluminium.

Self-interest is not the only factor biasing our evaluation of economic research. An institutional factor, in combination with asymmetric information, adds to the bias. To be a first-rate economist usually requires both imagination and insight, as well as technical skill. The technical skill of a new Ph.D. is easy to judge; his or her imagination and insight are not; any insight contained in the dissertation may well be that of the thesis supervisor. Hence, those who have consummate technical skill tend to get better initial jobs than those who have consummate imagination and insight. (Cf. Goodwin, 1991, pp. 146–7) Given the strong autoregressive element in the academic job market (see Ault, Rutman and Stevenson, 1982), such differences in initial placement tend to persist. The resulting tendency for those whose comparative advantage lies in technical skills to be at the better universities then lends prestige to these technical skills, and to those topics that require such skills. Imagine, for example, that the economics department of Duke, which has a first-rate programme in the history of economic thought, were at Harvard or Yale. Economists would then treat history of economic thought as a more important subject than they do now.

CONCLUSION

I have treated the methodology of economics as a problem in public choice theory, and discussed how self-interest is likely to bias the methodological choices that economists make, particularly in the direction of over-using mathematics and formalism. But it is worth noting what this does *not* imply. First, it does not imply that economists have consciously skewed their methodological preferences in that direction: such biases can operate entirely unconsciously. Second, it does not necessarily mean that these biases are large enough to make much difference. That remains to be demonstrated in the subsequent chapters. Third, it does not necessarily imply that mathematical techniques and formalism are over-used in economics. The bias in favour of using mathematics may merely offset the bias against mathematics that results from the limited mathematical aptitude of many economists. To decide whether mathematical formalism is over-emphasized one must look at actual instances of what economists do.

Finally, even if a self-serving wish to be seen as similar to physicists has caused us to over-use mathematics and formalisms this is not *necessarily* bad. Suppose that we did not do so. Would we then adopt an unbiased, and hence appropriate methodology? Surely not. Public choice theory suggests that we would still try to distinguish our wares from those of non-economists, probably by relying on a wide knowledge of esoteric trivia, or on copious citations from obscure sources. As George Stigler (1982, p. 77) notes: 'A lesser, related scholarly value is the emphasis upon the paraphernalia of scholarship. The form of work takes on a value independent of its content: a scholar should be literate, and his work should be pursued with non-vulgar instruments.' Something like that has apparently happened in jurisprudence where there have been complaints about the excessive use of footnotes in law review articles (see Barrett, 1988). Nor are legal scholars the only ones to abuse footnoting. Price (1986, p. 69) has written about 'the practice of first writing the paper and then adding for decoration some canonical quota of a dozen references – like Greek pillars on a Washington D.C. building'.

Werner Sombart in his De*r Moderne Kapitalismus* (1916), published when wide-ranging scholarship rather than mathematical sophistication was the ornament of choice, quoted without translating passages in, if I remember correctly, eight foreign languages, including Portuguese. Presumably he thought that by acting as though he expected his readers to know all these languages he was showing his own erudition. If we economists did not signal by excessive formalism, perhaps we would signal in even more dysfunctional ways. There is conspicuous production as well as conspicuous consumption.

NOTES

1. Applying economic analysis to economists' work is not new. Thus Peter Earl (1983) argues that self-interest provides economists with a strong incentive to conform to the accepted paradigm and procedures. But he overstates the costs of unorthodoxy – producers of orthodox papers have a readier market, but also face more competitors in that market. David Colander (1991, p. 104) claims that in the economist's maximization of his own welfare the search for truth is 'relatively unimportant' because of the difficulty of determining what is true. Arthur Diamond (1988) formalizes the problem whether to devote one's time to enhancing the scope or the elegance of a theory. Susan Feigenbaum and David Levy (forthcoming) investigate the role of self-interest in exercising care in empirical work and in making one's data available. Richard Whitley (1986, p. 197) attributes the emphasis on theory to economists' self-interest.
2. This does not require a conspiracy theory of editing. Each individual editor could have strong prejudice against mathematical papers. In response, readers would drift towards those journals that have the least prejudice, since those would publish better papers. In this way journals would eventually be disciplined, but the process could take a long time.
3. D. Wade Hands (1985, p. 3) argues that a major reason why economists feel attracted by Lakatos' methodology of science is that it de-emphasizes the role of external factors in the growth of a discipline.
4. This is by no means just a matter of laying false claims for purpose of self-enhancement. If physicists find particular modes of thinking useful, it is surely worth seeing if these are also useful in economics. I am certainly not arguing that attempts to copy physics or other hard sciences are useless, but only that the self-interest of economists will induce them to go too far in this direction, and also that they will lay claim to act like hard scientists when they do not (see Mirowski, 1989).

5. Craufurd Goodwin (1988, p. 216) states that in reports to the Ford Foundation during the 1960s and 1970s economists repeatedly tried to 'identify economics with hard sciences both by describing comparable "tools" among them and by eschewing any substantial remaining links with the humanities.'
6. As Hands (1984) pointed out, Rosenberg's argument is erroneously based on an identification of economic theory with formalist economic theory.
7. Indeed A.K. Dasgupta (1968, p. 4) advocated the use of mathematics as a way of sheltering economics from intrusion by the untrained.
8. Herbert Grübel and Lawrence Boland (1986) have used public choice theory to attribute the increased mathematization of economics to mathematical economists being more effective rent seekers. One reason is that they have a greater incentive to enhance their role in universities, since they have fewer other employment opportunities. Second, they receive support from those in other fields who use mathematics. Third, once they capture commanding positions on committees, they use these to enhance their role. Fourth, there are no or few market tests to check rent seeking. Finally, mathematical ability is easier to determine than other ability. These arguments are not entirely convincing. First, mathematical economists can get jobs other than teaching if they are willing to turn their mathematical skills into econometric skills. Second, it is not clear how much help mathematicians in other departments can provide to mathematicians in economics departments. Third, the absence of a good market test does not establish that mathematical skills are overvalued. Fourth, the control that can be exercised by capturing university committees could also be used by those opposed to mathematization. However, the point that it is easier to test for mathematical skills is valid, and surely does help young mathematical economists. Grübel and Boland support their argument with a survey showing that economists think mathematical skills are overrated by editors. But that may merely reflect that editors are better judges than the average economist.
9. I am indebted for this example to James Booth.

3. Two Types of Mainstream Economics

> The path to success in theoretical biology is thus fraught with hazards. It is all too easy to make some plausible simplifying assumptions, do some elaborate mathematics that appear to give a rough fit with at least some experimental data, and think one has achieved something. The chance of such an approach doing anything useful, apart from soothing the theorist's ego, is rather small, and especially so in biology (Francis Crick, 1988, pp. 113–14).

We would all like to solve – with complete rigour and utter precision – important and relevant problems. But in most cases we must make trade-offs between the relevance of the problem and the rigour and precision of its treatment. This is well known. What is less well appreciated is that often there is also a conflict between truth and accuracy on the one hand, and precision on the other – hence the title of this book. Precision and accuracy are *not* the same thing. Andrew Kamarck (1983, p. 2) provides a nice illustration:

> On Cape Cod where the pace of life is unhurried and casual you may ask a craftsman in June when he will come to repair your fence. If he answers, 'Sometime in autumn', he is being accurate, but not precise. If he answers 'Ten a.m., October 2', he is being precise, but not accurate – it is almost certain that on October 2, the fish will be running and he will be out on his boat.

Here is another example. In the paper and pencil days before PCs I once asked a research assistant to calculate per capita GNP from the data I gave him. Being a graduate student in mathematics he believed in precision and calculated per capita GNP to the nearest cent.

We can trade off the precision of our statements against the probability that they are correct, as we do when we decide to how many places of decimals to state a result. We can also trade off both precision and the probability of being correct against the difficulty of the problem we tackle. Much confusion and ill-feeling is caused by failure to appreciate that many of our colleagues make different trade-offs than we do, and hence should not be judged by the criteria we apply to our own work.

The fields that are often loosely referred to as 'the sciences' divide their subject matter not only horizontally by fields, e.g. biology and geology, but also vertically by the level of abstraction, e.g. physics and engineering, and physiology and medicine. In doing so they make room for different criteria at each level. An engineering paper need not be as rigorous as a physics paper, and a physics paper is usually not as rigorous as a mathematics paper.[1] In the social sciences we divide fields horizontally, but not vertically, so that economics comprises mathematical formalism, empirical science work, and applications to specific practical problems. Hence we are tempted to apply inappropriate standards of rigour.

FORMALIST AND EMPIRICAL SCIENCE THEORY

The term 'theory' encompasses a broad range of statements: some theories are low-level generalizations of observations: others are highly abstract formulations. Although there is a continuum, it is useful to draw a distinction between what can be called 'formalist theory' and 'empirical science theory'. This distinction is based largely on the criteria that are used to evaluate theories. It is not a difference in logic, but a difference in rhetoric, in McCloskey's (1985) sense of the term. that separates these two types of economic theory.

In formalist theory logical rigour and elegance play a much larger role than they do in empirical science theory. In its pure state formalist theory is a set of theorems. Results are rigorously derived from assumptions whose validity is, at least for the purposes of the particular theory, simply asserted. If the assumptions are wrong, the theory itself, as an 'if ... then' statement, is still correct. Since the rules of deduction are beyond reasonable doubt, a theory that uses these rules correctly provides results that are also beyond doubt. But they are model-specific in the sense that their validity is demonstrated only for a given set of assumptions. Plane geometry is not refuted by the fact that the familiar world has more than two dimensions, though it may be dangerous to rely on plane geometry when navigating on a sphere.

Formalist economists use mathematics and logic as their exemplars. While most economists employ mathematics, formalists do not treat mathematics as just a convenient tool. Instead, they place great weight on the mathematical virtues: elegance, generality, parsimony and formal demonstration. While they are certainly not entirely indifferent to the practical importance of the problems that they deal with, the criteria by which they judge economic research are, to a large extent, those of mathematicians. As McCloskey (1991, p. 9) notes, they '*define* the economic problem as dealing with a certain kind of (easily manipulable) mathematics'. Brian Loasby (1976, p. 13) described what I am calling formalist economics as a research programme that 'seeks to emulate the mathematicians by the careful construction of watertight logical systems from a brief but comprehensive axiom set.'

Several results follow from using mathematics as a model, and not just as a tool. First, if one's exemplar of science is geometry, then all theorems have to be derived from a few axioms, and parsimony of axioms is elevated to a central concern. Second, empirical evidence plays little, if any role. A geometrician in the Greek mode does not waste time measuring the sum of the angles in many triangles to confirm that they all have 180 degrees. Third, knowledge is built up methodically by deriving the implications only of steps that have already been proven or of axioms.

In contrast to formalist economists, there are the empirical science economists, who take as their model the natural sciences; not only physics, but also the less highly developed sciences, such as geology and biology. These fields, too, use mathematics, but only as a convenient tool. They are much less concerned with mathematical virtues, and more concerned with empirical testability, and with the extent to which a theory enhances our understanding of what we actually observe. Karin Knorr-Cetina (1991, p. 114) describes how particle physicists trade off considerations of 'scientificity' for 'money, time, competitiveness, manageability and other "nonscientific" – yet necessary – goods.' Moreover, empirical scientists are not in the thrall of first principles. As Karl Brunner (in Klamer, 1984, p. 195) remarked:

> Science rarely progresses by working 'down from first principles'; it progresses and expands the other way. We begin with empirical regularities and go backward to more and more complicated hypotheses and theories. Adherence to the Cartesian principle [of insisting on the derivation of all statements from a small number of axioms] would condemn science to stagnation.

Sir Karl Popper (1961, p. 111) wrote:

Science does not rest upon rock bottom. The bold structure of its theories rises, as it were, above a swamp. It is like a building erected on piles. The piles are driven down from above into the swamp, but not down to any natural or 'given' base; and if we cease our attempt to drive the piles into a deeper layer, it is not because we have reached firm ground. We simply stop when we are satisfied that the piles are firm enough to carry the structure, at least for the time being.

Another philosopher of science, Ian Hacking (1983, pp. 263–4), reports that in particle physics:

> Various properties are confidently ascribed to electrons, but most of the confident properties are expressed in numerous different theories or models about which an experimenter can be rather agnostic. Even people in a team, who work on parts of the same large experiment, may hold different and mutually incompatible accounts of electrons. That is because different parts of the experiment will make different uses of electrons. Models good for calculations on one aspect of electrons will be poor for others. Occasionally a team actually has to select a member with a quite different theoretical perspective simply in order to get someone who can solve those experimental problems. You may choose someone with a foreign training, and whose talk is well nigh incommensurable with yours, just to get people who can produce the effects you want.

This is a mind-set far different from that of formalist economics, with its insistence on first getting the fundamentals right. The work of formalists is certainly not irrelevant to the world of empirical science economists – the latter use some propositions that the formalists prove. The difference is that empirical science economists do not consider these proofs all that vital. They are willing to proceed on the basis of what is merely 'highly plausible', rather than only on the basis of what is established beyond doubt. The next three chapters justify this procedure, and show why such an attitude is not 'unscientific'. In the meantime, here is an excerpt from George Bernard Shaw's *Caesar and Cleopatra* (1971, pp. 251–2). Cleopatra hears a slave playing the harp:

> Cleopatra [to the old musician]: I want to learn to play the harp with my own hands. Caesar loves music. Can you teach me?
> Musician: Assuredly I and no one else can teach the queen. ...
> Cleopatra: Good: you shall teach me. How long will it take?
> Musician: Not very long: only four years. Your Majesty must first become proficient in the philosophy of Phythagoras.
> Cleopatra: Has she [indicating the slave] become proficient in the philosophy of Phythagoras?

Musician: Oh, she is but a slave. She learns as a dog learns.
Cleopatra: Well then, I will learn as a dog learns; for she plays better than you.

I have drawn the distinction between formalist economists and empirical science economists very sharply. Many economists cannot be classified as definitely in one camp or the other. But the distinction does catch the essence of a central methodological division amongst mainstream economists. Thus Gerard Debreu's (1991, p. 5) presidential address to the American Economic Association put the formalist position as follows:

> In the past two decades, economic theory has been carried away further by a seemingly irresistible current that can be explained only partly by the intellectual successes of its mathematization. Essential to an attempt at a fuller explanation are the values imprinted on an economist by his study of mathematics. When a theorist who has been so typed judges his scholarly work, those values do not play a silent role: they may play a decisive role. The very choice of the questions to which he tries to find answers is influenced by his mathematical background. Thus the danger is ever present that the part of economics will become secondary, if not marginal to that judgment.

By contrast, here are statements of the empirical science position by some of its leading practitioners. Maurice Allais (1990, p. 5) in his Nobel lecture warns us:

> When neither the hypotheses nor the implications of a theory can be confronted with the real world, that theory is devoid of any scientific interest. Mere logical, even mathematical, deduction remains worthless in terms of an understanding of reality if it is not closely linked to that reality. Submission to observed or experimental data is the golden rule which dominates any scientific discipline. Any theory whatever, if it is not verified by empirical evidence, has no scientific value and should be rejected.

Phyllis Deane (1990, p. 12) writes:

> Putting the arguments into mathematical terms clarifies them only to those readers already fluent in that language. Even for those who are fluent, getting the logic of an economic theory watertight is an exercise of limited value unless it is obvious that the theory applies to the real economic system it purports to depict.

Similarly, Robert Solow (1985, pp. 328–9) points out that:

> economics is a social science. ... [S]ubject to Damon Runyon's Law that
> nothing between human beings is more than three to one, ... the interests
> of scientific economics would be better served by a more modest ap-
> proach. There is enough for us to do without pretending to a degree of
> completeness and precision which we cannot deliver. ... The true func-
> tions of analytical economics are best described informally: to organize
> our necessarily incomplete perceptions about the economy, to see connec-
> tions that the untutored eye would miss, to tell plausible – sometimes even
> convincing – casual stories with the help of a few central principles, and
> to make rough quantitative judgments about the consequences of economic
> policy and other exogenous events.

George Stigler (1988, p. 71) states:

> At leading centers of economic theory, such as MIT, it has been the
> practice to ask: is the new theory logically correct? That is a good question
> but not as good as the second question: Does the new theory help us to
> understand observable economic life? No one will deny the desirability of
> eventually asking the second question, but many economists prefer to
> leave that question for a later time and a different person to answer. That
> division of labor is quite proper, but until the second question is answered,
> a theory has no standing and therefore should not be used as a guide to
> policy.

Martin Bronfenbrenner (1991, p. 604) tells us: 'Meanwhile we go
our merry ways, debating questions nobody has asked with rigour only
a mathematician could appreciate, at the expense of real policy issues.
Pirandello writes of a character in search of an author; we offer techniques in search of an application.'

Finally, here are two examples of the empirical science position
from specialists in the natural sciences. Michael Ghiselin (1989,
p. 130) writes: 'We cut corners. The economic optimum is to understand
a theory just well enough to solve the problem at hand, and no better.'
A leading philosopher of science, Karl Popper (1983, p. 7) states: 'The
doctrine that there is as much science in a subject as there is mathematics
in it, or as much as there is measurement or "precision" in it, rests on a
complete misunderstanding.'

The methodological pronouncements of economists are hardly an
unfailing guide to their actual practices (see Blaug, 1980, Ch. 15). So
let us look at these practices. How close to the formalist end of the
spectrum many economists are was demonstrated when the Santa Fe

Institute invited a group of natural scientists and mathematicians to meet with a group of economic theorists recruited by Kenneth Arrow. At this meeting:

> the physical scientists were flabbergasted to discover how mathematically rigorous theoretical economists are. Physics is generally considered to be the most mathematical of all the sciences, but modern economics has it beat. Palmer, a condensed matter physicist, says economists use much more 'fancy mathematics' and hard to understand notation than physicists. 'You can't publish in an economics journal without theorems,' he adds. ... The mathematical rigor of today's theoretical economics, Arthur [an economist] explains, can be traced to the 1950s ... 'A whole generation of mathematical economists joined in a movement that believed in spelling out the assumptions that were being made,' he says. 'Now that's become the only way you can do economics, and physicists ... find that surprising.' The flip side of the physicists' surprise at the rigor of economists was the economists' astonishment at the physicists' lack thereof. ... Arthur says physicist Per Bak spoke at the institute about self-organizing criticality. ... [A]t the end of his talk an economist stood up and asked Bak about his proofs. Bak replied that the results were all from experimental work done on a computer. 'You can whip up theorems, but I leave that to the mathematicians,' he said. Arthur comments: 'The economists could not believe that constituted research. We found it shocking that you could do science that way. This difference in approach arises, Anderson [a physicist] says, from the difference in the amount of data available to the two fields. [Physicists can be secure that experimental data] will not allow them to wander too far off course. ... A related difference between the disciplines is illustrated by a recent incident. ... A group ran across a problem ... That night Palmer set up a computer program to approximate the answer, while Geanakoplos (an economist) solved it exactly with pencil and paper. ... [They reached the same solution.] The economists in the group were taken aback by Palmer's computer short cut – they would never have thought of it (Robert Pool, 1989, p. 701).

Had the economists been selected not by Kenneth Arrow, but by some outstanding empirical science economist, such as Milton Friedman or James Tobin, the physicists would have got a very different impression of economists.

For a further illustration of how sharply formalist theory and empirical science theory differ consider Milton Friedman's work. In 1957 he published *A Theory of the Consumption Function*. Although called 'A Theory', most of the book is taken up by empirical tests, and the theoretical chapters contain only simple mathematics. Friedman is content to demonstrate his theory for a simple two-period case, illustrated by an indifference-curve diagram. Friedman decided to spend most of his time on showing the consistency of his theory with a wide range of observed phenomena, rather than to demonstrate it rigorously and elegantly in an infinite-horizon model. He did so presumably because anyone disposed to doubt the theory is much more likely to be sceptical about its consistency with the data, than about whether it can be generalized to the infinite-horizon case.

This attitude is alien to formalists. In reviewing a collection of Friedman's essays, *The Optimum Quantity of Money*, Hahn (1971, pp. 61, 62, 65) writes:

> Friedman neither has, nor claims to have a monetary theory. His strong and influential views are not founded on an understanding of 'how money works', but on what his empirical studies have led him to believe to have been the course of economic history. He himself, at least in this book, claims no more. His celebrated policy recommendations themselves depend on a plea of ignorance. ... To justify the dependence of the demand for money on 'permanent prices' he is satisfied with the following: 'holders of money presumably judge the "real" amount of cash balances in terms of the quantity of goods and services to which the balances are equivalent, not at any given moment of time, but over a sizable and indefinite period' (p. 121). The force of the word 'presumably' here is obscure. ... Here I simply note the casual theorizing. There are many other instances of this lack of seriousness. ... But the general point is an important one, for we all know the difficulties of statistical inference in the absence of a precisely articulated theory, and it is on the statistics that Friedman in the final analysis rests his case. ... I conclude that the 'empirical hypothesis' in question [the stability of the money demand function] is nothing more than a claim that empirically established demand functions for money have behaved 'better' than empirically established consumption functions. It is puzzling that such a claim should be the basis of a school of economic thought. ... It is also possible that I have misunderstood him ... that he has in mind a well-founded theoretical framework. ... If so, it really is rather important that he should produce it.

Hahn's criticisms that Friedman has no monetary theory, that he lacks an understanding of the workings of money, and that he bases his views merely on what he sees as the course of monetary history, illustrate well the difference between the criteria used by formalists and by empirical scientists. The latter would argue that Friedman certainly has a monetary theory, since he has a coherent explanatory framework that predicts the effect on income of changes in the quantity of money. An empirical scientist would hardly be surprised that the claim for the validity of a theory is based on the lessons of economic history, or that the claim to greater predictive power forms the foundation of a school. That is what empirical science is all about. As long as an economic theory explains the 'course of economic history' it is a good theory, even if it is expressed in casual, common-sense terms. A deeper understanding, while certainly not worthless, is not of dominating importance. For instance, what economist would doubt Friedman's statement that, with a lag, holders of money judge the adequacy of their cash balances by the real rather than the nominal value of these balances? Whether or not this should be called 'casual theorizing' does not matter; what matters is whether it generates correct results in a plausible way or not. By contrast, to a formalist like Hahn, it is the rigorous derivation of the demand for money from the underlying microtheory that is central.

Moreover, Friedman's policy conclusions are not based on a plea of ignorance or entirely on a belief in the stability of velocity, a belief that it is relatively easy to evaluate with the tools of economics. As Friedman has often stated, he objects to discretionary monetary policy on two grounds. First, he believes that the central bank cannot predict accurately enough both future GNP and the impact of its policies on GNP. Second, he thinks that the central bank lets its own bureaucratic interests and political pressures interfere with stabilization policy. Such hypotheses about central banks are harder to test than are hypotheses about the stability of the demand function for money. A strengthening of the microfoundations of this demand function would therefore not raise by all that much the probability of a joint hypothesis that contains both Friedman's money demand function and his hypothesis about central banks. Hence, an empirical science economist may consider it more useful to work on how the central bank functions than on the microfoundations of the money demand function.

Neil Wallace provides another example of a strongly formalist stance when he discusses how one can explain the coexistence of low-yielding money and higher-yielding securities. After pointing out that either a cash-in-advance model or a model that has money in the utility function would provide such an explanation, he writes:

> Consider the money-in-the-utility function model. Suppose someone could issue liabilities backed by holdings of interest-bearing securities that would compete with outside money in yielding utility. Such liabilities could arise in the cash-in-advance model. ... So we are left in these models with the question: what thwarts these profit opportunities? *A boorish response* to these concerns consists of simply repeating the assumptions: outside money is an argument of utility functions. ... This is a *boorish* response because it

stops conversation and leaves us at an impasse (Wallace, 1988, p. 25, italics added).

He then discusses two possible answers, that inside money is not trusted, or that issuers of inside money need to hold a reserve of outside money. He finds neither of these answers satisfactory since usually 'both money-in-the-utility function and cash-in-advance models have perfect security markets. If trust is not a problem in those markets, why is it a problem for securities that are to be exchanged for goods?' (p. 26).

The use of the word 'boorish' illustrates the aesthetic heuristic of formalists. So does the emphasis on the simplicity of assumptions: either security markets are perfect, or they are not. It is not an atmosphere receptive to such an inelegant assumption as: 'Security markets can generally be approximated by a model of perfect markets. However, the market in which one type of "security", money, is traded for goods is not perfect, because the prices of goods are sticky.' By contrast, to someone with an empirical science orientation such a complex assumption seems acceptable. Markets vary in their degree of perfection, with a 'perfect market' as a limiting case. When analysing some markets the assumption that they are perfect is convenient and does no harm, but for other markets this assumption would lead to wrong results. Friedman (1953), for example, has stated explicitly that for some purposes we may consider an industry to be competitive and for others treat it as monopolistic.

A further illustration of the split between formalist and empirical science economics is the situation in monetary economics. Formalist monetary theory, that deals with how money fits into the general equilibrium model, or the type of monetary theory discussed by Nagatani (1978) in his textbook *Monetary Theory*, differ sharply from the type of theory that guides empirical work in monetary economics. The problems that formalist monetary theory addresses are mainly to demonstrate the coherence and rigour of our general maximizing paradigm in a world that contains money, and to explain the existence of money. For empirical monetary theory these are at most quite subordinate problems. Instead, it tries to explain the influence of changes in the supply of money on prices and output, and that problem can be discussed without any deep understanding of why money is used. More generally, empirical monetary theorists, such as Friedman, would offer the same answers as they do now to the questions they pose if formalist monetary theory did not exist. Conversely, formalist monetary theory is unaffected by what empirical monetary theory has to say, or by what econometric studies of the demand for money show.

As another example of the distinction between empirical science economics and formalist economics consider the status of the rationality assumption. To formalists it is an axiom, and hence no concessions to irrational behaviour are allowed, even when observed behaviour can be reconciled with rationality only by making highly implausible assumptions. By contrast, to mainstream empirical science economists' rational behaviour is an extraordinarily useful working hypothesis that should generally be adhered to, but that can be relaxed if all else fails. For example, when all other ways of explaining the stickiness of interest rates on credit cards failed, Ausubel (1991) could invoke irrational behaviour by card holders. With economic theory thus resting on a working hypothesis rather than on an axiom, a formal derivation of the results from rational utility maximizing is not all that attractive.

The distinction between the formalist and empirical science mind sets also shows up in econometrics. Lawrence Summers (1991) clearly explicates the distinction between formalist econometricians who seek deep parameters and empirical science econometricians who look for regularities in the data. He shows that it is the latter and not the former who have produced the evidence that empirical science economists find convincing.

Finally, here is a more personal example. My former colleague Ross Starr once told me with great exhilaration that he had found a way of determining the optimal allocation of consumption over time (later published as Heller and Starr, 1979). When I replied that Friedman had already done this with a simple diagram, Starr was shocked, probably rightly so, at my philistinism in not appreciating the importance of the greater rigour and elegance of his proof. But I thought that the probability that Friedman's indifference-curve proof is wrong is so low, that I did want to sit still for a more elegant proof. (Starr is right, I am a philistine.)[2]

What divides economists here is not a disagreement about objective reality that can, at least in principle, be settled by rational argument or empirical investigation. Nor is it a matter of explicit methodological positions consciously derived from different philosophies of science, which again would, in principle, be amenable to settlement by discussion. Instead, it is a difference in mind-sets, that is in scientific tastes, in what we are trying to accomplish.[3] Hence, what is called for is the degree of tolerance that marked Debreu's (1991, p. 6) presidential address, where he remarked, 'Our profession may take pride in its exceptional intellectual diversity, one of whose clearest symbols is an Ely lecture given by an economic historian at a session chaired by a mathematical economist.' A failure to show such tolerance can lead to serious misunderstandings. As discussed in the Appendix to this chapter, this has happened with respect to general equilibrium theory.

ALTERNATIVE WAYS OF CLASSIFYING ECONOMICS

The distinction I have drawn between economics as formalist science and as empirical science differs from several common ways of classifying economics. Thus it does not correspond to the old-fashioned distinction between mathematical and 'literary' economics. Some empirical science problems cannot be resolved without a great deal of complex mathematics. Conversely, though examples would be hard to find, it is possible to imagine a purely verbal treatment of a formalist problem. Michio Morishima (1984) has argued cogently that mathematical economists should pay much more attention to the institutional details of the economy, and advocates, in effect, that they use empirical science criteria. The distinction between formalist economists and empirical science economists is therefore a more subtle matter than whether ones uses mathematics.

Economists are sometimes classified as 'empiricists' or as 'theorists'. This too does not correspond to the distinction I am drawing, because it does not distinguish between those who do empirical science theory and those who do formalist theory. Nor am I distinguishing between 'pure theory' and 'applied theory'. Pure theory is defined as a theory for which applications and empirical relevance do not matter (see Balzer, 1982, p. 41). But many formalist economists do claim *some* empirical relevance for their work.

The frequently drawn contrast between those interested in theory (and hence in 'science') and those concerned with policy is also not relevant here. Where does this leave someone who is interested neither in elegant theorems, nor in policy, but in understanding the world around us, even in cases where this understanding does not lead to policy conclusions? Here are two simple examples. In January Christmas cards are sold at a discount of up to 50 per cent or so. In the

United States gas stations set a per gallon charge for service rather than a fixed dollar charge. Someone might seek explanations for these puzzling observations even though these explanations have no policy implications.[4] Surely in economics, as elsewhere, at least some empirical research is the result of curiosity unmotivated by practical considerations.

Moreover, the frequent identification of formalistic work with 'science' and policy with non-science is ill-founded. The work that is required for good policy, that is the formulation and empirical testing of hypotheses, is similar to the work done in the fields that are generally considered to be the paradigms of science. Indeed if one defines science narrowly enough to encompass only empirical science, as is often done, then it is formalistic economists not policy-oriented economists whose membership in the scientific club should be questioned.

Hahn (1990) draws a distinction between what he calls the British and the American tradition of economics. He attributes to the British tradition the following two characteristics, both of which correspond to what I am calling the 'empirical science' approach:

> The study of economics is not to be regarded as an end in itself. It lacks the beauty of mathematics or art or the possibilities for precision and prediction of physics. The main motive for its study must be the improvement of the condition of mankind. The ... complicated analyses which economists endeavor to carry through are not mere gymnastic. They are instruments for bettering human life. It is pretentious to use mathematics when words will do and it is equally pretentious to use 'highbrow' mathematics when more elementary methods will do almost as well (Hahn, 1990, p. 539).

Granted that the characteristics Hahn describes are more prominent in British than in American economics, I suspect that the majority of American economists adhere to what Hahn calls the British tradition.

My distinction between formalist and empirical science economics is quite similar to Friedman's distinction between Marshallian and Walrasian economics, since Marshallians are much more in the empirical science camp than are Walrasians. As A.W. Coats (1988, p. 76) remarked:

> The Marshallian style can be maddening to economists who value logical rigor over realism, whose ideal in economics is mathematical formalization, complete specification of all terms and steps in the argument, and

conclusive empirical tests. No wonder they prefer the precision and apparent completeness of general equilibrium analysis rather than Marshallian partial equilibrium analysis, the successful application of which depends on the analyst's skill in distinguishing relevant from irrelevant variables, and in knowing how far to pursue the implications of a given problem.

But the distinction between Marshallian and Walrasian economics could be misleading because it is not just a matter of general versus partial equilibrium. Although general equilibrium analysis is usually more rigorous and formal than partial equilibrium analysis, one can also provide an informal analysis of general equilibrium. Similarly, although rigour usually requires general equilibrium analysis, it does not always do so; some discussions of the time inconsistency of monetary policy provide a counter-example.

The dichotomy between formalistic science and empirical science has much in common with the frequently drawn distinction between 'high-brow' and 'low-brow' theory. However it differs in two ways. First, empirical science economics obviously includes empirical work along with theory. Second, the terms 'high-brow' and 'low-brow' are often used in an invidious and in a sometimes even sneering manner that is entirely inappropriate. Once one realizes that the difference between high-brow and low-brow theory is essentially the distinction between formalistic science and empirical science, it should be apparent that this difference is not one that can be ranked on a value scale. Some high-brow tastes, such as preferring Hamlet to a soap opera, may indicate superior intellectual status, but preferring mathematics to physics or logic to chemistry does not.

CONCLUSION

Although there is no sharp line of demarcation between hypotheses that are close to the observational level and those that are at a high level of abstraction, it is useful to classify the work of economic theorists into two categories, formalist theory and empirical science theory, because economists invoke widely different criteria in evaluating theories. Much misunderstanding is caused if one type of theory is judged by the criteria applicable to the other type. The next chapter argues that both formalistic economics and empirical science economics make valuable contributions, but that the formalist criteria for evaluating theories are given too much weight.

APPENDIX – GENERAL EQUILIBRIUM THEORY

The distinction between formalist theory and empirical science theory has played a major role in the debate about general equilibrium theory. Thus Alan Coddington (1975, p. 555) wrote about the

> Procrustean temptations that are held out to the practitioners of GE: to consider arguments not on their own merits, but only to the extent that they can be reformulated within ... the GE framework. The refutations of the arguments concerning foreign aid, balanced budgets and floating exchange rates succumb to just the same Procrustean temptations. What is refuted in each case is not the guarded argument which typically is put forward, but a quite unguarded one resulting from chopping off everything that does not fit neatly into the GE framework.

Frank Hahn (1985, pp. 20–21) responded to such criticisms by arguing that general equilibrium theory does elucidate how an actual economy operates:

> In giving us this precise formulation and these existence proofs Arrow and Debreu vastly increased our understanding of what had gone before and ... provided the first essential step in any serious discussion of the Invisible Hand. ... The elegant definition of a good made it clear to the naked eye that the market structure would have to be much richer than in fact it is if an actual economy in equilibrium should correspond to theirs [Arrow and Debreu's]. The fundamental theorem of welfare economics then underlines the message that, even if actual economies are in equilibrium, they may be inefficient. ... Who can read the Core theorem without even a flicker of pleasure in the beautiful and not obvious role of the Arrow–Debreu equilibrium? Who can read them without finding their understanding of market power and the role of markets deepened? ... We understand a basic problem with public goods because of our understanding of the private goods case. ... Is our understanding of Keynesian claims not deepened and modified by making the connection to missing markets? If we did not have the Arrow–Debreu theory it would be priority number one to construct it.

If Hahn is right, my distinction between formalist and empirical science economics is invalid. But Hahn claims too much. His argument that the absence of some markets invalidates the *identity* between Pareto equilibrium and the equilibrium achieved by the invisible hand is certainly correct. But whoever claimed that market allocations are perfect? Adam Smith certainly did not. As Coddington (1975, p. 554) pointed out, we do not need the Arrow–Debreu analysis to know that market solutions are imperfect. Those who advocate them do not do so because they claim to have a theorem establishing the identity between market solutions and Pareto-optimal solutions. Rather, they believe, as an empirical hypothesis, that the allocation provided by the invisible hand is in most cases superior to that provided by government intervention. To determine if they are right one has to quantify the losses from the inefficiencies of both processes. But general equilibrium theory merely tells us that in the absence of complete contingent markets the invisible hand suffers from some inefficiency.

Moreover, it does not take a technical general equilibrium model to demonstrate that the absence of some contingent markets creates problems. Surely everyone analysing the impact of inflation is aware that there is no perfect inflation hedge. Anyone working on health-care economics knows that insurance markets are imperfect because of moral hazard, and that asymmetric information bedevils a fee-for-service system, so that the market solution to health care is not ideal. Similarly, anyone familiar with elementary Marshallian welfare economics will not say that 'only investment profitable to private investors can be beneficial.' To be sure, there may be some ideologists who deny that the market system has any imperfections. But surely there are easier ways to bring such people to their senses than to make them read Arrow–Debreu.

To an empirical scientist the absolute truth of statements is unimportant. What matters is whether they are sufficiently accurate for the purpose at hand. Thus an ecologist concerned about pollution may treat the Black Sea as a closed body of water, the Straits of Marmara being sufficiently narrow for that. But someone considering how to ship goods from London to Odessa should not.

Hahn's claim that our understanding of market power, public goods and Keynesian theory is 'deepened' by general equilibrium theory invites a related response. Is the deepening cost-effective? Would we not learn more about public goods and Keynesian theory by studying them at a lower level of abstraction? The foundations of mathematics are currently in disarray (see Kline, 1980). Hence, one might claim that our understanding of, say industrial organization theory, which uses some mathematics, would be deepened by research in mathematical philosophy. But that would hardly be an efficient way of improving the administration of the anti-trust laws. Not all round-aboutness is productive. Hence, from the viewpoint of empirical science economics, it

is hard to agree with Hahn that if we did not already have Arrow–
Debreu theory, constructing it would have to be our first priority.

Weintraub (1985) presents a more subtle argument than Hahn's, one
that focuses not on general equilibrium theory per se, but on the
broader neo-Walrasian tradition. He treats Walrasian theory as the
Lakatosian hard core of neo-classical theory.[5] Since that theory makes
a significant contribution to understanding the economy, it seems to
follow that Walrasian theory is part of what I have called empirical
science economics. But improving the intellectual coherence of a
theory's hard core may not be a cost-effective way of improving the
theory's predictive and explanatory powers. Suppose that we had no
coherent proofs of existence and uniqueness, but relied on mere sur-
mises. How much would this change what we say when we try to
explain relative prices?

Weintraub's (1988a) response is to point to a set of papers on the
economics of households as examples of empirical applications of
Walrasian theory. But it is far from clear that these papers, which use
game theory to investigate allocation problems within a household, are
Walrasian in the sense that to write them required facility with advanced
Walrasian theory (see Birner, 1988, p. 48). The evidence that Weintraub
(1988a, p. 49) cited for this is that when one of the authors was a
graduate student he proposed the topic of the paper as his Ph.D. dissertation, and Becker and Heckman rejected it because it was 'too general
equilibrium in character. ... Moreover ... [the other author's] contribution ... came out of a seminar I taught, and she was trained as a neo-
Walrasian.' This argument has some force, but to go from a willingness to work with many parameters to full-scale Walrasian theory
involves a large jump. Similarly, that an author was trained in Walrasian
theory does not mean that all the papers he or she writes are part of
Walrasian theory.

Blaug (1991) draws a useful distinction between Walrasian general
equilibrium *theory* which deals with the existence, uniqueness and
stability of multimarket equilibrium, and the general equilibrium *model*
which solves for the value of several endogenous economic variables.
He points out that, while the model has empirical content, the theory
does not. Hence, although the theory 'is the most prestigious economics of all and ... has absorbed an entire generation of the finest minds
in modern economics ... it is extremely questionable, to say the least,
whether ... [it has] thrown any light at all on the way economic
systems function in practice. Worse still, it has fostered an attitude to

economics as a purely intellectual game' (Blaug, 1991, pp. 508–9). Blaug rejects Weintraub's claim that general equilibrium theory represents the 'hardening of the hard core' of neo-classical economics, and can therefore lay claim to a share of the empirical successes of neo-classical economics. As he points out, general equilibrium theory does not make precise 'an economic tradition that is as old as Adam Smith's invisible hand', because Adam Smith referred to the 'dynamic process of competition and not to the static end-state conception of perfect competition ...' (1991, p. 508).

In any case, my argument does not depend on whether Walrasian theory has any empirical content at all, or on whether it is progressive. Even a highly formal theory can have an empirical science by-product. All I am saying is that to aim for empirical science results by using general equilibrium theory is often a too round-about process. Hence, general equilibrium theory should be understood primarily, though not entirely, as formalist economics.

NOTES

1. The story is told about a committee to select a new university president. Before interviewing various faculty candidates, a committee member suggested that, to probe a candidate's common sense, they all be asked the simplest possible question, 'how much is two plus two?' The first candidate, a mathematician, replied: 'I am glad you asked that question. I have just developed a more elegant proof than one based on Whitehead and Russell,' and he proceeded to cover two blackboards before triumphantly concluding that two plus two equals four. The next candidate, an engineer, looked thoughtful and said: 'Well I guess two plus two is pretty close to four. If you treat it as four, you'll be alright.' The third candidate, an accountant, got up, closed the door, faced the committee and said, 'Well, ladies and gentlemen, what would you like it to be?'
2. Starr pointed out to me that formal methods have two advantages over geometric ones. First, a geometric 'proof' has the problem that one cannot be sure that one has drawn the curves in the only permissible way, and hence that one's results are general. Second, algebraic treatment allows one to extend the analysis by adding or relaxing constraints in a way that a geometric treatment does not.
3   Such differences in mind-sets among practitioners is not unique to economics, but shows up also in medical research as a clash between scientists and physicians (see Natalie Angier, 1990).
4. Such a sharp cut in the price of Christmas cards can hardly be due to the carrying cost of an inventory. A more plausible explanation is that if a certain type of card is left over after Christmas this signals its inferior quality. Moshe Adler (1989) has suggested that gas stations impose a per gallon charge for service because with a fixed dollar charge, employees could simply pocket the payment for service.
5. Imre Lakatos (1978) developed an approach in which a scientific research programme consists of a central core that is not tested itself, or even testable. This core is used to generate hypotheses in the 'protective belt' that are tested.

4.   Honour Them Both

> But a thriving subject will know at each stage of its development what the
> next crucial questions are. Pure theory is no exception. But it so happens
> that it is becoming ever more clear that almost none of them can be
> answered by the old procedures. Instead of theorems we shall need
> simulations, instead of simple transparent axioms there looms the likeli-
> hood of psychological, sociological and historical postulates. ... [I]t is
> unlikely that those with the temperament and facilities of mid-twentieth-
> century theorists will find this a congenial road. ... [E]conomics will
> become a 'softer' subject than it now is (Hahn, 1991, p. 47).

Those who insist that 'if it isn't mathematics it isn't economics' are
wrong, and so are those who think formalist theory is useless. For an
economist maths phobia is a crippling disease – and so is word phobia.
Both formalist theory and empirical science theory are legitimate
branches of economics and should co-exist peacefully.

IN DEFENCE OF FORMALISTIC THEORY

Post-Keynesians and institutionalists reject both the formalist theory
and much of the empirical science theory of mainstream economics.
Much of their campaign has relied on generalized charges. They have
spent much too little time showing that specific theories are invalid in
the sense that there exist rival theories that predict better. Their criticism
has therefore met with the correct response that, although *homo
economicus* with an 'impassionate passion for impassionate rationality'
does not exist, by assuming that he does we can generate many useful
and valid hypotheses.

But formalist theory has also met with telling criticism from mainstream economists. Terence Hutchison (1988, pp. 170–71), citing J. R.
Hicks's statement that 'much of economic theory is a good game',
points out that most economic research is supported by public funds.
Hence economists have a duty to provide something useful, and should
not just play games for their own amusement.

41

Is it possible that economists' applications for financial support might not have been as successful as they have been if it had been evident that the kinds of claims for the subject on which these applications are based resembled those of physicists and natural scientists much less than they did the kinds of claims relevant for applications for sponsorship from artists, poets, rhetoricians, or game players and sportsmen of one kind or another (Hutchison, 1988, pp. 174–5).

It would be hard to quarrel with Hutchison's stricture that grant applicants should not make misleading claims. Nor can one doubt that if granting agencies realized the irrelevance of some formalist grant applications to practical problems, they would fund fewer formalist research projects.[1] Similarly, suppose universities could allocate different teaching loads, and hence different amounts of time for research to faculty members working on various problems. It is likely that, at least in US state-supported universities, less research time would be allocated to economists working on formalist theory. In Britain in the 1980s, the Thatcher government pressured universities and polytechnics to focus more on applied, and less on pure research.

But that does not mean that no or only extremely little formalist research would be supported. Formalist research does produce knowledge, and knowledge is valued, quite apart from its instrumental practicality. One can plausibly argue that if the public were completely unwilling to pay for 'impractical' research, it would by now have found some way of controlling the research that universities do. Moreover, the US National Institute for the Humanities does support research in fields like classics that promise results that are no more 'practical' than are elegant proofs of existence theorems in general equilibrium theory. George Stigler (1988, p. 89) conjectured that 'the public wishes to admire superior performance in every legitimate calling'. Ghiselin (1989, pp. 194–5 and 197), despite his clear empirical science orientation, writes:

We derive pleasure from understanding the world around us. Why should this pleasure be any different from that which we derive from eating? It is conceivable that we deal here with a maladaptive or adaptively neutral aspect of our biology. But all too often adaptively neutral features turn out to be failures of the imagination. ... A sense of curiosity would seem to be a normal part of our adaptability as organisms. ... We all know how much pleasure children derive from acquiring knowledge, in spite of educational practices. ... Pure science plays a central role in all aspects of intellectual culture.

All the same, it seems plausible that if those who directly or indirectly pay for academic research did not face a severe principal/agent problem less formalist research in economics would be undertaken. One might, of course, respond that because these principals are ignorant, or for some other reasons, their preferences should not dominate those of their agents. This argument raises deep philosophical issues, and I will pass it by. All I need to maintain is that *some* amount of formalist research can be justified as a 'good game', because enjoying and hence being willing to pay for a 'good game' are part of being human.

A second defence of formalist research is that it is more than merely a 'good game'; it is often directly or indirectly practical. What characterizes *some* formalistic economics is not a frivolous disregard of the severe economic problems facing the public, but a belief that to alleviate these problems we must start our thinking from firm foundations, plus a (more questionable) identification of firm foundations with formally derived results (see Katzner, 1991). Thus Robert Lucas demonstrates as much dedication as does anyone to resolving genuine policy problems.

A principal theme of this book is that, at the margin at which we are currently operating, formalist research is an inefficient way of obtaining empirical science knowledge. But low productivity does not mean zero productivity. Thus formalists can, to some extent, use that standard defence of basic research, that it can have totally unanticipated practical pay-offs. When imaginary numbers were developed, who would have supposed that this research could save sailors from drowning? But the theory of imaginary numbers was needed to develop radio, and radio communication has saved many a sailor's life. When Einstein developed relativity theory non-Euclidian geometry turned out to be more than the merely idle speculation it had previously seemed.

Hutchison (1988, p. 173) questions the applicability of this argument to economics because:

> multiplying highly abstract formulas or models on the possibility that one day some kind of real-world application *might* (one never knows) turn up does not seem to be a convincing additional justification for an activity that was otherwise, or initially defended as a good game. Some limited concession might, however, be made. But before any such is granted it would be reasonable to ask for convincing examples from the history of economic thought, which do not seem easy to find [emphasis in original].

Hutchison is, of course, right in saying that the ultimate practicality of pure research in economics should be neither assumed, nor argued for merely by analogy with other fields. But examples of pure research in economics that have, or may have, important practical implications do exist. Thus, highly abstract work on aggregation theory has led to a new measure of money (Divisia money) that could perhaps improve monetary policy. Real business cycle theory, which developed out of a formalist mind-set, if correct, has obvious practical implications. Martin Shubik (1988, p. 1517) points out that, while only the less abstract aspects of game theory have practical applications, these aspects 'would hardly exist' if it were not for the more abstract models. Similarly, abstract research on the meaning of causality may make an important contribution to the question whether money is exogenous, and hence to applied macroeconomics.

Furthermore, even if the 'economic theory game' does not itself generate practical knowledge, it could still be a useful mind-set to counteract the natural tendency to rush to the solution of practical problems with insufficiently thought-through ideas. Soldiers are taught close-order drill, even though it is no longer used in combat.

IN DEFENCE OF EMPIRICAL SCIENCE ECONOMICS

If, as some believe, economists accept the positivists' emphasis on the empirical basis of knowledge, then defending empirical science economics would be like watering the lawn during a downpour.[2] But by now formalist criteria have infiltrated the theory evaluation of economists to such an extent that empirical science economics needs to be defended against two related charges. One is that it lacks rigour and is little better than guesswork. The second is that it is not and cannot be a genuine science. Economists who try to copy the procedures of the empirical sciences ignore the much greater recalcitrance of the material dealt with by the social sciences than by the natural sciences. The nature of their material does not permit them to develop many nontrivial hypotheses that are able to withstand hard-nosed empirical testing. Besides, by pretending to understand much more than we actually do, we encourage a belief that we know how to manipulate the economy, and that often leads to disastrous results Hence we should give up the pretence of being almost-physicists. Instead, we should concentrate on what we can do well, that is formulating and solving purely logical problems. Economics will then be of virtually no use to policy makers, but at least it will do no damage, and will provide intellectual excitement.[3]

Most economists reject both of these arguments, and rightly so. There are 'real world' problems out there about which someone has to make decisions. If we economists do not provide advice, we leave the field open to journalists and politicians who know even less. And they are at least as likely to advocate ill-founded interventions as are economists. Besides, some of our hypotheses *do* stand up to hard-nosed testing. Granted that empirical testing is more difficult in economics than in physics, this does not necessarily mean that we should devote more of our efforts to formal theory than physicists do. Just the opposite might be the case. The higher cost of empirical results should perhaps induce us to devote more time to empirical work; not all price elasticities exceed unity.

BUT HOW MUCH?

To say that both empirical science theory and formalist theory are justified is not sufficient. The economist's question is: 'How much of each do we want?' By 'how much' I do not merely mean how much effort should be devoted to solving formalist problems relative to empirical science problems, but also the relative weight to be given to formalist and empirical science criteria when dealing with any specific piece of research. The latter is not as apparent an issue as is the type of problem to be investigated, but it could well be more important.

The relative emphasis that should be given to the two types of research is an extremely difficult question, because it involves tastes. I know my own tastes, but I very much doubt that anything I could say would change the reader's. So I will try a different tack. Instead of using my own evaluation I will try to deduce the socially optimal trade-off by using the trade-off made by the profession as a guide.

If one takes the opinions of the profession as the guide, must one not conclude that the current emphasis on formalism is correct? No, because several factors bias the economist's judgement. Three factors may induce many economists to undervalue formalist research. One is that they might lack the necessary mathematical training and aptitude. But this is much less likely now than it was, say, thirty years ago. Moreover, the relative volume of research done by empirical science economists and by formalist economists depends less on the training and preferences of the average economist than on the training and preferences of those who, being better trained, publish more.

A second factor that might induce economists to do empirical science research rather than formalist research is that more financial support is available for the former. But much of the support for academic research takes the form of low teaching loads, and hence is not restricted to practical problems. Besides, the National Science Foundation supports formalist research as well as empirical science research. Hence differences in financial support probably do not distort the choice between formalist and empirical science research very much.

Third, as already discussed, economists might feel overly attracted by the sense of satisfaction and power that flows from giving policy advice. But those who have a strong urge to give policy advice are more likely to be employed in government than in academia, and hence have little influence on academic research. And most of us in academia know that our advice is not likely to be heeded, so that we do not have all that much of an incentive to offer it. Thus, while there are three factors that induce economists to overdo empirical science economics, they are probably not very strong.

By contrast, there are two factors that push economists in the direction of formalist economics. And these seem stronger. One is that, as discussed in Chapter 2, emphasis on formalism is in the self-interest of the profession, and the refereeing process transmits that into the self-interest of the researcher. Second, as discussed below, formalist economics has more prestige than it deserves relative to empirical science economics. And that is likely to exert a powerful influence both on the type of problems studied, and on the criteria used to evaluate these studies.

MIRROR, MIRROR ON THE WALL, WHO IS THE FAIREST OF THEM ALL? ARE YOU SURE?

The prestige ranking of economics runs: first, formalist theory; second, empirical science theory; third, policy-advising and data gathering, and fourth, history of economic thought and methodology. The Appendix to this chapter shows how the ranking of various sub-fields of economics mirrors this ordering.

There are several explanations for the high prestige of formalist theory. One is that, as discussed in Chapter 2, a formalistic methodology enhances the prestige of economists. A related, but more questionable, explanation is that a bias towards formalism reflects a basic attitude in our culture, going back at least to Descartes (see Davis and Hersh, 1986). Thus Whitley (1977, p. 154) reports that '[i]t is not at all unusual when talking to experimental physicists for them to say that they are not intelligent enough for work in theoretical physics.' Similarly, scientists both social and physical, teaching in professional schools claim superior status to their more applied colleagues (Schön, 1983, pp. 26–7). We often seem to rank a science with a highly developed formal structure, such as physics, ahead of one with a less developed structure, such as zoology or geology. But it is not certain that this explanation of the great prestige of formalism in economics is valid. Do we really rank mathematics and logic above, say, astronomy and chemistry? Or, for that matter, does mathematical economics rank above geology? Another, more natural explanation of the prestige of formalism may be that formalist economics deserves its greater prestige because formalist economists are better. But are they?

Are Formalist Economists Better?

The belief that formalist theorists are abler than empirical science theorists is widespread among academic economists. Thus Klamer (Klamer and Colander, 1990, p. 181) reports that MIT students believe that 'policy is for simpletons'. As one student put it: 'those who can't do economics do policy'. Most abstract theorists probably think that they could easily do first-rate applied work, if they could just find time for such a pedestrian activity. But why should one accept this claim?

Only under two conditions could one rank these two types of economists unequivocally. One is if, say, formalists have an absolute advantage in both fields. But there is no evidence for that. Casual impression, admittedly based on an extremely small sample, suggests that good abstract theorists are not particularly good at less abstract economics. The other condition is that we have some metric for comparing the relative difficulty of making contributions to formalist theory and to empirical science theory. But no such metric exists.

A somewhat better, though loose argument for the superiority of formalists is that, due to its greater prestige among academic economists, formalist theory attracts abler students. But does it? One cannot support this argument by empirical observation of the students who specialize in formalist theory, unless these students are better in every subject, and I know of no evidence for this. If John gets an A in art history and a C in calculus, while Mary receives an A in calculus and a C in art history, how can one say who is abler? Nor can one claim that fewer students are good at mathematics than at, say, art history because, again, there is no metric that allows us to define 'good' in an objective way. More students can pass a set-theory course than become art historians on a par with Bernard Berenson.

A more plausible argument is that economic theory, being more prestigious, attracts a disproportionate number of those students who have a high opinion of their abilities. Since presumably estimated and actual abilities are positively correlated, one would expect formalists to be abler than applied economists. But there are two problems with this argument. First, the difference may well be minor, since it is the product of two correlations: the correlation between actual and estimated abilities, and the correlation between estimated ability and the propensity to enter the more prestigious field. Neither of these correlations need be high. Graduate students evaluate their abilities, in good part, on the basis of their grades, but grades are not such a reliable measure of capability, since it is hard to test creative thinking. And the correlation between a student's perception of his or her ability and the decision to become a theorist may also not be all that high. Many students enter economics to influence policy. In so far as this attitude survives the contrary indoctrination of graduate school, some who could become formalists will prefer not to.

Second, it is quite possible that there is only a fairly small correlation between ability at formalist theory and at empirical science theory. If so, then despite the great prestige of formal theory, there will be only a small drain of potentially first-rate empirical scientists into formalist science, and hence little reason to think that formalists are significantly better when measured by their abilities at both tasks.

Presumably the belief that mathematical economics is more difficult than applied economics, so that mathematical economists must obviously be abler, has two main sources. One is a comparison of the ability of mathematical and of applied economists at each other's tasks. Thus a mathematical economist might respond by saying: 'O.K., Mayer, let's assume that I know less than you do about monetary policy, and that even if I were to devote much time to it, your work on monetary policy would still be *slightly* better than mine. But even if you were to devote great effort to studying mathematics, your work in mathematical economics would be vastly inferior to mine. Therefore I am abler than you.' But why should ability at a task that one does not undertake matter? More generally, why should vast inferiority at one task be a more serious problem than slight inferiority at another? Where do the market prices needed to compare the two products come from? Imagine that a third person, a tight rope walker, joins the discussion and says to the mathematical economist: 'Well, with a great deal of effort I could learn almost as much maths as you did, but you lack totally the innate ability necessary for tight rope walking. Hence I am abler than you.'

In summary then, given the great prestige of formalist theory, one cannot entirely dismiss the argument that it attracts students who are abler by some objective standard, whatever that might be, though the difference, if any, may not be large. But regardless of objective truth, as long as economists believe that formalists are abler, they will try to claim formalist status for themselves. In the process they will give formalist problems and criteria more emphasis than is justified.

Formalism as the Beneficiary of some Confusions

But even if the high status of formalism has some slight justification in the quality of the students it attracts, its status is enhanced by several widespread confusions. One is a confusion of mathematics with empirical science. If one thinks of mathematics as the stigmata of science then it is indeed easy to conclude that formalist economics with its high degree of mathematization is scientific economics. The usually much less mathematically sophisticated work that I have called 'empirical science economics' is then merely an inferior imitation produced by less skilled craftsmen that should be allowed to fade away as inadequately trained economists make way for those with adequate mathematical training. By no means all formalists reason that way, but this type of argument has been a powerful weapon in the struggle to expand the formalist empire.

Mathematics is indeed the language of science, but just as speaking Italian does not make one an Italian, speaking mathematics does not make one a scientist. Horoscopes cast with computers and with algebra are just as much humbug as horoscopes cast the more traditional way.

In browsing through the journals in the physical sciences library of my university I was struck by how little mathematics some of these journals contain. Even in the physics journals the mathematics is less formal than that often used in economics journals with their infestation of lemmas, thus confirming the impression physicists received of economists at the Santa Fe conference, and Rosenberg's previously cited belief that (formalist) economics is mathematics rather than science.

An additional reason for the high status of formalism may be a confusion about the role of lower-level hypotheses. Many people seem to believe that those fields that deal with hypotheses that are more abstract, and hence more formalistic, generate the theory that is then put to use in the applied fields. Hence, a breakthrough in economic theory has a much greater effect than does a breakthrough in an applied field. But the assumption that in science forward linkages are stronger than backward linkages is questionable. Thus Gordon Tullock (1966, p. 18) argues that the 'spearheads of advance are probably normally in the applied fields rather than in pure science.' Similarly, Derek de Solla Price (1986, pp. 239–40) remarks:

> Another remarkably widespread wrong idea ... holds that science can in some mysterious way be applied to make technology. Quite commonly it is said that there is a great chain of being that runs from basic science to applied science and thence to development in a natural and orderly progression that takes one from the core of science to technology. Historically, we have almost no examples of an increase in understanding being applied to make new advances in technical competence, but we have many cases of advances in technology being puzzled out by theoreticians and resulting in the advancement of knowledge. It is not just a clever historical aphorism, but a general truth that 'thermodynamics owes much more to the steam engine than the steam engine to thermodynamics.'... Historically the arrow of causality is largely from technology to science.

Moreover, even if in the natural sciences progress were to come mainly from the theoretical core, it is by no means clear that in economics abstract theory deserves to be held in more esteem. First, the general laws that natural scientists praise are laws that usually predict as well as the lower-level hypotheses, because they are not accepted unless they do. That is not always so in economics.

Second, while high-level hypotheses do indeed have an honoured place in science, and theorists are ranked above experimenters (Hacking, 1983), lower-level hypotheses and even 'mere' observations are also held in esteem, at least when they have a bearing on higher-level hypotheses.[4] Good empirical science demands a subtle and extensive interplay of observation and low-level theory, and of lower-level theory and higher-level mathematized theory. It can benefit from the accumulation of observation statements with little theory attached. As Oskar Morgenstern (1972, p. 701) pointed out, Tycho Brahe, who patiently accumulated the observations that allowed Kepler and Newton to formulate their laws, is considered by astronomers to be a great scientist. By contrast, many economists tend to sneer at a colleague who 'merely' gathers facts as someone who is not doing 'science'.[5] Indeed, economists often use the term 'theory' to denote only formalist theory. An economist who develops a theory explaining the observed correlations between, say, the money stock, prices and interest rates, would usually not be called a theorist. By contrast, his colleague who presents a new proof of the uniqueness of general equilibrium is called a theorist. As McCloskey (1991, p. 14) remarked, 'The leading middle-aged economists laugh when Gary Becker is described as a "theorist" ... and the leading young economists do not even think it funny.'

But Ian Hacking (1983, pp. 248–9) tells us:

> What is characteristic of the scientific method? It brings ... [pure theory and empirics] into contact. ... Even pure mathematics benefits from this collaboration. Mathematics was sterile after the Greek era until it became 'applied' again. ... But many of us experience a sort of nostalgia, a feeling of sadness, when we survey social sciences. Perhaps this is because it lacks what is so great about fairly recent physical science. Social scientists don't lack experiment; they don't lack calculation; they don't lack speculation; they lack the collaboration of the three.

The interplay of observations and hypothesis that Hacking advocates requires more emphasis on lower-level hypotheses, and on empirical science economics in general, than is now fashionable.[6] As already mentioned, Summers (1991) shows that economists have found lower-level work more convincing than more abstract econometric results.

An additional confusion that has fostered the emphasis on formalist economics is a misreading of Friedman's influential essay on positive economics, with its advocacy of 'as-if' reasoning. Friedman's argument that hypotheses do not require realistic assumptions has been treated as a carte blanche for making whatever assumptions provide a tractable model. Formalists have found this highly convenient, since it seems to imply that their 'if-then' reasoning can by itself solve empirical science problems. But those who have embraced Friedman's permissive message in this fashion disregard his equally important prescriptive message: that the implications of hypotheses must be tested. Friedman, who has spent most of his professional life testing hypotheses, sometimes by econometrics, and sometimes by economic history, should not be cited in support of purely deductive analysis (see Hirsch and de Marchi, 1990). Indeed, he wrote his methodological essay as a criticism not just of institutionalism, but also of formalism.

More specifically, Friedman's argument that a hypothesis should be tested only by the validity of its implications, rather than by the validity of its assumptions, does not give one complete freedom to choose assumptions just for tractability. Sometimes an assumption is also an implication, and hence can be used under that label to test the hypothesis (see Mayer, forthcoming). For example, the homogeneity of agents' expectations may be both an assumption and an implication of a hypothesis. If so, evidence that agents hold (sufficiently) different expectations disconfirms the hypothesis.

Still another confusion that has caused economists to disregard the difference between formalist and empirical science economics is the identification of the rigour of an argument with the rigour of the strongest link in its chain, which I discuss at length in the next chapter. When attention is focused on the strongest link, formalism comes into its own, because it is precisely the use of formalist theory that makes this link so strong. But to deal with empirically relevant problems the strongest link usually has to be supplemented by other steps, and it is here that empirical science economics comes into its own.

CONCLUSION

Economists who are strong advocates of one type of economics, be it mathematical formalism or institutionally grounded economics, sometimes dismiss the other type of work with the words: 'This is not economics'. There is no reason why they should be allowed to thus practise lexicography without a licence. We need both formalistic theory and empirical science theory. How much of each is more difficult to decide. While there are some reasons suggesting that formalist economics currently receives too little emphasis, there are stronger reasons to think that the opposite is true. Professional self-interest, a belief that formalist economists are much abler, and certain confusions all induce our profession to over-emphasize the importance of formalist theory relative to empirical science theory.

APPENDIX – THE RANKING OF VARIOUS SUB-FIELDS

The status of the various sub-fields of economics shows how the focus on formal theory dominates economics. Benjamin Ward (1972, p. 10) classified various sub-fields into the following prestige categories:

A. Microtheory, macrotheory, econometrics
B. International trade, money and banking, public finance
C. Industrial organization, labour, economic history
D. Economic development, history of economic thought, comparative economic systems.

By now this ranking seems outdated in two respects. First, due to its use of game theory, industrial organization has probably moved up a notch, and the disarray in macroeconomics may have moved it down a notch. Second, formalist theory has invaded the applied fields, and such work is highly prized, regardless of its field. But even so, what does Ward's ranking tell us about the criteria by which economists evaluate their work?

The main criterion cannot be the extent to which various sub-fields have developed validated results. There is no reason to think that those whose field is the history of economic thought have less empirically validated specialized knowledge than do other economists, or that macrotheorists have more than do labour economists.

Could the ranking instead reflect the extent to which various sub-fields meet the criterion that economists use to decide whether a theory is scientific? The majority of economists, if asked for their criterion of science, would probably mention something along the lines of falsificationism.[7] But that criterion cannot explain the ranking of sub-fields. Neither microtheorists nor macrotheorists can claim that their hypotheses have survived more stringent tests than those in, say, international trade or industrial organization. Indeed, there is much debate whether a highly prestigious component of microtheory, general equilibrium theory, meets falsificationist criteria at all.

Thomas Kuhn (1977, pp. 272–6) has advocated another criterion for demarcating science from non-science: the existence of an invisible college of scientists that agrees on what constitutes puzzles that should be solved, and possesses a sufficiently articulated theory to provide criteria for an acceptable solution. But this criterion is met about equally well by all the sub-fields of economics so that it, too, cannot explain the prestige rankings.[8]

Ward (1972, p. 10) suggests that what governs the prestige rankings is the relatedness of a sub-field to the central theoretical core of economics:

> The highest status fields, those in Class A, define the nature of the acceptable research problems in economics and the approximate procedures to use in attempting to solve them. The remaining fields are classified in terms of the extent to which practitioners actually make use of the class A framework. ... The class D fields, for example, require a good deal of research borrowing from outside economics and contain a relatively large number of practitioners who are not well versed in class A topics.

A somewhat more accurate view is that we rank sub-fields by the extent to which their theory is general and abstract, and thus 'highbrow'. Whether such abstract and complex theory comes from economics itself does not matter all that much. A sub-field that uses, say, chaos theory or the latest developments in differential geometry would probably rank highly, even if it made little use of the core theories of economics. An evaluation of sub-fields by the elevation of brows is therefore similar to evaluating them by their use of mathematics. Economists are not the only ones who have such a value system: it is also common elsewhere (see Mirowski, 1986, p. 193, Caldwell, 1991b).

NOTES

1. To be sure, many empirical science projects would not be funded either if the granting agency were wise.
2. Positivism is a doctrine that higher-level statements have to derive in some way from direct observations.
3. The Austrian school is a particularly strong advocate of such a position.
4. Taxonomy is held in low esteem by scientists, and sometimes not considered 'real science' because it is descriptive and does not use modern techniques (Luoma, 1991). Its low status may also be due, in part, to a lack of relatedness of its descriptions to higher-level hypotheses. Its tools are not as modern as those used even in low-level economics.
5. I once wrote a paper (Mayer, 1990, Chapter 10) on the so-called monetarist experiment in which I presented a decomposition of the variance of the M-1 growth rate, and pointed out that the results were different from what both monetarists and anti-monetarists claimed. A referee complained that, since it contained no theory, it was not a scientific paper.
6. By insisting on differentiating formalist from empirical science economics I am not advocating the type of divorce between theory and empirical work that Hack-

ing deplores. On the contrary, by shielding empirical science theory from formalistic criteria I am freeing it to have a more intimate relation with empirical work.

7. Falsificationists argue that we should look for observations that might disconfirm our theory. If none turn up the theory can be tentatively accepted.

8. Still another, though hardly legitimate, reason why 'high-brow' theory may seem more prestigious is that it has little direct practical use. Attributing value to uselessness may seem paradoxical to some economists. But it should not surprise those who have read Veblen's (1899) *The Theory of the Leisure Class*. There is a long tradition that only those pursuits that have no practical use are fit for a gentleman. Finally, the absence of empirical relevance has a practical benefit. As Robert Merton (1957, p. 543) pointed out, lack of applicability protects scientists from the pressure of outside agencies, and thus 'from the invasion of norms which limit potential advance and threaten the stability and continuance of scientific research as a valued mental activity.' *Perhaps* this justifies a 'possibly apocryphal toast at a dinner for scientists in Cambridge' cited by Merton (1957, p. 543): 'To pure mathematics and may it never be of any use to anybody.'

5. Truth versus Precision

Our discussion will be adequate if it has as much clearness as the subject-matter admits of, for precision is not to be sought for alike in all discussions, any more than in all products of the craft (Aristotle, 1941, p. 936).

It is better to be vaguely right than precisely wrong (old proverb).

The typical paper in economics has a theoretical core in which each of the steps is worked out with great precision, along with other parts in which the argument is much less precise. As McCloskey (1990, pp. 73–4) has remarked: 'The extreme explicitness of modernist reasoning under the lamp-post is accompanied by extreme vagueness outside its range.' Many economists act like the person who, when asked about the age of the Amazon river, replied that by now it is one million and three years old, because three years ago he was told that it was a million years old.

Consider the following story. Two men on a train saw some sheep grazing on an adjacent hillside. One said to the other, 'All the sheep are shorn'. His friend, who was extremely cautious, replied, 'At least on one side'. 'Well', replied the first man, 'the probability that, if they are shorn on only one side, we just happen to see that side is small, isn't it, probably no more than 10 per cent?' At this point an economist who had overheard their conversation broke in and said: 'You can be much more precise and rigorous than that. There are eight sheep; if they are all shorn on just one side, the probability of us seeing the shorn side of all the eight sheep is 0.5^8, which is less than 0.4 per cent.' The economist was precise, but wrong!

The probability of seeing only the shorn side of all the sheep, if they are indeed shorn on just one side, depends not only on the number of sheep, but also on the probability that, perhaps due to the direction of the wind, they are not behaving randomly, but tend to turn the shorn side towards the train. Hence the chance that the sheep are shorn on only one side is probably closer to the non-economist's 10 per cent than to the economist's 0.4 per cent. The economist had fallen into the trap of working out rigorously and precisely what can be quantified, while ignoring that which cannot be so treated.

THE PRINCIPLE OF THE STRONGEST LINK

I call this procedure of focusing attention on the strongest part of an argument, and then attributing its strength to the entire argument, the 'principle of the strongest link'. It abounds in our journals. A typical paper starts with the utility and production functions of agents and derives from them in great detail a quite obvious step of the argument, such as that under perfect competition, etc. agents will consume various products until the elasticities of substitution equal the relative price ratios. Simply to assert that this is so is not considered rigorous enough; it has to be proven. But surely, if the argument of the paper contains an error, it will not be at that point. Proving this point is merely the ceremonial activity of strengthening what is already a totally persuasive link. Even in 1964, when formalist criteria did not exercise nearly as much influence as they do now, Hahn and Matthews (1964, p. 890) wrote about growth theory:

> ... While not disparaging the insights that have been gained we feel that in these areas the point of diminishing returns may have been reached. Nothing is easier than to ring the changes on more and more complicated models, without bringing in any really new ideas and without bringing the theory any nearer to casting light on the causes of the wealth of nations. The problems posed may well have intellectual fascination. *But it is essentially a frivolous occupation to take a chain with links of very uneven strength and devote one's energies to strengthening and polishing the links that are already strong* (Emphasis added).

More recently David Colander (1991, p. 157) compared physics, in which all calculations are carried out to the same level of exactness with mainstream economics in which 'certain aspects ... are carried out to twenty digits, while other aspects are rounded off at two.' Similarly, Henry Woo (1986, p. 47) wrote:

> Consider ... the theory of economic growth. Adam Smith first outlined several, crucial dimensions. ... Among these three main features capital accumulation is the most readily quantifiable and formalizable. So in time, the structure of analysis grew around the formal analysis of capital accumulation while the other factors faded into the background.

Yet it may seem that strengthening an already strong link can be justified. Suppose that somehow it were costless to raise the probability that step A is correct from 0.9998 to 0.9999. Then, even if the joint probability that all the other steps of the argument are correct is only 75 per cent, raising the probability of the first step would still enhance the probability of the entire argument, albeit slightly. But raising the probability of the strongest link is generally not costless. The more time one spends on increasing the precision and rigour of any one step, the less time one has available to verify the other steps. Similarly, too much of the reader's time is spent on considering the strong parts of the argument and too little time on thinking about the weaker parts. The next chapter discusses several other costs.

The time that authors spend on polishing the strongest link to shining perfection could often be better spent on one of the weaker links.[1] To be sure, one should generally not allocate one's time to make the probabilities at each step equal, because it may take more effort to raise the probability by a given amount at one step than at another. And there are surely cases where almost nothing can be done to enhance significantly the probability of those steps where it is low to start with. But cases in which it takes more effort to raise the probability by a percentage point for the low probability steps than for the high probability steps are not likely to predominate. An economist's training biases him or her to focus attention on those components of the argument where economic theory can make a substantial contribution, and these tend to be the strong parts of the argument. Moreover, standard procedures exist for making certain steps, which are already fairly rigorous, even more so, and they are likely to be used. If not, then on the general principle that other people's time is costless, referees are likely to demand that they be used. By contrast, the less rigorous steps often involve problems that are not as amenable to economic theory, and hence referees are less likely to see an obvious way of improving them. Authors are therefore tempted to misallocate their efforts by spending too much time on steps that are already strong, and the marginal social productivity of additional effort at these steps is likely to be low.

That such misallocation can be important becomes obvious once one considers the resource constraint. Rigour and precision are not free goods. Suppose that journals publish n papers, and that economists have available h hours for research. If n and h are determined exogenously, then each paper embodies h/n hours of effort regardless of how much rigour editors insist on. The time spent on polishing one part of the argument comes from the time that would otherwise be spent on verifying another part. To be sure, *n* may be endogenous. If editors insist on explicit formal derivations, papers may contain the same informal material as they otherwise would, but be longer. In that case the cost of formalization is that fewer papers are published. The time spent on research, *h*, may also be endogenous. If formalistic papers take longer to read than others, the more formalism the journals require, the less time economists have for their own research. With the number of papers that are published being fixed, each paper then received fewer hours of work.[2]

Although I cannot document this I have the impression that thirty years ago economists spent more time considering their results from various angles, 'kicking tyres' so to speak, than they do now. As Sheila Dow (1985, p. 14) points out, the type of thinking whose ideal is axiomization is not the only valid mode of thought. There is an alternative mode that prefers 'to employ several strands of argument which have different starting points and which, in a successful theory, reinforce each other.' That type of thinking seems less common now.

So much for generalities. To document my argument requires examples. Hence, the next section provides several brief examples of the principle of the strongest link, and the subsequent section considers in more detail a single example, time inconsistency theory as applied to monetary policy. Chapters 7 and 8 deal with another example, new classical theory. In Chapters 9 and 10 I provide additional examples in connection with modelling and econometrics. These examples do not, of course, show that economists *always* reason according to the principle of the strongest link. Such a claim would be silly. What I do claim is that this principle does show up often enough to seriously distort economic analysis.

SOME EXAMPLES

One way in which the principle of the strongest link frequently biases research is when a paper demonstrates that some puzzling phenomenon, say credit rationing, can be explained by some factor, say asymmetric information. Having rigorously shown that asymmetric information provides an incentive to ration credit, the paper then claims to have explained why credit is rationed. But this is a big leap of faith. Although the model explains why *some* credit rationing occurs, this reason for credit rationing may account for only a small percentage of the observed amount of credit rationing. But with the wondrous display of pyrotechnics in the step that relates asymmetric information to credit rationing, the step needed to go from *an* explanation to *the* explanation is easily forgotten.

My point is not that such a paper is of little or no use. It may be highly useful. Nor is it that authors of such papers should try to do better – perhaps one cannot determine how important asymmetric information is for credit rationing. All that it may be feasible to establish is a possibility argument, that is an argument showing that much credit rationing could be due to that type of asymmetric information. Rather my purpose is to point out two things. First, the seeming precision of the model gives a quite misleading impression of what it actually accomplishes. Second, reallocating some effort from the refinement of the model to a discussion of how important this particular explanation is relative to other explanations may well improve our understanding. It might require adding some steps that are far from precise. That is hardly ideal, but it is better than passing these problems by in discreet silence, as is often done for fear of polluting a seemingly precise argument by explicating some less precise steps. The rigour of a paper is all too often judged by what is explicit in it, and not at all by what it leaves implicit.

The second example comes from the debate about monetary policy. As discussed in Chapter 3 monetarists advocate stable monetary growth, both because they doubt that the central bank has the requisite knowledge for a successful stabilization policy, and because, along public-choice theory lines, they distrust its motives. Keynesians have pointed out that there exists a discretionary policy that is better, or at least as good, as a monetary rule. That they can show rigorously (see Goldfeld, 1982). But they cannot show rigorously that the monetarist conjecture about central bank behaviour is wrong, so they just ignore it.

Baumol's (1952) classic paper on the transactions demand for money furnishes another example. In the first part of this elegant paper Baumol, using only elementary calculus, develops a square root rule for the demand for money; that is, that the income elasticity of the transactions demand for money is 0.5, and that the interest elasticity is –0.5. These remarkable results are widely cited. But to obtain them Baumol had to assume that all payments are received not in the form of money, but as bonds, and also that brokerage costs are strictly proportional to the volume of transactions. Hence, in the second part of his paper he presents another model that does not make these extreme assumptions. In this more realistic model, the square root rule does not hold. Subsequently Karl Brunner and Alan Meltzer (1967) showed that in the second, more realistic model the departure from the square-root rule is very substantial. But since the conclusions of this second model are not as elegant as those of the first model it is often ignored, and Baumol is cited as having shown that the interest elasticity of the transactions demand for money is –0.5. Thus several textbooks present Baumol's square-root model without stating the assumptions and warning students that this is a special and unrealistic case (see for instance Hall and Taylor, 1991; Jaffe, 1989; Dornbusch and Fischer, 1990).

Moreover, even empirically oriented discussions of the interest elasticity of the transactions demand for money usually deal with the Baumol model, the closely related Tobin (1956) model or their derivatives, such as the Miller–Orr (1966) model. Yet there is another source of the interest elasticity of the transactions demand for money that is mentioned only rarely. This is that banks often require business borrowers to keep compensating balances, that is demand deposits on which they earn no explicit interest. At least for large firms, the amount they are required to keep is a negative function of the interest rate, with the interest elasticity under certain conditions being minus one.[3] This institutional detail could well be a more important source of the observed interest elasticity of the demand for money than are the factors dealt with in the Baumol–Tobin-type models. But it has received almost no discussion, presumably because it does not lend itself to sophisticated modelling.

An additional example is the choice of a monetary policy target. In a seminal paper William Poole (1970) compared a policy of targeting the money stock with one of targeting the interest rate and showed that, under certain conditions, the Federal Reserve should target the money stock if the unpredictable shocks are greater for the IS curve than for the LM curve, while in the opposite case it should target the interest rate. In the extensive and highly sophisticated literature that grew from this paper many economists blamed the Fed for not following this rule, and for targeting the interest rate when it should be targeting the money supply. That soon became a major, if not *the* major criticism of the Fed. But what was more important is a much simpler point that does not lend itself to formal analysis. This is that the Fed was not targeting the interest rate in the sense of setting it at the level appropriate for stabilizing GNP. Instead, it was trying to hold the interest rate more or less stable at its prevailing level, whatever that happened to be, instead of setting it at the level required to attain its GNP target. Although there was much evidence for this simple point, it took a long time until the confusion between stabilizing the interest rate and targeting the interest rate was appreciated. In the meantime, by focusing the discussion on the choice between targeting money or interest rates, economists distracted attention from what the Fed was actually doing, and hence failed to criticize monetary policy on the right grounds.

Here is a more recent example. Matthew Shapiro (1987) presents a test of the relative importance of cyclical demand and supply shocks to productivity. He develops his theoretical analysis in a rigorous manner. But in his empirical test he uses as his dependent variable residuals from a production function. Even though it is well known that residuals may be sensitive to some of the more or less arbitrary specifications of the function that has been fitted, Shapiro does not mention whether he undertook sensitivity tests to see if his results hold up when a slightly different function is used.

A further example is the use of Granger tests of money-income causality to evaluate the monetarist hypothesis that money causes income. There has been much debate about subtle and complex issues that may invalidate Granger tests. This discussion has ignored a simple point – many monetarists do not deny that changes in income often cause changes in the money supply. Indeed, they strongly criticize the central bank for accommodating changes in the demand for money as income changes. They just claim that at certain times, when the central bank steps sharply on the brake (or the accelerator), it generates a recession (or inflation), and that prolonged changes in the price level cannot occur unless accompanied by corresponding changes in the money supply. Hence, Granger tests should not be used either to criticize or to defend monetarism.

Still another example is Richard Todd's (1990) VAR test of the quantity theory. In discussing whether his monthly or his quarterly models are more reliable he points out that the monthly models are based on less reliable data than the quarterly models, but that the quarterly models suffer more from aggregation bias. The error that results from the use of less reliable monthly data cannot be estimated, but Todd did estimate the error due to aggregation bias. He then concludes:

> A precise and well-known effect, temporal aggregation, seems to be able to account for most of the differences between monthly and quarterly models. The corresponding effects of data measurement errors are not well understood in this context and have not been explicitly modeled. Therefore I conclude that the quarterly models' evidence against Sims is suspect ... (Todd, 1990, p. 33).

In other words, what cannot be modelled and measured is ipso facto of little importance and can be ignored!

Meanwhile in microeconomics, Franklin Fisher (1989, p. 123) concludes his survey of application of game theory to industrial organization as follows:

> There is a strong tendency for even the best practitioners to concentrate on analytically interesting questions rather than on the ones that really matter for the study of real-life industries. The result is often a perfectly fascinating piece of analysis. But as long as that tendency continues, those analyses will remain merely games that economists play.

TIME INCONSISTENCY AND MONETARY POLICY

In recent years the traditional arguments for eliminating central bank discretion, i.e. long and variable lags, forecast errors, and the central bank's self-interested behaviour, have been pushed aside by a new literature that applies time inconsistency theory to the choice between monetary rules and discretion. Using game theory, it has replaced vague and discursive discussions with precise modelling. As Stanley Fischer (1990, pp. 1169 and 1181) remarks, it 'completely changed the debate. ... The pre-1977 arguments ... lacked any convincing demonstration that rules might systematically be better than discretion.' Similarly, David Papell (1989, p. 1106) wrote that as a result of the work on time inconsistency, 'the proposition that monetary policy should be conducted according to a rule has achieved widespread acceptance.'

What is remarkable about this turn in monetary policy discussions is that it took place without any evidence that the previously discussed problems with discretionary policy are less important than time inconsistency, and indeed without any evidence that time inconsistency matters empirically. Time inconsistency became the central issue because it allows precise modelling of *some* of the steps in the case for a monetary rule. This prime example of the principle of the strongest link shows how the use of game theory can add an illusion of rigorous scientific truth.

Essentially the time inconsistency case for a monetary rule is that the central bank has an incentive to trick agents into expanding output beyond what is optimal for them individually, because higher employment and output have the positive externalities of greater tax revenues and reduced welfare-type expenditures. Hence the central bank generates inflation to fool agents into overestimating their real wages and therefore increasing work effort. (In another version the central bank generates inflation to counter the nominal wage stickiness that generates unemployment.) The central bank balances at the margin the benefits from this increased output with the loss from a higher inflation rate.

But this policy does not work in the long run as expectations adjust. Since the central bank knows this, it may seem as though it would not play this game. But even a policy that does not try to fool agents may generate inflation. Suppose that the central bank cannot convincingly signal its intentions. If agents believe that it is trying to fool them into increasing output they will raise wages and prices. With inflation thus being unavoidable the central bank realizes that it might as well adopt a policy that is expansionary enough to generate high employment at this inflation rate. One can, of course, also tell a story with a different outcome: the central bank may be able to signal its anti-inflationary stance, and thus prevent agents from raising wages and prices. There are numerous game-theoretic models that analyse the various potential outcomes (see Blackburn and Christensen, 1989).

This time inconsistency literature has made little contribution to empirical science economics because it has not paid sufficient attention to the empirical evidence. It has simply assumed that the central bank has an inflationary bias. But Fed policy was not inflationary from the end of the World War I inflation to the 1930s. It was then, on the whole, deflationary in the 1930s. Following the war-related inflation of the 1940s, it was, except for the Korean War period, essentially not inflationary until the mid-1960s. (From the first quarter of 1954 to the first quarter 1965, the mean annual inflation rate was 2.1 per cent for the GNP deflator, and only 1.4 per cent for the consumers' price index.) The subsequent period of high inflation unconnected with a

major war is unique in American history. Whether since then the Fed
has been too inflationary, or has tried to reduce the inflation rate too
fast, is open to debate.[4] And as Stanley Fischer (1990, p. 1173n) points
out, the long-term historical record for Britain, Germany and Switzer-
land also shows that 'inflation is only a sometime thing'.

One might argue that this record *suggests* that the Fed has an inflationary bias, but one might also argue that the secular inflation in the
United States since World War II could be due to unbiased errors in
monetary policy in a world in which excess demand leads to inflation,
and insufficient demand to falling output rather than to falling prices.
Whether this is a plausible story or not does not matter for my purpose.
All that matters is that, in acting as though an inflationary bias by the
central bank were a well established fact, the time inconsistency literature has, in accordance with the principle of the strongest link,
combined rigorous game-theoretic analysis with a well known theorem by Arm-waver.

Moreover, suppose that there is an inflationary bias. Why attribute
that to the central bank wanting to raise output above the agents'
equilibrium level to the socially optimal level? Why is this a better
explanation than political pressures? Is there any reason except for the
urge to settle for the most technically complex explanation that is
available?[5]

All that the extensive literature on the time inconsistency of monetary policy has contributed to empirical science ·economics is that a
central bank *might* aim at too high a level of output, and that, as we
know from the Phillips-curve literature, this would lead to higher
inflation instead of higher output, and also that the central bank's
credibility, and hence its independence, matters. These are certainly
things worth knowing. But they could have been established by a brief
verbal discussion, with almost no loss in the probability of obtaining
the correct conclusion. And the time saved by not building game-
theoretic models could then have been used to see whether time inconsistency actually plays a significant role in central bank policy and in
inflations. Introducing such messy empirical issues would lead to results
that are far less precise than those of the current game-theoretic discussions, but they would provide much more reliable answers to the
questions whether central bank discretion is desirable, and what explains
observed inflations.

CONCLUSION

In previous chapters I have argued that economists have a bias towards excessive formalization. In this chapter I have shown that one form this bias takes is to lavish tender loving care on those steps of the argument that are rigorous, while paying little attention to the other steps. Such a distortion of research effort is just one of the problems that arises when formalist criteria are allowed to invade what should be the domain of empirical science economics. The next chapter discusses others.

NOTES

1. One reason for this is simply a matter of arithmetic. Suppose that an argument consists of three steps with independent probabilities, step A with a probability of 0.98, step B with a probability of 0.95, and step C with a probability of 0.90. Raising the probability of step A by one percentage point to 0.99 raises the joint probability of A, B and C from 0.8379 to 0.8464, that is by 1.01 per cent of the joint probability in the original case. By contrast, raising the probability of step C by one point raises the joint probability by somewhat more, 1.11 per cent. This difference becomes more pronounced the lower is the probability of step C. If it is only 0.70 instead of 0.90, then a one percentage point enhancement of the probabilities at step C raises the joint probability from 0.6517 to 0.6610, a 1.43 per cent increase, while raising the probability of step A by one percentage point results in only a 1.03 per cent increase.

2. Another, though probably unimportant possibility, is that if papers require more effort, then foundations will provide more support for economic research as applicants ask for more time off from teaching. But unless the supply curve of grants is infinitely elastic larger grants will not offset all the increased time required for formalism. It is, however, possible that increased use of formalism shifts the supply curve outward by impressing granting agencies with the 'scientific' nature of economics. But by fostering abstract research that is not appealing to foundations, formalism may also shift the supply curve inward. That seems more likely.

3. At least for large firms, banks multiply the firm's deposit by the Treasury bill rate to calculate the free services to which the firm is entitled. For firms that need at least that amount of bank services and do not want to pay for them directly, the interest elasticity of the demand for money is minus unity.

4. This failure of the time inconsistency hypothesis to predict the behaviour of prices cannot be ascribed to the Fed being constrained by balance-of-payments considerations, since the results are essentially the same if one looks only at periods in which there was no balance-of-payments constraint (see Mayer, 1991, Appendix B). David Romer (1991) has tried to provide empirical support for the time inconsistency of monetary policy. He tests a prediction he derived from this hypothesis: that there is a negative correlation between an economy's openness and its inflation rate, because the benefit of unanticipated inflation is less the more open the economy. But this negative correlation is also consistent with just about any reasonable theory about why countries choose a particular inflation rate, and hence provides no reason to accept the time inconsistency theory.

5. Almost verbatim records of FOMC meetings are available until early 1976. The level of discussion makes it most unlikely that the FOMC took account of anything as subtle as the distinction between the optimal output levels for agents and for society.

6.   Other Types of Damage

As a mathematical discipline travels far from its empirical source, or still more, if it is a second or third generation only indirectly inspired by ideas coming from 'reality', it is beset with grave dangers. It becomes more and more purely aestheticizing, more and more purely *l'art pour l'art*. This need not be bad if the field is surrounded by correlated subjects, which still have close empirical connections, or if the disciple is under the influence of men with an exceptionally well developed taste. But there is a grave danger that the subject will develop along the line of least resistance, that the stream, so far from its source, will separate into a multitude of insignificant branches. ... In other words, at a great distance from its empirical source, or after much 'abstract' inbreeding, a mathematical subject is in danger of degeneration (John von Neumann, cited in Dore, Chakravarty and Goodwin, 1989, p. xiv).

The harm done by the principle of the strongest link is not the only damage that results from confounding formalist and empirical science economics. This chapter describes several other types of damage.

SPURIOUS AND UNNECESSARY CLAIMS FOR PRECISION

One result of applying a formalist mind-set to empirical science economics is that empirical science economists try to lay claim to a degree of precision that is both unnecessary and unrealistic. If precision were indeed the hallmark of science, then evolution and cosmology would be bad science, and creationism would be good science. Cosmologists estimate the universe to be ten to twenty billion years old. A creationist, Archbishop Ussher, dated it more precisely: 4004 BC!

As Sir Karl Popper (1962, vol. 2, pp. 19–20) tells us:

In science ... we are always conscious that our terms are a little vague (since we have learned to use them only in practical applications) and we reach precision not by reducing their penumbra of vagueness, but rather by keeping well within it, by carefully phrasing our sentences in such a way that the possible shades of meaning of our term do not matter. ... The view that the precision of science and of scientific language depends upon the precision of its terms is certainly very plausible, but none the less, I believe, a mere prejudice. ... In physical measurements, for instance, we always take care to consider the range within which there may be an error; and precision does not consist in trying to reduce this range to nothing, or in pretending that there is no such range, but rather in its explicit recognition.

Another leading philosopher, Paul Feyerabend (1989, p. 117), characteristically took an even stronger stand:

We must not attach too great an importance to 'what we mean' by a phrase, and we must be prepared to change whatever little we have said concerning this meaning as soon as the need arises. Too great concern with meanings can lead only to dogmatism and sterility. Flexibility and even sloppiness in semantic matters is a prerequisite of scientific progress.

The unrealistic element in our drive for precision shows up most clearly in the way we usually present empirical results. Elementary arithmetic provides rules about the number of significant digits to which results should be expressed. But in the pursuit of alleged precision we usually express our results to more significant digits than that (see Kamarck, 1983, Technical Appendix). Perhaps the most discouraging experience I have had in economics was in some seminars I gave in the late 1960s or early 1970s on tests of the permanent income theory, in which I used a 'prediction coefficient', defined as $(MP-A)/(MM-A)$, where A, MM and MP were respectively the average propensity to consume, and the marginal propensities to consume out of measured income and permanent income. Given the errors that result when one divides one small residual by another small residual, both of which are estimates from data subject to sampling and other errors, I measured the prediction coefficient to only one significant figure. I was much criticized for being vague.

Does it matter that we express our results with spurious precision? After all, we economists all know when we read about an MPC of 0.7854, that this figure is not correct to the fourth place of decimals, and non-economists do not pay much attention to econometric results in any case. Yes, it does matter. First, we are sometimes taken in by spurious precision. Thus we sometimes claim success for our hypothesis because its standard error is slightly lower than that of its rivals, without investigating whether the data are precise enough, and the techniques robust enough, for such a small difference to matter. Second, spurious precision is bad for the soul; a mind-set that permits the sacrifice of truth in one way encourages sacrificing it also in other ways.

DON'T JUST STAND THERE
AND DESCRIBE, THEORIZE

The formalist is commanded by Science (with a big S) to search for high-level laws that link lower-level hypotheses, or else to derive lower-level hypotheses from higher-level ones. Yes, somewhere in the background there should probably be some observations, or stylized facts, but they belong in the background where dunces may want to play with them, or even generate them. But for minds as good as thine and mine theory is worthy, observations are not.[1]

This is a tenet of formalism that economists have taken up with great enthusiasm. As Alice Rivlin (1975, p. 4) stated in her Ely lecture: 'Disdain for data collection is built into the value and reward structure of our profession. Ingenious efforts to tease bits of evidence from unsuitable data are much applauded; designing instruments for collecting more appropriate information is generally considered hack work.' Similarly, James Bonnen (1975, p. 761) noted in his presidential address to the American Agricultural Economics Association that: 'Agricultural economists have a tradition of inquiry that prevents innocence of the empirical. Even we, however, are increasingly failing in individual and institutional research to do the hard, unglamorous slogging in data collection that often is the most productive of new knowledge.'

The typical academic economist's disparaging view of those who bother to make observations is due partly to his or her orientation towards mathematics rather than empirical science. He or she feels less like a scientist when gathering data, or thinking about data, than when doing the mathematics of a paper. Some reading in the history of the empirical sciences would quickly dispel that view. Moreover, since we treat the gathering of data as a less scientific activity, we do not teach it in our graduate programmes. As a result, students absorb the naive belief that making observations and gathering data are simple-minded activities that anyone who has enough patience (that is a low enough marginal productivity of time) can do as well as anybody else. Thus they never learn that developing a framework for data gathering or drawing up good questionnaires are demanding skills. Economists are in this respect in a low-level equilibrium trap. Until they realize that making good observations is a demanding task it will not be part of our graduate programmes, and until it is economists will not learn it, and hence find out that it is not a task for simpletons. (Change 'demanding skill' to 'useful skill', and you have the situation that for a long time retarded the growth of mathematical economics.)

As already discussed in Chapter 3, natural scientists take a different view of observations and of those who gather them. Norbert Wiener (1964, p. 90) wrote: 'Very few econometricians are aware that if they are to imitate the procedure of modern physics and not its mere appearances, a mathematical economics must begin with a critical account of these quantitative notions and the means adopted for collecting and measuring them.' Wiener may be wrong in referring to mathematical economics, but his criticism does apply to empirical science economics.

Such a dismissive attitude towards observations has several unfortunate results. One is the obvious point that too little effort is allocated to generating new data sets. Indeed data not readily available in one's data base may be ignored. Detailed scrutiny of data sometimes helps scientists to discover low-level hypotheses. Those who fear to be caught looking at data forego this useful technique. If graduate students spent some time looking at data, they might find dissertation topics sooner. Summers (1991) makes a cogent case for deriving hypotheses by looking at data rather than at textbooks in set theory.

Second, chasing after 'rigour' results in work that economists do not find all that convincing. Thus Summers (1991), after considering a wide variety of research projects, concludes that those that have changed economists' opinions have used simple theories and simple techniques.

[W]hile formal econometric work has had little impact on the growth of economic knowledge, I believe that any history of macroeconomics would have to give great weight to informal pragmatic empirical approaches to economic problems. I think of Friedman's (1957) and Modigliani and Brumberg's (1955) treatments of the consumption function as obvious examples. Other examples might include Friedman and Schwartz (1963), Solow (1957) and Denison (1967); Phillips (1958) whose empirical finding had profound if largely unanticipated effects; and the large body of work summarized in Fama (1970) on stochastic properties of speculative prices. ... [C]onsider two issues where today's macroeconomics textbooks present a radically different picture than did the macroeconomics textbooks of the 1960s – the long-run neutrality of inflation and the relative importance of monetary and fiscal policies in affecting economic behavior. Changes in opinion about inflation neutrality resulted from theoretical arguments about the implausibility of money illusion that became compelling when inflation increased and unemployment did not decline during the 1970s. Formal statistical tests contributed almost nothing. Surely, *A Monetary History of the United States* (1963) had a greater impact in highlighting the role of money than any particular econometric study or combination of studies. It was not based on a formal model, no structural parameters were estimated, and no sophisticated statistical techniques were employed. Instead, data were presented in a straightforward way, to buttress verbal theoretical arguments, and emphasis was placed on natural experiments in assessing direction of causality (Summers, 1991, pp. 130, 140).

Summers concludes that these examples of successful research have three characteristics in common: first, they address 'a stylized fact or a collection of stylized facts characterizing an aspect of how the world worked' (p. 140); second, the empirical work results in regularities that theory can explain; and third, there is no scientific pretence; one starts 'from a theoretical viewpoint, not a straightjacket' (p. 140).

Summers contrasts this type of work with the theoretically much more sophisticated work of Hansen and Singleton on estimating deep parameters:

They rely on new estimation techniques to build a bridge between a fully articulated stochastic theory and data. Given the dominant professional view of what constitutes high quality empirical work, it is easy to understand why their paper was awarded the Frisch medal. ... Hansen and Singleton have estimated the utility function parameters the importance of which Lucas stressed. Would anyone genuinely interested in predicting the effects of a tax cut make use of their estimates of representative consumers' utility functions? To my knowledge no one has used these estimates for this or any other purpose. It is not difficult to understand why. The uncertainties about the discount rate of the representative consumer upon which Hansen and Singleton's empirical work can potentially shed light are dwarfed by uncertainties about other nontaste variables. For example, many consumers may be unable to borrow. ... These consumers will spend all the proceeds of a tax cut. Others may lack the information processing skills necessary to distinguish the reasons for changes in their take-home pay. ... Still others may revise their expectations about future income. ... None of these uncertainties can be addressed by estimating the utility function of the representative consumer. Nor, I suspect, will anyone modify their view about the empirical importance of these considerations when and if someone gets a representative consumer model to fail to reject its overriding restrictions. I find it hard to escape the conclusion that Hansen and Singleton's work creates an art form for others to admire and emulate but provides us with little new knowledge (pp. 134, 136–7).

Last, but not least, serious errors can result from not paying enough attention to the quality and the meaning of the data. Leontief (1971, p. 3) rightly complained that:

> in all too many instances sophisticated statistical analysis is performed on a set of data whose exact meaning and validity are unknown to the author, or rather so well known to him that, at the very end he warns the reader not to take the material conclusions of the entire 'exercise' seriously. ... While the quality and coverage of official statistics has recently been permitted to deteriorate without eliciting determined protest on the part of their potential scientific users, masses of concrete, detailed information contained in technical journals, reports of engineering firms and private marketing organs are neglected.

Though better known as a theorist, Oskar Morgenstern (1963) wrote the classic indictment of the quality of our data that uncovered shocking errors. More recently Kamarck (1983), a former director of the World Bank's economics department, toured the dangerous wasteland we call economic data and discussed the horrors encountered therein. As he points out:

> [I]t is necessary to do systematic work on using the concepts of economic theory to specify what we want to measure: to investigate how closely the existing measures correspond to the concepts of theory; to determine whether, how and to what extent the concepts are measurable in the real world; and to establish what the consequences are for the theory and applied economics of the deviations between the measures that are or can be produced and what is required by existing theory (Kamarck, 1983, p. 118).

Zvi Griliches (1986, p. 1507), too, has warned us about the unreliability of our data, pointing out that the US trade deficit with Canada in 1982 'was either $12.8 or $7.9 billion depending on whether this number came from U.S. or Canadian publications.' As Cornelis Los (1986, p. 6) reminds us, 'most sciences have shown their greatest rate of improvement when the quality of their data improved. Kepler and Newton could make their highly successful inferences only after Tyhe Brache [sic] had painstakingly collected reams and reams of data.'

It is tempting to reply that there is nothing we can do, given the great expense of gathering data. But this response is totally invalid. First and foremost, if our data are not adequate for what we do with them, the correct response is not to shrug our shoulders and go on with the work, but to cease doing that work. The truth value of work based on inadequate data is not improved in some magic way by the fact that better data are not available.

Moreover, if our data are poor we should try to find out just how poor they are, and then warn the reader, something now done only rarely. Furthermore, if we let policy makers know how seriously the quality of our data may distort the advice they receive, perhaps we could get better data. In addition, we should develop some techniques for estimating how robust various econometric techniques are to data errors, and use primarily the more robust ones. Thus despite the problems created by a common trend, it *may* sometimes be better to regress the levels of the data rather than their first differences, because taking first differences can greatly exacerbate the influence of errors in the data.[2] In all of these ways a more serious attitude towards the data would improve economics.

WARPED POLICY ADVICE

The amount of space that journals devote to a topic is not, and should not be, proportional to its empirical importance. There is, however, the danger that those topics that are much discussed in the journals will play too large a role in the policy advice that economists give, because we naturally tend to confuse what is much discussed with what is important. This would be a problem even if research in empirical science economics were not unduly influenced by formalist criteria, but the large role that these criteria do play makes it worse. To the extent that the papers which journals publish on empirical science topics are selected, in part, because they are analytically 'sweet', certain ideas will be over-represented relative to their substantive importance. There is then the danger that those who advise policy makers interpret the large number of papers on such an idea as indicating that this idea is very important, and let it play too large a role in the advice they give. For example, economists advising on setting up the 'Euro-Fed' might pay too much attention to time inconsistency theory. Franklin Fischer (1989) gives examples of similar dangers from the application of game theory to industrial organization. Such a tendency need not be confined to economics; two military historians, Eliot Cohen and John Gooch (1991, p. 86), refer to what they call the '"55/95 problem" – the tendency to see that element of military difficulty that bulks largest (55 per cent of your problem) as the whole of it (95 per cent).'

In addition, theoretically 'uninteresting' problems receive insufficient attention from economists, and are relegated to the attention of those with little training in economics (see Bronfenbrenner, 1991).

DE-EMPHASIS OF CIRCUMSTANTIAL EVIDENCE

The formalist vision is that of a proof so compelling that no reasonable person can reject it. Fine and good, within the confines of formalist economics whose task it is to find truth that is akin to beauty. But empirical science is not built that way. Compelling proofs, in the form of crucial experiments, play only a subordinate role in empirical science. Thomas Kuhn (1977, pp. 327–8) tells us that:

> books and articles on the philosophy of science refer again and again to the famous crucial experiments. ... These experiments are paradigms of good reason for scientific choice; they illustrate the most effective of all sorts of arguments which could be available to a scientist uncertain which of two theories to follow ... . But they also have another characteristic in common. By the time they were performed no scientist still needed to be convinced of the validity of the theory their outcome is now used to demonstrate. Those decisions had long since been made on the basis of significantly more equivocal evidence. The exemplary crucial experiment ... provides needed economy to science pedagogy, but they scarcely illuminate the character of the choices that scientists are called upon to make.

Closer to home, McCloskey (1985) rightly points out that what persuades us economists is often something that does not conform to the rule of evidence that we consider 'scientific'. I suspect that the 1987 stock market crash persuaded more economists to reject efficient-market theory than did any single 'scientific' paper.

Yet journal referees, and perhaps readers too, judge empirical tests in economics by standards that are more or less appropriate to a crucial experiment.[3] Thus perhaps the most common reason an empirical paper is rejected is something along the following lines. The author shows that his or her hypothesis implies that a certain coefficient is positive, and then shows that this coefficient is indeed positive. The referee then points out that there is a rival hypothesis that also implies that this coefficient is positive. Hence, the coefficient being positive does not confirm the author's hypothesis.

This is an entirely valid reason for concluding that the paper does not provide compelling evidence for the hypothesis, but it does not necessarily mean that it is of little worth. It may still be worth publishing, because it provides useful circumstantial evidence. Suppose that the rival hypothesis is an implausible one, with a probability of, say, only 10 per cent. If so, the author's evidence, while not conclusive, is still persuasive in establishing a high degree of plausibility for the hypothesis.

Similarly, the convention that coefficients must be significant at the 5 per cent level, or at the very least at the 10 per cent level, *may* be too constrictive and pretentious. As McCloskey (1985, Chapter 9) points out, we should think about the appropriate loss function for Type I and Type II errors. Besides, how many readers of an applied econometrics paper really believe that the probability that its results are correct is 95 per cent, or even 90 per cent? Moreover, suppose that, say, six economists working independently with entirely different data sets all find that the coefficient is significant (with the right sign) only at the 20 per cent level. Surely valuable information is lost if none of these five papers is published. One need not go all the way with Ward's (1972) argument that economics should model itself on law rather than on the natural sciences, to conclude that in economics too, circumstantial evidence can be valuable.

The insistence on strong evidence means that economists disregard available information on issues on which strong evidence cannot be obtained. For example, about 70 per cent of US corporations value inventories on a FIFO (first in – first out) basis, even though this generally raises their tax burden. Although valuing inventories on the alternative LIFO basis is more complex, this does not seem a plausible explanation for the prevalence of FIFO. Another explanation is that switching to LIFO would reduce reported pre-tax profits, even though it raises actual after-tax profits. This explanation, if correct, would have an important implication since it is inconsistent with the efficient market story we usually tell. Hence it is worth investigating. Suppose that this cannot be done with the standard econometric tools, but can only be done by seeking the opinion of business managers. Suppose that such a study points to the reduction of reported pre-tax profits as the explanation for the use of FIFO. Suppose further that the degree of credence one should give to such survey evidence is only 70 per cent. It would still provide useful information on market efficiency. By itself it would not be enough to reject the efficient market hypothesis, but in the presence of other weak disconfirming evidence it might be enough to tip the balance. Yet most journals would probably reject a paper based on such survey evidence.

FORMALISM AND THE LOSS OF INSIGHT

Woo (1986, Chapter 3) argues that a theory starts out as a 'coarse structure' which embodies a particular insight. It then goes through a stage in which it is related to the empirical evidence. If it survives, it passes to a stage of axiomization, in which it becomes fossilized as it loses much of the insight that it had originally. Woo believes that economic theory is in that third stage. As a result, there is a big gap between the sophistication of high theory and the naive theories used in empirical work (Woo, 1986, p. 96). This is a hypothesis that historians of economic thought and specialists in the history of other sciences should test.

FORMALIST CRITERIA AND
EFFECTIVE COMMUNICATION

Formalist criteria also interfere with the effective spread of empirical science economics in several other respects. One is that in some ways formalism hinders the winnowing out of invalid hypotheses. By drawing the readers' attention to the technical aspects of the paper, it reduces the attention paid to the often more questionable less technical aspects. If a paper presents a simple story, it is often easier to notice if a critical aspect of the problem has been omitted. It is usually much harder to notice such an omission if one is given no 'story', but just a deluge of algebra. Thus in refereeing papers I usually read the paper twice, first very rapidly, skipping the technical apparatus, and then more carefully. In roughly half the cases where I detect a serious flaw it is in the first, rapid, reading. I suspect that in empirical science economics it is, on the whole, more dangerous to accept a hypothesis for which one has not been given the intuition than one for which one has not been given the algebra.

Another way in which the focus on formalist criteria protects a paper from criticism is by making it more time-consuming, and hence more costly, to write a critical comment on it. It is not just a matter of forcing one's way through the barbed wire entanglement of mathematical notation. The flaw in the paper may be simple and obvious. But to meet the critical standards of the journal a comment usually has to be presented in formal dress, and hence takes much time to write. I sometimes refrain from writing comments on a paper that seems to contain a simple, but fatal error. Although my point may be straightforward and could be presented in a paragraph or two, adding the elaborations required by the journal would take much time.

Formalism also inhibits communication by excluding from the discourse those who are stymied by the mathematics. The facile reply, that this is their own fault, that they should learn more maths, will not do, because it does not matter whose fault it is. Producers of research should, within obvious constraints, provide what the consumer wants. Learning maths, like anything else, is not costless. Moreover, even for those who can follow the analysis, unnecessary formalist decorations often make for slow reading, thus wasting time readers could use to study other papers.

As I shall discuss in Chapter 11, excessive formalism also degrades a particular type of communication, graduate education. Moreover, the failure to distinguish between formalist and empirical science economics can make it difficult for economists to clarify their message. The next two chapters illustrate this with the debate about new classical theory.

CONCLUSION

Adherence to the principle of the strongest link is not the only way in which the misapplication of a formalist mind-set distorts empirical science economics. It induces us to work on problems that are difficult rather than important, and warps what we tell policy makers. Misleading claims for precision abound, while the search for data and concern about their reliability are disparaged as unworthy of a 'scientific mind'. Much potential information is lost because it cannot be dressed up in the white coat of 'Science'. All this in the name of science.

NOTES

1. A leading theorist of the last generation, Abba Lerner, who then held a fellowship in empirical economics, once walked into an office which he shared with a colleague. When he saw his colleague working with data, he said: 'Ugh, data', and walked out.

2. Suppose, for example, that a certain variable is measured as 100 in the first quarter, 102 in the second quarter, and 103 in the third quarter. Suppose further that, while the first and third quarter figures are correct, the second quarter figure should have been 101 instead of 102, a small percentage difference. The correct first differences are then 1 and 2 instead of 2 and 1, a substantial percentage difference. All this is obvious, but that is no reason to disregard it.

3. I say 'more or less' since a 5 per cent significance level is not consonant with a crucial experiment.

7. New Classical Theory – General Characteristics

The new classical coup d'état is a striking attempt to impose a formalist regime on what was previously largely an empirical science domain. It is what Blinder (1988b, p. 278) has called a 'triumph of a priori theorizing over empiricism'. Since the new classicals do not acknowledge that their opponents use different criteria, and implicitly claim to do 'good economics, period', their claims have generated much puzzlement and confusion. If my distinction between formalist economics and empirical science economics is valid it should have something useful to say about that debate. And I should be able to show that the new classicals have failed to bridge the gap between formalist and empirical science economics; that as far as the latter is concerned, their seeming rigour is largely an illusion based on the principle of the strongest link. Since I am primarily concerned with the new classicals' methodology and not with evaluating new classical theory per se, I will take up only a few components of this theory that I need to illustrate my argument and will focus essentially on methodological rather than substantive issues.

Much, though certainly not all, of the debate about new classical theory is grounded in a disagreement about what is an acceptable style of argument. This has been concealed by the dramatics of the policy invariance proposition that has drawn so much attention. While to many economists this proposition is the essence of new classical economics, it is much less important to the new classicals themselves.[1] Thus Lucas and Sargent (n.d., p. 69n) point out that Sargent and Wallace derived the policy ineffectiveness proposition

> in the context of a standard macroeconomic model, but with agents' expectations assumed rational. ... The point of this example was to show that within *precisely* that model used to motivate reactive monetary policies, such policies could be shown to be of no value. It hardly follows that *all* policy is ineffective in *all* contexts (p. 69n, italics in original).

Moreover, Sargent (in Klamer, 1984, p. 70) stated: 'most of my recent work wouldn't have any reason for existing if I took the neutrality proposition seriously.' Similarly, Robert Townsend (in Klamer, 1984, p. 845) remarks that, 'One can write down explicit dynamic models that allow for uncertainty and include rational expectations, but produce the result that money matters.'

Instead of the policy invariance proposition, the new classicals themselves stress a basic methodological feature of their work: their insistence on the formal derivation of propositions. Thus, in summarizing his interviews with new classical economists and with their critics, Klamer (1984, p. 239, 245) concludes:

> [T]he main disagreement may well be not what to say, but on how to say it; if so, the distinctive claim of new classical economists would concern style, not substance. ... [The new classicals] seem to imply that precision is the foremost standard of scientific arguments. ...

An insistence on formal derivations is not all that unusual in microeconomics, but it was unusual in the context of macroeconomics. Much of the new classical debate is therefore a debate about the technical rigour that should be required in macroeconomics. What divides macroeconomists is not whether macroeconomics needs microeconomic foundations, but the thoroughness with which these microfoundations should be explicated. Can one simply rely on a plausible, but vague statement that a particular macroeconomic proposition, say a declining marginal propensity to consume, is consistent with agents maximizing their utilities, or does it have to be derived formally from a utility-maximizing model? Long before the rise of new classical economics it was generally agreed that macroeconomic propositions need *some* microeconomic foundations – I remember teaching this in the late 1950s. But what I, and presumably others, meant by this was just that one should ensure in a common-sense way, that what one said about the behaviour of agents in a macroeconomics class is consistent with what one might say in a microeconomics class. It did not imply, as new classicals now insist, that all macroeconomic propositions have to be formally derived from a strict utility-maximizing model that makes no allowance for systematic human error and foibles. It is just such adulteration of logic with common sense, with casual observations and with merely suggestive empirical evidence that new classical economists want to replace with what they consider 'serious economics'.

Is this a reasonable endeavour? Or is it an example of excessive ambition and hubris? I will argue that to undertake empirical science economics, which is what macroeconomics has traditionally attempted, with the rigour that it rightly demanded of formalist economics does show hubris, and that the new classicals' claim of success is based on the principle of the strongest link. In this chapter I consider the new classical methodology as a whole before taking up specific new classical hypotheses in the next chapter. I start with three features of new classical theory: its claim to rigour and the hubris that this claim involves; its aesthetic; and its treatment of the realism of assumptions.

HUBRIS

A salient characteristic of new classical economists is the elan with which they press their claims. They frame the debate as a dispute between the enlightened few who believe that arguments should be rigorous versus primitives who do not care about rigour, between those who 'take economics seriously' and those who do not. Thus new classicals tend to characterize casual reasoning as mere 'coffee-break conversation' that has no place in the brave new world of 'serious economics'. What hubris! While it is true that many 'old-fashioned' economists are incapable of working out a rigorous model, others can do so. If they do not, it is because they are more aware of the distinction between formalist science and empirical science. Being less in the thrall of the principle of the strongest link, they spread their efforts more evenly across the various links in the chain of their argument. And some of these links neither they – nor the new classicals – can discuss in a rigorous manner. If nothing except casual evidence is available, those with an empirical science orientation use it in the absence of anything better; those with a formalist orientation add an axiom to their model.

But the new classical hubris is not just a matter of rejecting casual evidence. New classicals also reject as ad hocery anything, such as wage and price stickiness, that may be observed, but that does not fit into their own microeconomic theory. In doing so, they assume that their microtheory contains everything worth knowing about the economy, that whatever their theory does not explain, ipso facto, does not matter. This is an appropriate procedure in formalist science, but not in empirical science, and amounts to taking economic theory, but not the economy itself, seriously. Even physics has to allow for what we do not yet understand. As Hoover (1988, p. 60) points out, if what we cannot explain does not exist, then 'we would all be able to fly because physicists do not fully understand gravity'. New classicals remind me of a ditty about the great classics scholar and Master of Balliol College, Benjamin Jowett:

> I come first, my name is Jowett
> There's no knowledge, but I know it
> I am Master of this college,
> What I don't know isn't knowledge.

The hubris that lurks behind the new classicals' conviction that economics can dispense with casual evidence becomes clearer when one considers how the empirical sciences have evolved. One need not agree with Feyerabend (1975) that in science just about 'anything goes', to wonder what would have happened to the natural sciences had they accepted the new classicals' austere and demanding methodology when they were at a stage of development similar to where economics is now. As developed by Darwin the theory of evolution lacked a basic step, and not until Mendelian genetics came to its rescue was it completed. Relativity theory and quantum mechanics are known to be inconsistent. Yet physicists use both (Hawking, 1988). Feyerabend (1975) provides numerous other examples.

The new classicals' hubris also shows up in the extreme wording of their claims. Thus Sargent and Wallace (1976, p. 169) declared that: 'There is no longer any serious debate about whether monetary policy should be conducted according to rules or discretion.' Lucas and Sargent (n.d., pp. 49–50), in discussing the predictions made by Keynesians in the 1970s, wrote:

> That these predictions were wildly incorrect, and that the doctrine on which they were based is fundamentally flawed, are now simple matters of fact, involving no novelties in economic theory. The task which faces contemporary students of the business cycle is that of sorting through the wreckage, determining which features of that remarkable intellectual event called the Keynesian Revolution can be salvaged and put to good use, and which others must be discarded.

New classicals are prone to extreme claims, not only for the success of their substantive work, but also for their methods. Thus, on the importance of mathematical modelling Sargent (in Klamer, 1984, p. 77) proclaimed victory:

> The controversy about these things is over. ... I am talking about what young people are working on. That's the tip off. Look at what assistant professors are working on at the best places. ... Schumpeter and other people have said that the revolutions in science are brought about by young men. ...

This is hardly a compelling argument. As discussed in Chapter 2, the invisible hand that guides academic research is shaky. Furthermore, as described in Chapter 1, Klamer and Colander's interviews with graduate students show much dissatisfaction with the prevailing mathematization of economics. It may be more a realization of what pays off in professional stature than a conviction about the scientific superiority of formal modelling that induces young economists to model, model and model.[2]

Not all new classicals are as hubristic as appears from their previously cited claims of victory and their implicit assumption that they know all they need to know about microeconomics. To accuse all new classicals of over-reaching would itself be over-reaching. Thus Patrick Minford (1991, p. 262) wrote that:

> there are horses for courses. The New Classical methodology is a powerful new tool kit for attacking theoretical issues – institutions (why is money/government debt used? what would a cash-less economy look like?) ... It has created a new industry and industry standard. It is the only theoretical game in town. What NC methodology is not (yet at least) is an alternative to normal applied economic analysis. This still has to be built around estimates we have – whether micro elasticities, or macro models of demand /supply/wages, etc. That horse is still best for the normal course.

I do not want to give the impression that hubris is entirely bad. It is not. It contributes to what are some of the most admirable characteristics of new classical theorists: an infectious enthusiasm, a dedication to the advancement of economics, and an obvious sense of mission that conveys the impression of a research programme on the move. One can only be thrilled when one reads statements such as Sargent's (in Klamer, 1984, p. 74): 'When you do research, the idea is that you don't produce a finished product. You produce an input. You write the paper with the hope that it will be superseded. It is not a success unless it is superseded.' No wonder that their work excites the young. And even the old! Recently, when reading in Lucas's text I found myself carried away by its rigour and elegance. This is what economics should be. I had to remind myself constantly of how much such neat formulations leave out. The new classicals' vision of what economics should be is noble. It is therefore not surprising that they 'occupy the high ground', and 'set the agenda for modern macroeconomics' (Hoover, 1990, p. 1). When I criticize them it is because I believe that their methodological programme is utopian at this stage of the development of economics, so that their intolerance of the string and sealing-wax devices that are needed for empirical science economics is ill-founded and is based on the principle of the strongest link. Such a judgement is entirely consistent with an admiration for the panache as well as for the expertise with which they undertake their task.

AESTHETICS

Scientific theories, and not just art and literature, have their aesthetics. It would be naive to argue that the acceptance of scientific theories depends solely on their 'truth', and hence is entirely a factual matter.[3] Thus Kuhn (1970, p. 158), in describing paradigm shifts, remarks:

> Something must make at least a few scientists feel that the new proposal is on the right track, and sometimes it is only personal and inarticulate aesthetic considerations that can do that. Men have been converted by them when most of the articulable technical arguments have pointed the other way. ...

To speak of the aesthetic of new classical theory is therefore not to derogate it or to deny its scientific status. Instead, if one builds a reasonable case for the aesthetic of new classical theory, one has gone a long way towards justifying it; of course, the opposite holds true too. I will discuss three characteristics of the new classical aesthetic: its emphasis on rigour; its focus on technique; and its downplaying of empirical tests. These three characteristics place it firmly in the formalist camp.

Rigour

New classical models pay much more attention to the formalist's dominating criterion, rigorous derivation, than most other macroeconomic models do, though Hahn (1983) argues that even so, they are not rigorous enough. In its quest for rigour new classical theory is less constrained by other considerations than is true of traditional macrotheory.

One of these constraints is expository simplicity. Certainly not all papers written by traditionalists (as from now on I shall call Keynesians and monetarists) are easy reading. Yet, by and large, they are much easier to read than are new classical papers. Such pedagogic simplicity should not be dismissed as mere catering to intellectual laziness. As discussed in Chapter 6, the easier it is to grasp an idea the easier it often is to see its faults as well as its virtues, and as Popper has taught us, theories should be easily falsifiable. Moreover, time is not a free good.

Another constraint that their aesthetics imposes on many traditionalists is that the story that accompanies a model should have some resonance with personal experience and casual observation. To be sure, Keynesians have their 'paradox of thrift', and Friedman stresses that surface plausibility is often an unreliable guide (Hirsch and de Marchi, 1990). All the same, traditionalists generally avoid stories that are clearly inconsistent with what we observe as participants in the economy. This acts as an informal and inchoate constraint on the models they build. By contrast, new classicals build some models of the labour market that assume a system of almost complete unemployment insurance. Similarly, they often think of wages as highly flexible. In sharp contrast to the informal and mostly tacit but important role that personal experience and introspection play in traditionalist thinking by limiting the hypotheses to be considered, new classicals look upon themselves more like disembodied technicians. Thus Willem Buiter (1989, pp. 8–9) has remarked that:

> Direct observation, introspection and common sense, as well as hundreds of empirical studies of market structure and consumer and firm behavior, should, however, suffice to reject ... [the new classical] tool kit. For some reason this has not happened (yet). The most plausible reason for this is the increasingly *self-referential* nature of much of modern economic analysis and by no means just the ... [new classical theory]. Models are judged and evaluated not in terms of their success in explaining or predicting real world behavior, but in terms of their internal consistency and the extent to which their construction and design is true to some *a priori* set of rules and characteristics. Disciplines develop according to their inner logic without reference to economic reality ... (italics in original).

Focus on Technique

A prominent component of the new classical aesthetic is its great emphasis on technique, something that fits in well with the formalist mind-set. Thus Lucas (1987, p. 35) tells us that 'technique is interesting to technicians (which is what we are if we are to be of any use to anyone.)' If technique is interpreted broadly enough to mean any specialized knowledge, then clearly, if we are to be of any use, we must be technicians. But the new classicals interpret the requirement for technique in a narrower way. Thus they would not consider someone who has little mathematical training, but is thoroughly familiar with the pricing practices of many industries, to be a good technician. But they would call a good technician someone with highly developed mathematical skills, and little knowledge of pricing practices or other institutional detail. It is by no means clear why we can only be useful if we are technicians in this peculiar sense of the term. Such a narrow emphasis on formal, mathematical technique, while it is certainly not confined to the new classicals, is not characteristic of most traditionalists. Thus Robert Solow (in Klamer, 1984, p. 143) complained about the new classical econometrics that:

> many of the empirical things that the [new classical] school has done strike me as unserious in the particular sense that the results are so fragile, so tied to particular sample periods, particular methods, and so on, that even the authors of the papers don't really tend to believe in their results. They are writing these papers to get across the message that it can be done technically; that's all.

Empirical Testing

An additional way the aesthetic of new classicals differs from that of traditionalists is in the role the new classicals assign to empirical tests. At least in principle, though much less so in practice, traditionalists attribute a dominant role to empirical tests, more specifically to goodness of fit. Not only must a model predict or retrodict well but, within broad constraints, one should choose the model that predicts best.

While new classicals agree that economics is a predictive science, they seem to be satisficers rather than maximizers with respect to prediction. Indeed, instead of fitting regressions, some rely on calibration which does not provide any standard test statistics.

Since predictive success is only one of the appropriate criteria for choosing among theories, in principle there is nothing wrong with satisficing rather than maximizing goodness of fit. But new classicals are satisficers who are easily satisfied. As long as the prediction of their model is not, in Sargent's (1976, p. 233) words, 'obscenely at variance with the data', they seem satisfied. Their model does not have to fit better than rival models. Indeed, despite their claim to being more rigorous than thou, new classicals often follow the common practice of not comparing the fit of their model to the fit of rival models. Nor do they set out what their criterion for an adequate fit is. In the calibration clan of the new classical tribe this approach is made explicit by Kydland and Prescott (1991, pp. 171, 174) when they write:

> The issue of how confident we are in the econometric answer is a subtle one which cannot be resolved by computing some measure of how well the model economy mimics historical data. The degree of confidence in the answer depends on the confidence that is placed in the economic theory being used. ... [T]he model economy which better fits the data is not the one used. Rather currently established theory dictates which one is used.

Even those new classicals who rely on estimation rather than on calibration seem to pay less attention than do traditionalists to predictive tests. One reason may be that they impose tighter limits on the models that they allow into the race. Traditionalists, too, impose constraints on the admitted models: models may not contain logical contradictions and, at least when aided by (limited) ad hoc fudge factors, they must be consistent with general economic theory. New classicals impose much narrower constraints on the horses that they allow into the race, since anything they consider an ad hoc fudge factor disqualifies a horse. With so many horses thus excluded, the race is less interesting. Second, and more generally, the new classicals' formalistic mind-set assigns a low priority to empirical testing. Put rather strongly, being able to pass empirical tests is merely frosting on the cake. It is rigorous derivation that matters. This is, of course, entirely appropriate for formalist theory, and as such new classical theory is an outstanding achievement. But that does not, as new classicals seem to think, make it a substitute for traditional macroeconomics.

TREATMENT OF ASSUMPTIONS

As already mentioned, many traditionalists are uneasy about assumptions (stories) that are sharply at variance with what we observe around us. By contrast, the new classicals, while requiring consistency with microeconomic theory, are willing to make strong assumptions about matters on which microtheory is silent. Those they treat as institutional details that are of little interest, and about which one can make totally ad hoc assumptions. Thus in overlapping-generation models they assume money is the only asset that the old can pass on to the young, and in some of their models the rich hold only bonds and the poor only money (Hoover, 1988, p. 126). They are not bothered by such ad hoc assumptions, but defend them as needed for tractability, and presumably also on the grounds of as-if methodology. If assuming that leaves want to grow on the sunny side of trees allows us to predict the position of leaves correctly, why not make this assumption?

Neither claim is convincing. First, constructing and solving a certain model may require a peculiar assumption. But is that an argument for making this assumption, or for not building that model? Again the distinction between empirical science economics and formalist economics is central. If a model is technically interesting a formalist economist prefers making a bizarre assumption to giving up the model. An empirical science economist prefers to abandon the model.

Second, to invoke Friedman's as-if methodology as a defence for some of the strange assumptions of new classical theory is to misinterpret that methodology totally because, as discussed in Chapter 4, it requires serious testing of predictions. Hence, if the new classicals want to defend their unrealistic assumptions as harmless because they lead to correct predictions, they have to pay much more attention to predictive tests.

For the assumptions about the behaviour of agents that are basic to microtheory, the situation is very different. Here it is the traditionalists who are more relaxed about their assumptions. Although they will usually not work with assumptions that are flagrantly at variance with microtheory, they do not insist that all assumptions agree precisely with simple microtheory. To them microtheory, with its assumption of rational income maximization, while it is a highly useful approximation, is just that, an approximation. Hence what may be a useful assumption for one problem may not be a good assumption when dealing with another problem (see Friedman, 1953). Besides, there are many versions of microtheory, e.g. the theory of competitive markets and the theory of monopolistic competition, that may have different implications.

The new classicals take a very different position. To them any assumption that diverges from the implications of an austere utility-maximizing model is anathema. Their ideal is to develop, not theories, but theorems. And theorems, unlike theories, are inflexible; there is no room for saying that what is a convenient way of thought at one level of abstraction is a less convenient way at another. Hence, a major charge they bring against traditionalist macroeconomics is that it is ad hoc.

AD HOCERY AND REDUCTIONISM

To dismiss traditional macrotheory as inferior to new classical theory because it is ad hoc, the new classicals must not only show that it is indeed ad hoc, but must also show that their own theory does not involve ad hocery that is just as bad, or even worse. To assess which theory suffers more from the fault of ad hocery, one must first see just what this fault is.

Two Types of Ad Hocery

Ad hocery has a very bad name. Some of this bad reputation is deserved, but some is due to a confusing terminology. Wade Hands (1988) distinguishes two meanings of the term. One, 'Popperian ad hocness' consists of protecting a hypothesis against empirical refutation by arbitrarily adding subsidiary hypotheses that immunize it against disconfirming evidence, without these subsidiary hypotheses themselves receiving any support from independent empirical evidence. Suppose, for example, that a theory predicts that the savings rate will fall. But instead of falling, it rises. One might try to salvage the theory by claiming that the savings rate would have fallen had it not been for a change in expectations, even though there is no evidence that expectations have actually changed. Popper rightly condemned such defensive manoeuvres.

Hands contrasts this way of using the term 'ad hoc' with one of the three ways in which another leading philosopher of science, Imre Lakatos, used it. To Lakatos a hypothesis needed to protect a theory is ad hoc if it does not grow naturally out of the main heuristic of that theory's research programme. Such ad hocness narrows a theory's scope. In this Lakatosian sense – but not in the Popperian sense – a hypothesis can be ad hoc even when there is much empirical evidence supporting it. For example, with respect to simple versions of price theory, price stickiness is an ad hoc hypothesis in the Lakatosian sense, but not necessarily in the Popperian sense, because there is some empirical evidence that prices are sticky. Within economics, methodologists generally think of ad hocness in its Popperian sense, while theorists generally, though not always, use it in a Lakatosian way (Hands, 1988, pp. 130–31).[4]

This distinction is crucial for evaluating the importance of the new classicals' claim that traditional macroeconomics is ad hoc. If certain traditionalist assumptions, such as price stickiness, are ad hoc assumptions in the Popperian sense, then traditionalists should be severely criticized for using them. But if they are ad hoc only in the Lakatosian sense, then traditionalists can reply that they are just incorporating into their theory some empirically established characteristics of the economy. If these characteristics are alien to microeconomic theory, then that is the fault of microeconomic theory. Or they might argue that leaving some issues unexamined and making ad hoc assumptions about them is useful because it frees time to deal with more interesting issues. To some extent – though certainly not entirely – the new classicals' charge of ad hocery and their insistence on micro*theoretic*, and not just microeconomic foundations, then comes down to a preference for formalist theory over empirical science theory.

Reductionism

The new classicals' insistence on reducing macroeconomics to its microeconomic foundations is part of a scientific tradition known as reductionism.[5] The extent to which all or most higher-level sciences should be reduced to more basic sciences is a complex philosophical dispute. It is connected to how one views scientific theories. One way, called 'scientific realism', is that a theory aims at discovering 'the truth', that it should hold up a mirror to nature. Another view, instrumentalism, treats theories as merely convenient instruments for predicting. In this view theories need not be 'true'. They are merely inference-tickets. This 'as-if' way of looking at theories became popular in economics with Friedman's (1953) famous essay, 'The Methodology of Positive Economics', which, rightly or wrongly, is usually considered an instrumentalist tract (see Mayer, forthcoming).

To a moderate instrumentalist reducing macroeconomics to microeconomics may be desirable, other things being equal, but it is not an absolute necessity. One theory may be more convenient for dealing with one set of problems, and another for a different set of problems. In building a bridge engineers rightly use a 'wrong' Newtonian theory rather than the 'correct' general relativity theory.

Economists often take a specific realist position, called methodological individualism. Only individual agents act, and hence we must explain the actions of groups by looking at the incentives and opportunities of individual agents, not of groups. An instrumentalist might reply that, while it is true that only individuals act, we may be able to predict the actions of groups better by formulating laws about aggregates, such as the propensity to consume, than by using laws relating to individual agents. Physicists can predict the behaviour of a mass of sub-atomic particles, but not of any single one.

Moreover, a thoroughgoing realism than eschews any and all instrumentalism would be fatal to neo-classical economics. The belief that man is a rational utility-maximizing entity is surely not taken from psychology (see Woo, 1990). Nor does personal observation or introspection justify the assumption of 'economic man'. Instead, we justify our assumption about rational maximizing agents by the instrumentalist argument that making this assumption allows us to generate fruitful and valid hypotheses that predict with sufficient accuracy. Hence, our microtheory, being derived from observations about the behaviour of groups of agents, i.e. market data, itself lacks microfoundations (see Nelson, 1992).

To be sure, a thoroughgoing instrumentalism is undesirable because we want to explain as well as predict (see Hoover, 1984), but even so, we do not want to get rid of all instrumentalist elements in our thinking. The new classical notion that all macroeconomics has to be reduced to microeconomics is therefore a questionable assertion, if it is meant to be a fundamental principle that simply must be obeyed.

It is thus not surprising that many economists are unconvinced by the new classicals' insistence on reductionism. As Solow (1986, p. 196) notes:

> I have no wish to argue in principle against the demand for micro-founda-
> tions, though I think it is worth pointing out that harder sciences than

economics do not always take such a high-and-mighty attitude. I suppose that, in principle, the behavior of the airplane in which I am scribbling these words, should be understandable molecule by molecule. But nobody believes that to be practical or necessary, and airplanes are designed, built and flown on the basis of highly aggregative engineering relationships.

Blinder (1987, p. 135), too, argues that: 'Thermodynamics and chemistry, for example, have done pretty well without much micro theory. ... And the microfoundations of medicine are often very poor.'

Moreover, even if one treats reductionism as in principle a sound scientific imperative, it is by no means obvious that it is appropriate at this stage in the development of economics. It was not until the 1920s that quantum mechanics made it possible essentially to reduce chemistry to the underlying physics. Yet chemistry had made much progress before then. Fortunately seventeenth century physicists were not imbued with the new classicals' insistence on reductionism and the avoidance of ad hocery. Otherwise there would then have been no Newtonian revolution with its ad hoc law of gravitation and its arbitrary constant of gravitation. Indeed, the idea that gravity could act on disconnected bodies, i.e., 'action at a distance', was a major problem. It was handled for a long time by what for many people was an exemplar of Popperian ad hocery: the assumption that space is filled with an ether through which gravity acts. Not until long after the Michelson-Morley experiment in 1887 was the ether theory abandoned. In the meantime it served a useful purpose.

To be sure, economics is not physics, so that these analogies are hardly convincing. Indeed one might argue, as did Fritz Machlup, that in economics, explanations must link up with our own perceptions as human beings (see Langlois and Koppl, 1991). But such an argument does not coexist peacefully with the new classicals' assumption of extreme rationality.

The Lucas Critique

But new classicals advocate reductionism, not just as a matter of principle, but also as a practical matter, as the only way to overcome the Lucas critique. The macroeconomic parameters we estimate depend upon particular institutions and policies that were in effect during the period of observation. For example, a marginal propensity to consume, estimated over a period during which tax cuts were more or less permanent, does not tell us how agents will react to a new policy of cutting taxes only temporarily in recessions. To assume that they will react the same way implies that they are not behaving rationally. This contradicts the assumption of rational behaviour that we make in other parts of our analysis, and hence involves a logical contradiction. To a formalist that is all there is to it.

It is not only formalists who are disturbed. Stanley Fischer (1988b, p. 302) called the effect of the Lucas critique on econometric policy evaluations and on the credibility of econometric models 'devastating', writing that 'such models are now routinely dismissed as "subject to the Lucas critique."...' But while many, though not all, empirical science economists find the Lucas critique disturbing, they do not throw up their hands and say that we can do nothing until we have reliable estimates of deep microeconomic parameters. To be sure, the Lucas critique may prevent us from using econometric models to predict the effects of policy changes but, as I shall discuss in Chapter 10, there is also a much more mundane reason why we should not use such models for predicting the effects of certain policy changes.

Moreover, when predicting the effects of a policy change in an informal way one can make some rough allowance for likely changes in parameters or in institutional constraints (cf. LeRoy, 1991). In addition, as Benjamin Friedman (n.d., p. 78) points out, we often want to discuss the effects of a particular, non-repetitive policy change, such as a once-for-all tax cut, that does not represent in any meaningful way a regime change of the type that alters the relevant deep parameters. Beyond this some, probably many, if not most, empirical science economists are more or less willing to live with the logical contradiction that results when one makes predictions not founded on deep parameters. We do not have such deep parameters, nor are we likely to obtain them soon, and beggars cannot be choosers. So we can continue to predict with shallow parameters and see if, despite this failing, our predictions are adequate for their purpose.[6]

Thus Stanley Fischer (1988b, p. 302) follows the above-cited passage on the Lucas critique with: 'remarkably, ... [the Lucas] critique has not been shown to be of any empirical significance in accounting for the failure of econometric models in the seventies.' Similarly, J.C. Siebrand (1988, p. 118) writes: 'for the bulk of the parameters of a conventional macroeconomic model the dependence of the values on policy regimes is only a remote possibility.' Even Sims (1982, pp. 118–19), who is essentially a new classical, argued that: 'permanent shifts in the policy regime are by definition rare events. ... Normally policy actions are generated by a mechanism that, from the point of view of the public, forms a more or less stable process.' Hence, as agents slowly change their understanding of the prevailing policy regime, coefficients are likely to change in a sluggish way which can be picked up by econometric studies. To Sims (1982, p. 122): 'The rational expectations critique is only a special case of the more general cautionary note – statistical models are likely to become unreliable when extrapolated to make predictions for conditions far outside the range experienced in the sample.'

Only empirical studies of specific regime changes can tell us whether such a dismissal of the Lucas critique is justified. The results of several, summarized in the Appendix, are mixed. They suggest that the Lucas critique is fully applicable to financial markets, but that its applicability to the labour markets is more problematic. All in all, while obviously valid and a major contribution to empirical science economics, and not just to formalist economics, the Lucas critique does not tell us that the inherent endogeneity of the usual macroeconomic coefficients is necessarily more serious than are the other problems we encounter in forecasting and in giving policy advice. It does not require us to abandon all macroeconomic predictions until we have reliable estimates of deep parameters. But it should make us cautious.

New Classical Ad Hocery: Representative Agents

Not only is the charge that traditional macroeconomics is ad hoc much weaker than the new classicals claim, but also, if interpreted as empirical science economics, new classical theory is itself open to the charge of ad hocery. In the next chapter I illustrate this with respect to some specific new classical hypotheses. Here I look at one instance of Popperian ad hocery that pervades nearly all new classical theory, the representative agent assumption.

As Gordon (1990b, p. 1136) has remarked: 'Professional microeconomists, as distinguished from macroeconomists who dabble in microeconomics modelling, find the failure to confront aggregation seriously to be the most critical flaw of representative agent modelling.' John Geweke (1985) has complained that, by modelling the economy as though it consists of representative agents, the new classicals make the ad hoc assumption that the aggregator function is structural. Geweke shows that this assumption can substantially affect the results obtained. Moreover, in using the representative-agent assumption, new classicals often assume implicitly that agents do not face a significant coordination problem. Yet there is no reason to assume this, either as an empirical generalization or as a natural outgrowth of microtheory. The proliferation of lawyers suggests that it is far from easy to write and police contracts that coordinate the actions of agents. Prisoner-dilemma models also suggest that coordination is not always feasible. Buiter (1989, pp. 12–14) cites a wide variety of different problems for which the representative-agent assumption is misleading. Hoover (1991a, p. 13) refers to the representative-agent device as 'pseudo-microfoundations'.

The representative-agent assumption plays a crucial role in new classical theory. The rationality of expectations is often defended by saying that it does not require all agents to know the true model, merely that agents do not make systematic errors. While some agents overestimate a particular coefficient, others underestimate it. Only the mean estimate of agents is correct. So far so good. But the strong representative-agent assumption is then used to impose a questionable symmetry in the reaction of those who overestimate and those who underestimate the coefficient. It is only if one assumes such symmetry that one can proceed as though agents know the true model.

Without this symmetry assumption, or certain other strong assumptions, that bête noire of new classical theory, the effects of a money illusion, cannot be dismissed merely by appealing to the rationality of expectations. Suppose that prices are declining by 10 per cent, but that half the employees think that prices are falling by 15 per cent, while the other half thinks that they are falling by only 5 per cent. The first group is then willing to take the 10 per cent wage cut that corresponds to the actual 10 per cent decline in prices. It even offers to work more hours at the new wage. But the second group objects to a wage cut of more than 5 per cent. If it simply offers fewer hours of labour, fine and good. But not if it withdraws its labour entirely to search for an employer willing to offer what it thinks of as the appropriate real wage. It would then take a peculiar supply curve of labour for the first group to work twice as many hours as before because it thinks that real wages have risen by 5 per cent.[7] But unless it does so, total hours worked fall as a result of a money illusion despite the rationality of expectations.

But could one not defend the symmetry assumption as a provisional assumption that will be discarded once the theory is further developed? Yes and no. New classicals are certainly right in stressing that initially a new theory should be protected against destructive criticism, and also that they have already succeeded in some models in weakening the representative-agent assumption to some extent. But such an infant industry argument has its limits. New classical theory has received so much nurturing from first-class minds over the last twenty years that it can no longer claim to be an infant. Besides, if this theory is to be granted a long grace period, should not traditionalists also be given a long grace period to meet the objections raised by the new classicals? Moreover, if new classicals are presenting their work as merely a promising line of research that may perhaps pay off in the future, then, to put it mildly, they have to tone down slightly their criticism of traditional macrotheory. All in all, it may be better to treat many of the models that make the representative-agent assumption as formalist economics rather than as empirical science economics.

CONCLUSION

All economists can be proud of what their new classical colleagues have wrought. It is an admirable intellectual achievement. But that does not necessarily mean that it is also good empirical science economics. Its aesthetics puts it firmly into the formalist tradition, in terms of its emphasis on rigour and technique, as well as its de-emphasis of empirical testing. The problem is that the new classicals have made the hubristic claim that their work can replace traditional macroeconomics as usually practised in the empirical science tradition. There, the microfoundations they have provided are not all that necessary, while the special assumptions they must make for tractability are a serious problem. Hence, as empirical science economists they have not been successful, though traditionalists do have to come to terms with the Lucas critique.

APPENDIX – THE EFFECT OF REGIME CHANGES

Not many empirical studies are available on the effect of regime changes on the coefficients of models, and not all can be discussed here. Several deal with the effects of the Volcker regime change in 1979.[8] In one, Phillip Cagan and William Fellner (1983) measure shifts in the Phillips curve by adding dummy variables. They conclude that the Phillips curve had shifted downward, though they concede that their finding does 'not add up to what one would consider a "proof"' (Cagan and

Fellner, 1983, p. 607). Similarly, Wayne Vroman (1983, p. 35), looking at the residuals from the Phillips curves of four major econometric models in 1981–82, comes up with the not very strong verdict that:

> [E]ven though the equations have been overpredicting wage increases in recent quarters, the average size of the overpredictions has not been consistently large relative to the basic error variances of the underlying equations. A rough test of the eight averages indicates that three were significantly negative at the 0.5 level and one more at the .10 level (Vroman, 1983, p. 36).

John Taylor (1984, p. 210) concludes that:

> wage inflation is much less persistent for the sample that includes the last three years. The impact of any shock to wages deteriorates more rapidly than in the pre-1980 sample. ... The initial and medium-term impacts of unemployment on wage formation are larger for the sample which includes the last three years. Eventually, however, the effect of the unemployment shock is smaller.

Preston Miller and William Roberds (1987) looked at the stability of the coefficients of a BVAR model for real GNP, the GNP deflator, the three-months Treasury bill rate, and the exchange rate, during two regime changes: the 1979 change in the FOMC's operating procedure, and the 1981 Reagan budget initiatives. They conclude that 'unpredictable coefficient changes were large and were primarily responsible for sizable prediction errors. ... These results suggest that the Lucas critique does have quantitative significance' (Miller and Roberds, 1987, p. 1).

On the other hand, Olivier Blanchard (1984, pp. 211–12), using the Phillips curve of the DRI model, finds that:

> There is extremely little change in the coefficients until 1982, thus no apparent direct (credibility) effect of the policy change. There is from 1982 on, some evidence of ... a decrease in the mean lag effect of price inflation on wage inflation. There is also, in the last regression, some evidence of a larger effect of unemployment on wage inflation: this is more likely due to the very high unemployment rate in 1983 than to direct policy-change effects. ... Overall, there is no evidence of a major shift in the Phillips curve (Blanchard, 1984, p. 213).[9]

George Perry's findings are similar. In his view:

Developments have certainly not supported the central promise of some classical models that once steady disinflationary policies are in place, disinflation will take place with little output loss. The disinflation that occurred was not exceptionally prompt, and when wages finally did slow by unusually large amounts in some manufacturing industries and construction, that development was accompanied by unusually large declines in employment. ... The result presented here suggests that we have gotten about what would have been predicted from past experience ... (Perry, 1983, pp. 600, 602).

Robert Gordon (1990a, pp. 7–8) notes:

The econometric version [of the Phillips curve], developed and refined in the late 1970s, has been validated in the 1980s. ... The predictive power of the mainstream model was demonstrated in 1981–87, when the actual sacrifice ratio (roughly six) turned out to be almost exactly what had been predicted in advance on the basis of parameters estimated through the end of 1980. ... This history of the triangle model [a Phillips curve model that included three sets of variables measuring demand, supply and inertia] reveals a wonderful irony. A central point of departure for Lucas' new classical revolution was the failure of the 1960s Phillips curve. ... The irony is that the triangle model was in print ... [at that time]. It has survived and thrived, while the wreckage consists of the empirical attempts by Robert Barro and others to validate the new classical policy ineffectiveness proposition, which ran aground on the bedrock of inflation inertia.

Steven Englander and Cornelis Los (1983) also tested the expectations-augment Phillips curve for four types of potential shifts: permanent deterministic, permanent stochastic, transitory deterministic and transitory stochastic. The Phillips curve for wages shows stability with respect to all four types of potential shifts, while the Phillips curve for prices shows instability only with respect to transitory shifts in one test, and marginal evidence for instability on another test.

The effect of regime changes on the Phillips curves of countries other than the United States has also been studied. For Canada Stuart Landon (1987), using a rational expectations natural rate model of the unemployment rate, found that unexpected monetary shocks played a larger role during the Bank of Canada's monetary targeting regime than during its exchange-rate regime. Michael Christensen (1987a), in studying the Danish Phillips curve during a regime change, found that for the inflation-augmented Phillips curve there was no strong evidence of a parameter change when a conservative government, pledged to reduce inflation, came into office. When he added the period after the new government took over, the coefficient of the unemployment rate changed by less than one standard error. This does not, of course, allow one to assert that the coefficient did not change, only that there is no convincing evidence that it did change. For the rational expectations natural rate version of the Phillips curve equation (which performed better than the inflation-augmented version), the results were more favourable for the Lucas critique in one of the two runs that Christensen tried, but even in this case the difference between the relevant coefficients did not quite reach significance at the 5 per cent level.

Not surprisingly the evidence for the Lucas critique is stronger for financial markets. Thus John Huizinga and Frederic Mishkin (1986) found evidence that the Fed's policy changes in 1920 and 1979 generated changes in the behaviour of real interest rates, though this evidence is disputed by William Schwert (1986). Gregory Mankiw, Jeffrey Miron and David Weil (1987) dealt with the effect of the establishment of the Federal Reserve System on the term structure of interest rates. They found that:

> These results show clearly the effects of regime changes predicted by Lucas. In particular, the relation between long rates and short rates changed when the process for short rates changed in the way that the expectations theory [of the term structure] predicts. ... The picture that emerges ... is that of a remarkably fast adjustment of expectations and behavior in the face of a major change in the economic policy regime (Mankiw, Miron and Weil, 1987, pp. 363, 371).

This regime change is, however, an easy test for the Lucas critique. As Mankiw et al. (1987, p. 371) point out, the implications that the establishment of the Fed had for the yield curve 'were not difficult to predict.'[10] By contrast, for the Volcker regime change, Blanchard (1984) concludes on the basis of informal evidence that 'it took more than a year to fully change the beliefs of financial markets'.

Christensen (1990) studied the change in the coefficients of a modified version of the Fisher-effect model that relates nominal interest rates to the inflation rate. He used this model to infer from the behaviour of interest rates whether expectations of inflation were affected by the government's decision to stabilize the exchange rate, and found that they were, thus supporting the Lucas critique (see also Christensen, 1987b).

Several papers have analysed how money market forecasters respond to changes in the Fed's operating procedures. They find that changes in these operating procedures affected the coefficients of the equations that explain how forecasters predict changes in the money supply (see Andreas Fisher, 1989; Gavin and Karamouzis, 1984).

At least two papers have looked at the stability of the coefficients of money demand functions and consumption functions during periods when there were large institutional or policy changes. Baba, Hendry and Starr (1992) conclude that the coefficients of the US money demand function were stable despite large institutional changes. Engle and Hendry (1989) and Hendry and Ericsson (1990) reach a similar result for Great Britain. For the consumption function Favero and Hendry (forthcoming) also find stability in the face of regime changes.

NOTES

1. Stephen LeRoy (1991, p. 39) has argued that 'the central project of new classical macroeconomics was to discredit discretionary macroeconomic policy and the associated mode of policy advice by economists. Analytical developments in new classical macroeconomics are best understood when situated in relation to this project.' This may well be the case, but I am dealing with new classical theory per se, and not with the motives of new classical theorists.
2. There might also seem to be circular reasoning if the best schools are defined as those in which young economists are developing new classical theory. However, one can estimate the quality of an economics department by the quality of a school's other departments.
3. As discussed in Chapter 2, the self-interest of the profession also plays a role. Moreover, a paradigm that opens up a rich mine of new research projects, particularly ones in which the younger members of the profession have a comparative advantage, will generate much enthusiasm. Harry Johnson (1971) noted this with respect to the ready acceptance of Keynesian theory after 1936, and it also seems applicable to new classical theory.
4. Thus Hands (1988, p. 132) writes: 'for economic theorists, the sin of ad hocness seems to be infidelity to the metaphysical presuppositions of the neo-classical program rather than face-saving adjustments in response to recalcitrant data.' Hands is using the term 'metaphysical' here in the sense of a Lakatosian metaphysical core.
5. For discussions of reductionism in economics see Nelson (1984, 1992) and Woo (1990).
6. There is also a question whether deep parameters would be sufficient (see Hartley, 1991).
7. Lucas has argued that the substitutability of leisure over time is high, but his evidence may not be applicable to a case where some people work more than, say, 60 hours a week.
8. In the postwar period the US inflation rate, not just the price level, had an upward trend. In October 1979 the Federal Reserve under Paul Volcker's leader-

ship decided to break this trend and adopted a disinflationary policy accompanied by a shift towards targeting the money supply.

9.   He obtained similar results using Perry's wage–wage Phillips curve.

10. Moreover, it is far from certain that the change in the serial correlation of short rates that Mankiw et al. discussed was due to the establishment of the Fed. See Mankiw et al. (1987, p. 359n).

8. New Classical Theory – Specific Hypotheses

> It is very difficult to defeat a research program supported by talented, imaginative scientists (Imre Lakatos, 1978, p. 72).

Many of the best minds of our profession have spent much effort developing new classical theory. If, despite this, it has relatively little to contribute to empirical science economics, then this suggests that the distinction I have drawn between empirical science and formalist economics is meaningful. Hence, it is useful to consider several new classical hypotheses in some detail.

I discuss only a few new classical hypotheses to illustrate my thesis. The first is rational expectations, and the second is rapid market clearing. In connection with the latter I briefly discuss real business cycles. Finally, I take up some components of new classical monetary theory. In Chapter 5 I have already discussed time inconsistency theory, which Hoover (1988) treats as part of new classical theory. Such a limited sampling is open to the objection not only that the sample is very small, but also that it may not be representative. Thus, I do not take up the new classicals' discussion of the termination of hyper-inflations, a discussion that is in the empirical science tradition. Indeed, I have not attempted to select a representative sample. On the contrary, I have selected hypotheses that illustrate my point. But since these include hypotheses that are basic to new classical theory, my selection bias does not invalidate my conclusions.

To claim that new classical theory is not good empirical science economics, I do not have to show that these hypotheses make no contribution whatsoever to that subject. Indeed, it would be surprising if any work done by as brilliant a group as the new classicals did not make some contribution to our understanding of empirical economics. Rational expectations analysis is a most significant contribution to empirical science economics. Though, as discussed below, the case for it is not compelling, the same is true for the alternative treatments of expectations. Another significant contribution is drawing the profession's attention to the potential importance of productivity shocks. All I have to show is that these contributions are much smaller than new classicals claim, and that they are limited when compared to the brilliant contributions that the new classicals have made to formalist economics.

RATIONAL EXPECTATIONS

For formalist economics the assumption that agents know the correct model, that is the model embodied within the paper, is appealing for two reasons. First, being what Lucas (1987, p. 14n) calls a 'consistency axiom', it fits in well with the over-arching assumption that agents behave rationally. Second, it is in some sense simpler than the assumption that agents have an alternative model in mind, particularly since such an alternative model would have to be chosen more or less arbitrarily.

In empirical science economics the rational expectations assumption has a less secure status. Here it functions as an empirical generalization that may, but need not be, a sufficiently accurate approximation. Hence, it is legitimate to write papers in which agents do not know the true model, i.e. the model presented in the paper. Indeed one might be tempted to argue that model-consistent expectations are often an inappropriate assumption because they evade the problem of learning. How long does it take agents to update their information set when conditions change? Moreover, as Hahn (1991, pp. 48–9) points out, in economic models the large number of possible situations in which everything has been learned, 'as well as the possibility that some of these allowed agents to live in an essentially fictitious world (sunspot equilibria) has convinced pure theorists (if not all macroeconomists), that the learning stage cannot be skipped.' Yet, as Alessandro Vercelli (1991, p. 155) points out in models built according to the Lucas heuristic, where only equilibrium conditions can be dealt with, there is no room for learning.

One might even put forward the following somewhat mischievous argument: Agents have not yet read the author's model, so how can he or she assume that they acted on the basis of something that was not in their information set during the period over which he or she tested the model? More seriously, even after the model is published its acceptance may be delayed, if not altogether prevented, by agents also reading rival models. The babble of economic analysis that pervades the media, as well as the professional journals, makes it hard for a new model or forecast to get much of an audience. The *Wall Street Journal* (1991, p. A2) in July 1991 listed the nominal GNP and CPI forecasts of 40 forecasters for the first and second halves of 1991. The forecasts of GNP growth for the two periods had means of 2.4 and 2.5 and standard deviations of 1.1 and 1.3 respectively, while the CPI forecasts had a mean of 3.6 and a standard deviation of 0.5 for both half-years. As I shall show in Chapter 10, forecasts of the effects of changes in monetary policy also diverge widely.

To be sure, this argument is not entirely persuasive. Agents may 'know' a model in an intuitive way without having read it, and hence follow rules of thumb that are consistent with it. And experience may have directed them to the right model. There is certainly something to this response, but it is less applicable in macroeconomics than in microeconomics. Agents, being specialists in a particular microeconomic activity, can be expected to 'know', at least by way of rules of thumb, as much, if not more, than the economist who studies the activity from afar. But few agents are specialists in macroeconomic problems. Here it is reasonable to expect economists to know more, so that agents do not always behave in accordance with the economist's latest model. As Hashem Pesaran (1987, pp. 270–71) notes in his comprehensive study of rational expectations theory, Muth's strong form of the theory requires the important and 'highly controversial' assumption that 'it is possible for individuals to learn the "true" model ... from their own experience, or perhaps from the experience of others.'

How then can the rational expectations assumption be justified in empirical science economics? One alternative is to replace the version in which agents know the true model with a weaker version in which they have only limited information, but use that information rationally. It is hard to object to that version. But unless the information set is specified, this version is vacuous. And how can it be determined empirically? Another alternative is to impose the assumption that agents possess all the relevant information, on the grounds that to exclude any specific information would be arbitrary and ad hoc (cf. Attfield, Demery and Duck, 1991, p. 221). Within the context of empirical science economics this is not convincing. Here one cannot justify the assumptions of a theory by saying that the alternative assumptions are ad hoc. First, the arbitrariness of one set of assumptions does not mean that another set of assumptions is empirically valid. It may be that we know too little to formulate a theory about this particular phenomenon. It may be more ad hoc to assume that the positions of certain planets at an entirely arbitrarily chosen date, say two days after one's fifth birthday, have more influence on one's life than their position at the date of one's birth. But that is hardly a strong argument for astrology!

Second, if the twin assumptions of rational expectations and full information are to be justified as the best we can do, we have to show, and not just assert, that indeed they are the best. This means primarily showing that models based on these assumptions predict better than models based on alternative assumptions, such as extrapolative or adaptive expectations, or models that use survey evidence on expectations. It is common to dismiss extrapolative and adaptive expectations models out of hand because they imply irrational behaviour. But where is the evidence that the assumption of some irrational behaviour leads to worse predictions than does the assumption that agents have expectations that fully correspond to those of the model? At the least, we should not rule out a priori that behaviour is not fully rational, given that considerable evidence for irrational behaviour does exist (see Boland, 1982, p. 80; Gerber, Singh and Frantz, 1990, p. 46; Kahneman et al., 1982).

Another justification given for assuming that agents possess full information is that they have an incentive to obtain any necessary information, so that the assumption that they have full information is likely to be closer to the truth than the assumption that they have no information at all (cf. Attfield, Demery and Duck, 1985, p. 193). This argument, too, is unconvincing. There are other alternatives, such as assuming adaptive expectations, that may be better than either of the polar alternatives of full information or no information at all. Again, whether these alternatives are actually better can only be decided empirically.

So what do the empirical tests tell us? Holden, Peel and Thompson (1985, p. 92), after reviewing a number of tests, state: 'in general, surveys of expectations do not support the rational expectations hypothesis.' Attfield, Demery and Duck (1991, pp. 224–5) conclude that:

> The evidence on the rational expectations hypothesis in macroeconomics is still very mixed. The direct tests summarized in Chapter 3, or the tests of the restrictions imposed by the hypothesis of rational expectations on the foreign exchange market or bond markets ... provide at best only very

modest support for the hypothesis. The early work by Lucas and Barro and others ... provides some support, although this has been seriously challenged by studies such as those surveyed in Chapter 7 and there is some evidence in favor of rational expectations from the studies of the consumption function ... although once again the evidence is by no means clear cut.

Buckle, Assendelft and Jackson (1990) discuss the rationality of expectations of manufacturers and builders in New Zealand about numerous variables. For most of the variables they analyse expectational errors are serially correlated. They conclude (p. 579) that the rational expectations hypothesis 'is rejected for most of the quantity variables but the case for rejection was not so clear for expectations of prices and costs.' Michael Lovell (1984, p. 205) summarizes his survey of the empirical evidence as follows: 'at the very least the weight of the cumulative evidence is sufficiently strong to compel us to suspend belief concerning the concept of rational expectations, pending the accumulation of additional evidence; rational expectations may be more myth than reality.' In a subsequent paper (1986, pp. 120–21) Lovell reports:

> My survey of a number of empirical studies of expectations is not supportive of the commonly invoked rational expectations hypothesis. Quite the contrary, if the cumulative evidence is to be believed, we are compelled to conclude that expectations are a rich and varied phenomenon that is not adequately captured by the concept of rational expectations; ... Nevertheless there are, I think, two important reasons that can be advanced for suspending judgement on the validity of tests of the rational expectations hypothesis: First, there is the problem of measurement error. ... Second, it must also be observed that departures from rationality may be a transient phenomenon arising because economic actors are learning to adapt to a shift in regimes; ...

Since then, much empirical evidence has appeared on the closely related efficient markets hypothesis. This evidence is also not very favourable to the rational expectations hypothesis. Thus, in his survey article LeRoy (1989, pp. 1609, 1614, 1616) writes:

> The consensus now is that the anomalies pose a serious problem which cannot be shrugged off. ... However attractive (to economists) capital market efficiency is on methodological grounds, it is extraordinarily difficult to formulate nontrivial and falsifiable implications of capital market efficiency that are not in fact falsified. ... Cognitive psychologists have

documented systematic biases in the way people use information and make decisions. Some of these biases are easy to connect, at least informally, with security market behavior. ... Economists have in the past confidently assumed that these biases would disappear in settings where the stakes are high, as in real-world securities markets. However, this line is beginning to wear thin, particularly in light of economists' continuing inability to explain asset prices using models that assume away cognitive biases.

All in all, it is hard to attribute the popularity of the rational expectations assumption to its empirical confirmation. At the same time one should not treat it as rejected and useless, if only because alternative ways of modelling expectations may do even worse. Moreover, it is not clear how seriously one should take the evidence that comes from surveys of expectations. As Holden, Peel and Thompson (1985, p. 93) point out, when filling out a questionnaire agents may not seek out all the information that they do when they make decisions. In addition, argue Holden, Peel and Thompson, aggregations over time and across agents, as are done in surveys, may not be legitimate when learning takes place. As Steven Sheffrin (1983) points out, the better informed agents control more resources. But, on the other hand, complementarities in the behaviour of agents give the views of uninformed agents a disproportionate influence (see Haltiwanger and Waldman, 1989). Thus all in all, rational expectations may still be a better assumption than the available alternatives, but for empirical science economics, there is not much more that one can say for it.

Hence, when using the rational expectations assumption in empirical science economics it would be useful to discuss how plausible it is in any particular case, to indicate how robust the results are with respect to departures from rational expectations, and to develop models that are relatively robust. Instead, rational expectations theory is frequently used in a mechanical way, as though it were well established empirically.

While not specifically a part of new classical theory, a good illustration of the excessive deference paid to rational expectations is the treatment of the traditional (Nordhaus) theory of political business cycles. This theory is often criticized because it assumes that the voter can be fooled. Nordhaus (1989, p. 25) considers this 'the most penetrating criticism' of the theory.

However, there is much less reason to assume that voters act rationally than that firms and households do. For firms there is a Darwinian argument for efficient behaviour, an argument which, though weak (see Winter, 1963), should not be dismissed entirely. Second, those who make decisions for firms have earned their positions by making correct decisions in the past. The more successful they are, the more resources they control. Third, the major decisions that households and firms make can have a substantial effect on their own welfare, so that they have a strong incentive to behave rationally. None of these considerations apply to voters. Moreover, voters would have to possess a great amount of information to eliminate the incentive for a political business cycle. They would need to differentiate those declines in interest rates and in unemployment that result from a temporarily more expansionary policy from those due to other causes. What variable should they focus on – M-2, interest rates or credit? More generally, with the professional literature disagreeing about the existence of a political business cycle, how can one expect most voters to know if it exists? In addition, with elections usually being as close as they are, governments may have an incentive to generate a political business cycle, even if most, but not all, voters are too well informed to be fooled.[1] Moreover, one can argue, along the lines of time inconsistency theory, that if the public believes that a political business cycle exists, then the government has an incentive to generate one. All this is simple and obvious. Why then does the rational expectations criticism of the traditional political business cycle theory persist?[2] It is probably due in large part to the technical sweetness of rational expectations theory and to the seductive appeal of formalism; in other words to the failure to distinguish between formal and empirical science economics.

MARKET CLEARING

As Hoover (1988, p. 225) has remarked, it is not rational expectations, but 'the Walrasian interpretation of the assumption that, to the limits of their information, agents are consistent and successful optimizers that is the distinctive feature of the new classicism. Rational expectations is but an implication of this assumption.' Due to transaction costs not all the rational expectations models must imply that all prices are flexible. Still, as McCallum (1989, p. 231) points out, the 'equilibrium models constructed to date have invariably featured fully flexible prices'. The new classicals share the belief that if no Walrasian auctioneer exists, then it is necessary to invent him.

New classicals claim that markets clear rapidly because otherwise agents would be foregoing mutually beneficial trades; there would be $5 bills lying on the pavement. And that is forbidden, not only by the new classical heuristic, but also by the heuristic of neo-classical theory in general. Indeed, some new classicals give the impression that adherence to the proposition that all profitable trades are carried out should be used as a loyalty test. Anyone who does not subscribe to it deserves to be read out of the economics profession, and to be branded with the dreaded S(ociologist) letter.

But the issue cannot be settled that simply. Surely the statement that all mutually beneficial trades are undertaken is not correct as it stands. Only those trades that are perceived as beneficial go through. Perceived by whom? Obviously by the potential traders, not by an economist contemplating the trade. New classicals dismiss this distinction out of hand because rational expectations theory tells us that the parties to the trade know the same as the economist knows. But is this correct? The parties know some things that the economist does not. And it may be precisely these things that prevent what would otherwise be a mutually beneficial trade.

Hence, the claim that all mutually beneficial trades are carried out does not allow us to insist that all markets clear. The latter is one of those potentially confusing statements that can mean two quite different things, and it is easy to slide from one meaning to the other. One of these meanings is tautological. In that sense all markets always clear at all times. If firms cannot sell as much as they want to, they either increase their inventories or cut production, and thus do what they 'want to'. If a worker cannot find a job at a wage greater than, say, one cent an hour he is not 'unemployed', but has left the labour force because his potential real wage is less than the marginal utility of leisure. If I hand over my money to a mugger it is a 'mutually beneficial trade'.

In this sense the statement that all markets clear is hardly informative. Surely, when they say that markets clear new classicals mean something more. Perhaps the way to interpret the new classicals' policy invariance proposition is the following simple and parsimonious story: expectations are rational and prices are flexible because there are no impediments that prevent firms from lowering prices until marginal revenue equals marginal cost, or prevent employees from cutting their wages until the real wage equals the marginal utility of leisure. If the government makes available all the information it possesses, and if private agents trust the government, then regardless of what the unemployment figures show, the economy is in Pareto equilibrium.

Such a theory can be challenged in only two ways. One is to develop a rival theory showing that there exist impediments to wage and price flexibility that inhibit market clearing. The other is to demonstrate that, regardless of our ability to formulate a theoretical explanation for it, the data do show that wages and prices are less flexible than new classical theory requires.

The latter is not as easy as might appear at first glance, because it is not clear by how much wages and prices would move if they were completely flexible. Suppose we observe output falling substantially and a big rise in the recorded unemployment rate, while both wages and prices fall slightly. This does not necessarily mean that wages and prices are inflexible. It could be a result of a high marginal rate of substitution between labour and leisure, and of numerous industries having steeply rising marginal cost curves. Some indirect evidence, cited by Blinder (1987, p. 131; 1988b, pp. 286–9), such as the proportion of total unemployment accounted for by the long-term unemployed, suggests that a voluntary leisure theory of unemployment is inappropriate. But even so, the main weight of the attack on the new classical proposition that markets clear must be carried not by data showing little movement in wages and prices in some absolute sense, but by a theory that shows plausible impediments to equilibrating movements in wages and prices.[3]

Theories of impediments to wage and price flexibility exist (see Dennis Carlton, 1989). New Keynesians have done much work on this topic (see Gordon, 1990b; Blanchard, 1990), though as Blinder (1991, p. 89) notes: 'Most economists would, I think, agree that we know next to nothing about which of several dozen theories of wage-price stickiness are valid and which are not.' One theory argues that price inflexibility is due to buyers preferring price stability (Okun, 1981; Rotemberg, 1982). Another theory points to long-term contracts. New classicals dismiss the latter with the assertion that contracts can be written contingent on various states of the economy, or can readily be revised. But do contracts actually contain many contingent clauses, and can they be readily revised?[4] Some can be, but can most?[5] Another approach attributes price inflexibility to oligopolistic behaviour. One variant stresses that oligopolists usually want to avoid price wars. Another variant states that oligopolists are reluctant to cut prices when costs fall, because they fear that their rivals would match their price decreases. Monopoly theory, as Carlton (1989, p. 930) points out, also suggests reasons for inflexible prices:

> To the extent that consumers adjust their future behavior in response to price changes today, a monopolist will take that adjustment into account in setting prices. ... This reasoning explains why a monopolist may not want to raise price of fear of inducing substitution away from his product in the long run. ... To the extent that consumers are uncertain about future prices, a monopolist might use his pricing path as a signal to tell consumers what prices they should expect in the future. This means that, if costs rise unexpectedly in the short run, but the monopolist knows that the increase will be only temporary, the monopolist might be reluctant to raise his price ... for fear that ... [consumers] will mistake the current price increase as being permanent and react to it in the long run by substituting away from the product. ... A monopolist who can hold inventory takes account of the relation between the marginal revenue curves at different points in time in setting his price. ... By taking account of these interactions, the monopolist is lead to choose a more stable price policy than the simple models of monopoly suggest.

More generally, Carlton (1989, p. 939) suggests that 'price alone may not be clearing markets and, instead, that price in conjunction with other mechanisms, such as a seller's knowledge of a buyer's needs, is performing that function.' If sellers ration supplies during shortages, or use various non-price inducements to encourage sales when demand falls, it is not obvious that the resulting market clearing – in the tautological sense – has the optimality characteristics that the new classicals ascribe to price-induced market clearing, and is therefore necessarily superior to government intervention. Perhaps it is, but that should be shown rather than just implicitly assumed.

Blinder (1991), in interviewing firms, found evidence for several of these theories. The four best explanations of price rigidity in his sample were:

1. price is not the only element that buyers consider;
2. the problems of coordinating price change with rivals;
3. prices change only as costs change; and
4. implicit contracts between firms and their customers.

Akerlof and Yellen (1985) and Mankiw (1985) have shown that the losses that a firm experiences if it refrains from adjusting prices when demand changes can be quite small. One might object that a profit-maximizing firm is eager to capture even a small potential gain. But if this gain is small, then it might easily be outweighed by the costs and risks of attempting to coordinate price changes with rivals, or by the losses from violating implicit contracts with buyers. Bruce Greenwald and Joseph Stiglitz (1989) show that price and wage rigidity can also arise as a response to uncertainty.

In sharp contrast to the literature just cited, the microtheory that new classicals use as the microfoundation of the policy invariance proposition is a simple theory that assumes competitive markets in which there are no significant impediments to changing prices. As Buiter (1989 pp. 10–11) notes:

> It is ironic that at the very time that microeconomic theory was abuzz with exciting new developments (the asymmetric information paradigm, principal agent theories, monopolistic competition, oligopoly and game-theoretic approaches to rivalry between firms, etc.) the ... [new classicals] should have opted for a recycling of the conventional pre-Seventies competitive paradigm. ... Macroeconomic modelling should start from the self-evident and crucial facts of (1) incompleteness of markets, (2) noncompetitive behavior in most of the markets that do exist and (3) essential heterogeneity among economic agents.

Extensive work has also been done on the reasons for wage stickiness. Much of it deals with implicit contracts, efficiency wages, and insider-outsider distinctions. But such work does not explain why nominal, as well as real wages, are rigid. However, models stressing long-term wage contracts with only limited indexing do. New classicals might argue that one should not take labour contracts as given, that they are the product of maximizing behaviour. They certainly are. But if we observe that few contracts are indexed, that is a fact we have to live with, even if we cannot explain it. Aerodynamic theory cannot explain how bumblebees fly. But that does not force them to walk.

Moreover, an old theory of wage rigidity, enshrined in the *General Theory*, can explain nominal wage rigidity, particularly when combined with the previously mentioned reasons for real wage rigidity. It does require the assumption that employees care about relative wages, and not merely about their own wages. But that is not a far-fetched assumption. The idea that relative as well as absolute income or wealth matters has a long history in economics, going back at least to Veblen. It was used more recently by Reuven Brenner (1983) and Robert Frank (1985) to explain a number of phenomena. Its acceptance is not confined to institutionalists, as the example of Hahn (1985, p. 64) shows. Some theorists have dealt with utility functions that take account of envy.

Another, rather unfashionable, explanation of wage rigidity may be a money illusion in the context of efficiency wage theory, once one drops the representative agent assumption. Suppose, for example, that 30 per cent of employees underestimate the magnitude of a price decline. If a firm cuts money wages while keeping real wages constant, a substantial proportion of employees would consider themselves unfairly treated. It seems plausible that these employees would reduce their efforts by more than those who overestimate the price decline would increase their efforts. If so, efficiency wage theory suggests that a money wage cut might well be costly for the firm.

Turning to the empirical evidence, Carlton (1989, pp. 921, 924) finds substantial price inflexibility in many industries, and much inter-industry variation in the degree of price flexibility. Bruce Greenwald and Joseph Stiglitz, too, point out considerable evidence for price stickiness.

The downward inflexibility of money wages is usually treated as a well established fact. However, Kenneth McLaughlin (1990) provides impressive evidence from four sources for nominal wage flexibility. One is the historical behaviour of aggregate wages. The second source is union contract settlements; the third, the distribution of changes in executive salaries; and the fourth is his analysis of data from the Panel Study of Income Dynamics. In the last of these the only sign of nominal wage rigidity is that the distribution of nominal wage changes has a small spike at zero.[6]

Where does this leave us? Economic theory, except in its simplest – one might even say most simplistic – version, does not impel one to believe that markets clear quickly and efficiently. On the contrary, it provides many reasons why they may not. Nor does the empirical evidence show rapid market clearing. For empirical science economics, a theory that assumes rapid market clearing is therefore ad hoc in both the Lakatosian and Popperian senses of the term. Such a theory could be justified on 'as-if' grounds, if, but only if, it predicts better than rival theories. But the new classicals have generally not registered a claim to superior predictive performance.

One possible response is to argue, as Lucas (1987, pp. 51–2) does, that dropping the market clearing assumption is a bad research strategy. It eliminates our ability to 'account for wage and employment determination in terms of preferences and technology'. Moreover, even if we drop the price flexibility assumption we still cannot go much beyond the confines of the Walrasian scenario because our theory still abstracts from the continuing relationship between agents. Furthermore, Lucas argues, abandoning the assumption that markets clear does not bring our theory into close contact with the data. What the data describe as 'unemployment' is an arbitrary concept that differs sharply from what we require for economic theory. Why should someone who works for 40 hours a week, and not for the remaining 128 hours, be classified as employed?

Lucas's defence of the market clearing assumption is entirely appropriate for formal science economics. Here we need to explicate carefully and precisely our microfoundations, and the various theories of price inflexibility do not provide these. Hence, it is better simply to assume that prices move enough to clear markets, and thus to avoid the ad hoc assumptions or vague formulations that are required to incorporate into the model the assorted complications that may prevent markets from clearing. Similarly, if the employment relation cannot be specified rigorously, then it is better to think in terms of self-employed barbers. Moreover, since our focus is on theory, making contact with data that do not measure something that corresponds precisely to our theoretical concepts is hardly worth doing.

For empirical science economics the story is very different. Here, while well explicated microfoundations would certainly be welcome, the need for them is not as pressing. One can just start with the observation that wages or prices are sticky. If challenged to provide a theoretical justification one can simply point to the various reasons discussed above, without having to explain how much of the observed price stickiness is due to each of them. Botanists study certain characteristics of the behaviour of plants for which the exact biochemical mechanism is still unclear.

Furthermore, while the theoretical import of the distinction between those who are unemployed for 168 hours, and those who are employed for the standard work-week, and hence are unemployed for 128 hours, is not clear, we *do* want to explain fluctuations in the proportion of the labour force that is unemployed for 168 hours rather than for 128 hours. This is, in part, because our clients, policy makers and the public, are interested in it. In addition, there are grounds for believing that the tastes of employees are such that they reflect the traditional definition of unemployment, illogical as it might seem.[7] Hence, the question whether the market clearing assumption is justified and appropriate cannot be answered in the abstract. It depends on whether we want to solve problems in formal science economics or in empirical science economics.

REAL BUSINESS CYCLES

New classicals explain business cycles as mostly due to supply shocks because a demand-side explanation is inconsistent with their chosen Walrasian market clearing paradigm. For formalist economics this is, of course, entirely sensible. But for empirical science economics more contact than that with the empirical evidence is needed. Real business cycle theorists have not provided enough such contact because they have usually not compared the fit of their models to the fit of demand-side models. Instead, they have generally proceeded by calibration. That is, they have tried to show that the values of certain coefficients required to generate real business cycles are in line with independent estimates of these coefficients.[8] Calibration is a legitimate procedure (see Hoover, 1991a), though whether calibration tests actually support real business cycle theory is a much debated issue (see Prescott, 1986 vs. Summers, 1986). But even if successful, calibration does not allow one to say whether real business cycle theory explains the data better than demand-side models do. At one time it seemed as though unit-root tests would provide at least a presumption for real business cycle theory. But unit-root tests have not furnished a useful answer (see Christano and Eichenbaum, 1990).

Hence, at present, the best one can say for real business cycle theory as a potential contribution to empirical science economics is that it has raised an interesting issue. All the same, it might turn out that subsequent research will confirm real business cycle theory. If so, then new classical economics will, under the inspiration of formalist economics, have made a fundamental contribution to empirical science economics. It would not be the first time in the history of science that what started out as pure research turned out to have highly important practical implications. But I doubt that this will happen for real business cycle theory.

NEW CLASSICAL MONETARY THEORY

There are many versions of new classical monetary theory. I shall deal only with the two most prominent ones, the overlapping generations model and the legal restriction theory of money.

The overlapping generations model is not monetary theory in the usual sense of the term, because it does not deal with money as it exists in actual economies. There, as in standard monetary theory, money is the most liquid of many durable assets. By contrast, in the overlapping generations model there is only a single durable asset – for some strange reason called 'money' – that the young can trade with the old.[9] The distinctive features of money, its provision of liquidity, and hence its transactions and standard of value services, do not appear in these models. With agents' transactions therefore not constrained by 'money' holdings, it is not surprising that strange results can appear; for example, that inflation can proceed without an increase in the quantity of 'money'. Authors are, of course, free to define their terms as they please, and in formalist economics they are also free to analyse any hypothetical economy they want. But then they should not be surprised if their results differ from the traditional ones, and should not claim that, since their results are more rigorously established within their model, these results should supersede the traditional results of empirical science economics. This is particularly so when their theory stays as far away from the empirical evidence as the overlapping generations model does. What empirical evidence would disconfirm it?

If overlapping generations models are intended as a replacement for traditional monetary theory, rather than as an analysis of a particular type of hypothetical economy, then they suffer also from a more technical problem. As Hoover (1988, p. 118) notes, they require, 'not only that the young correctly foresee future prices, but that they are also able to deduce from the infeasibility of the optimal choices of some future generations that their own choices should not be optimal.' The assumption that agents possess such knowledge cannot be justified by saying that they learn from experience. They must somehow know the true model of the economy (Hoover, 1988, p. 118). If one takes newspaper editorials as a rough guide to the economic sophistication of the public, such a strong rational expectations assumption seems bizarre. For formalist economics it is, of course, acceptable.

One overlapping generations model that illustrates well the new classicals' emphasis on formalism is Sargent and Wallace's (1982) attempt to rehabilitate the real bills doctrine.[10] They show that within their model, the price level fluctuations that under a real bills regime accompany changes in the demand for credit are Pareto-efficient. Their model makes no allowance for uncertainty. In their concluding section they state:

> Some may argue that our model is rigged against the quantity-theory view because it abstracts from uncertainty and from business-cycle phenomena. We doubt that merely complicating the model to deal with additional phenomena or generalizing it would change the basic message. Thus, for example, the mere presence of uncertainty does not destroy the underlying logic of the free banking position (Sargent and Wallace, 1982, p. 1233).

Compare this with the following passage in the 1979 *Economic Report of the President* :

> During an inflation individuals watch with frustration as the value of last week's pay increase ... is steadily eroded over the remainder of the year by a process that is beyond their individual control. All of us have to plan for the future. ... The future is uncertain enough in any event, and the outcome of our plans is never fully within our control. When the value of the measuring rod with which we do our planning – the purchasing power of the dollar – is subject to large and unpredictable shrinkage, one more element of command over our own future slips away. It is small wonder that trust in government and social institutions is simultaneously eroded (Executive Office of the President, 1979, p. 7).

As a contribution to economics as a formalist science, the *Economic Report* can hardly claim to compete with the Sargent and Wallace paper. Yet, viewed as empirical science economics, it may well have more to teach us. Although it contains no theorems and is 'mere words', it does suggest that, outside the narrow confines of the Sargent–Wallace model, uncertainty about inflation matters substantially. To be sure, since it appeals to a mixture of introspection and casual empiricism instead of to theorems and econometric results, one might reject it as not meeting the usual standards of scientific evidence. But that does not allow one to jump to the opposite extreme and to accept a hypothesis, such as Sargent and Wallace's, that requires the assumption that the uncertainty factor cited by the *Economic Report* is trivial and can therefore be ignored. This claim, too, is not based on well established theorems or econometric findings. A claim based on introspection and on casual evidence, while weak, is still better than a claim based merely on an arbitrary assumption.

Another major component of new classical monetary theory is the legal restrictions theory of money. This theory tries to explain the existence of a fiat money that does not bear interest, e.g. currency. It argues that this is due only to government restrictions on the issuance and circulation of small denominations of private interest-bearing debt, along with the government's unwillingness to issue such debt of its own. If interest-bearing debt, either private or public, were issued in small denominations, it would drive out fiat money that does not bear any interest. The existence of fiat money is therefore an artifact of government regulations that prevents the private sector from competing with the government.

This theory, too, demonstrates the new classicals' lack of regard for a basic rule of empirical science economics: the need for empirical testing. As Lawrence White (1987, p. 451) points out, in the nineteenth century neither England, the United States, Canada nor Sweden banned the private issue of interest-bearing notes of low denomination, but such notes were not issued. And even now, as Hoover (1988, p. 126) notes, the private production of low denomination notes is not entirely prohibited – travellers' cheques exist.

Moreover, someone imbued with the spirit of empirical science economics would look at the orders of magnitude involved.[11] As White (1987) points out the use of an interest-bearing currency would involve significant transactions costs as buyers and sellers calculate the interest due on each currency note. This would be worthwhile only for currency notes above a substantial threshold value, one that for historically observed interest rates exceeds the usual size of currency notes. White (1987, p. 453) calculated that 'On a note whose initial value equals two hours' wages, held one week while yielding interest at 5 percent per annum, accumulated interest would amount to less than 7 seconds' wages. ... To give a specific example, a $20 note held one week at 5 percent interest would yield less than 2 cents.' Thus even in the absence of large transaction costs, the social benefit of interest-bearing currency would be trivial. It is therefore surprising that Wallace (1983, p. 6), after agreeing that interest-paying currency would make it harder to control the price level, states that 'there is no complete argument leading to the conclusion that people are on average better off' with the greater price stability than with a currency that does not pay interest. A complete argument may not exist, but for empirical science economics, even an incompletely spelled out argument is better than just assuming that something does not matter.

CONCLUSION

This chapter has shown that, when evaluated as a contribution to empirical science economics, new classical theory has not been nearly as successful as its great technical virtuosity would seem to promise. The empirical evidence suggests that the rational expectations assumption is problematic, though it may well be superior to many other alternatives. The claim that wages and prices are highly flexible is even more problematic since it has neither solid microfoundations nor compelling empirical evidence to support it. Nor is there compelling evidence for real business cycles. Finally, at least those components of new classical monetary theory discussed here should not persuade one to abandon traditionalist monetary theory.

But such a negative verdict must be qualified in several ways. First, rational expectations theory, despite its weakness, is an important contribution to empirical science economics. Another contribution of new classical theory has been to force macroeconomists to reconsider their microfoundations, and thus to enrich both macroeconomics and microeconomics. (That task could, of course, have been accomplished with less formalism.) Third, it may turn out that real business cycle theory is correct. All the same, new classical theory is another example of the principle of the strongest link. Its advocates rightly take pride in the rigour of their deductive chains. But a rigorous deduction from a questionable premise, accompanied by no adequate tests of the conclusions, does not guarantee truth.

NOTES

1. A potential offset to the ability to fool *some* voters is that those who realize that the government is imposing a political business cycle on the economy might turn against the government.
2. While widespread, the rational expectations criticism of political business cycle theory has not gone unchallenged. Stephen Haynes and Joe Stone (1990, p. 443n) list several papers that challenge it.
3. All the same, it is quite likely that, whatever its weakness, it is the empirical

evidence more than theoretical arguments that induce so many economists to believe that prices are inflexible.

4. Here is an example of an inefficient contract from an industry with which many of us are familiar, the textbook industry. Contracts set royalties as a fixed percentage of the price of the book. Although these contracts are thus indexed, the indexing is crude. Changes in the price of paper affect royalties more than they should.

5. For examples of how flexible some actual contracts are see Goldberg and Erickson (1987).

6. McLaughlin also cites previous studies that show considerable wage flexibility. But does not the existence of substantial unemployment during recessions necessarily imply that wages are rigid, if one defines rigidity by a price not moving enough to clear the market? No, not necessarily, if one takes account of search unemployment.

7. There is a norm in our society that adult males should normally work about 40 hours or more per week, which may, in part, be due to legal arrangements. If they work less they risk being considered lazy, and if they do not work at all they may be considered incompetent. Such a norm provides an anchor for the traditional definition of unemployment.

8. King and Plosser (1984) do run some regressions, but downplay them.

9. One might wonder what would have happened to new classical monetary theory if Paul Samuelson (1958), in the classic article that started overlapping-generations models, had used the word 'heirlooms' instead of 'money'.

10. Laidler (1984) points out that Sargent and Wallace's view is quite different from the traditional real bills doctrine. That doctrine was not that price movements do not matter, but that they would not occur if the banking system obeyed the real bills doctrine. In general new classical theory does not deserve the title 'classical' (see Niehans, 1987).

11. Admittedly, failure to test one's hypothesis by simple back-of-the-envelope arithmetic is not confined to formalists such as the new classicals. An example occurs in the empirical science literature on the role of money in the production function (see Startz, 1984).

9.   Model or Die

> The hundredth possible world of international trade theory gives the impression of allegorical poesy gone wacko (McCloskey, 1990, p. 31).

Since so much of the work I have criticized in previous chapters consists of explicit models, it is useful to take an overall look at modelling as a technique for empirical science economics. It would be bizarre to assert that, due to some problem in its inherent logic, explicit modelling leads to invalid results. But it would also be bizarre to assert that it is the only way the human mind can obtain valid results. Any debate about the pros and cons of formal modelling should therefore focus, not on logic, but on whether modelling is a useful heuristic for discovering, verifying and communicating new results.

To many economists that question has already been answered with a resounding yes. David Colander tells a story about an economist who interrupted him when he presented a seminar and asked to be shown the model. When told that there was no model she walked out. Colander (1989, p. 35) also reports that when he described an informal idea to a graduate of a leading economics department, 'he asked if I had a formal model for it. When I said no, he said that he ... could not even think about' the idea without a formal model. While certainly not arguing for the elimination of formal modelling, which would be silly, I shall argue against this attitude of 'if no model, then no economics'. In doing so I shall not discuss formalist economics, where an explicit model is obviously needed, and shall postpone discussion of econometric models until the next chapter. First I take up the advantages of modelling and then turn to the disadvantages, and conclude with some specific examples.

ADVANTAGES OF MODELLING

The advantages of modelling can be dealt with briefly: why preach at length what is already fervently believed? Formal modelling makes explicit assumptions that would otherwise be hidden and hence unexamined. Vague and sometimes turgid prose is replaced by succinct equations. To be sure, some formal models are badly written, bristling with unnecessary symbols. But while bad writers can always make reading difficult, the spelling out of assumptions that formal modelling requires makes for transparency. Moreover, mathematical techniques can be readily applied. For researchers modelling can be a source of new ideas, while readers can garner aesthetic pleasure. A model is what Lucas (1980, p. 697) calls 'a mechanical imitation economy', within which we can be certain about our results, precisely because we exclude those elements that are not amenable to rigorous treatment, and because we reduce the great mass of variables that constitute reality to a number small enough, so that we can handle their interaction. Thus we can localize disagreement to elements outside the model instead of arguing about spurious issues. On a more mundane level, models lend themselves well to teaching and to examination questions.

THE COSTS OF MODELLING

The most obvious cost of formal modelling is that it reduces the time that researchers have available for other aspects of their papers. If, as I have argued previously, our profession overvalues the demonstration of technical proficiency, then economists have an incentive to spend too much time on the model itself, and too little of their fixed supply of research time on evaluating the model's applicability. Formal modelling is the main way in which the principle of the strongest link manifests itself. Instead of seeing whether the seemingly weak points of a hypothesis invalidate it, someone given to explicit modelling just models the hypothesis. Consider, for example, Ricardian equivalence, with its assumption that, on the average, the public estimates correctly changes in the public debt. A formal modeller derives this from the assumption of rational behaviour and goes on to build a model on that basis. A more traditional economist looks instead for evidence on the public's knowledge of the government debt.

Moreover, with modelling held in such high regard, there is the danger that a trivial idea, if it is accompanied by a large enough bodyguard of equations, will succeed in surmounting the refereeing process. Many published models merely 'algebray' the obvious. Such a misuse of mathematics to hide the lack of ideas reminds me of a famous *Punch* cartoon during World War I, in which a brash young infantry officer asks an older cavalry officer of what use cavalry is in modern warfare. 'Why, sir,' the cavalry officer replies, 'to add class to what otherwise would be a mere vulgar brawl.'

In addition, when handled badly, and it often is, modelling forces the reader to plough through an elaborate set of equations to get at what could have been said much more briefly. This is particularly bad if the intuition of the paper is not stated at the outset, so that some readers are trapped into ploughing through reams of algebra without learning anything they are interested in. Moreover, models are harder to remember than are intuitive explanations, and in that way are not a good expository device.

A more serious problem is that modelling tends to create tunnel vision, while good economics often requires peripheral vision. Like a searchlight a model throws a powerful but narrowly focused beam that plunges everything not caught by it into utter darkness.[1] Contrast an economist working with an explicit model to one who works more informally. The modeller decides at the outset which variables are relevant and important. He or she then works out the interrelation of these variables and tests the resulting model. If the result is successful even though, as discussed in the next chapter, it may have been subjected to only a weak test, he or she is not likely to step back and ask: 'Have I really got it right, or have I omitted some critical variables?' By contrast, an economist working without a formally explicated model will also work with just a few variables, but is more likely to keep in the back of the mind some thought about the variables he or she initially decided to omit, and hence is more likely to bring one or more of them back into the analysis. In this way the modeller is able to profit by learning as the work progresses and, what may be even more important, is likely to be aware of any relevant qualifications to the results.

Neva Goodwin (1991, p. 148) has raised a related point. Ambiguity may be a 'proper and useful reflection of a complex reality'. Formal modelling with its disdain for ambiguity may therefore be misleading at times. Not only does the modeller decide early on what variables to include in the analysis, but this choice is biased towards omitting those variables that are hard or even impossible to model. In Chapter 5, I cited an example of a measurement error being treated as less important than another error because, unlike the second error, it could not be modelled. In the preceding chapter I offered another example of how a variable that is not tractable, the uncertainty created by inflation, is simply left out of a model. Here is a further example. In contrasting the effects of the second oil shock on Britain and on Japan, Stanley Fischer (1988a) concludes that the attitude of workers was a major factor; that while Japanese workers responded to the deterioration in the terms of trade by accepting lower real wages, British workers were unwilling to do so. A variable such as workers' attitudes is unlikely to be included in a formal model. But if Fischer is right, then in this case such models give misleading answers.[2] And as Woo (1986, p. 48) points out, as economists build on each others' models the omitted variables are less and less likely to be taken into consideration.

It is tempting to respond that those models that omit important variables sooner or later succumb to empirical tests. But although these tests add some credence to the models that they accompany, econometric testing does not, by any means, conclusively validate formal modelling. Some papers are purely theoretical. To be sure, the author might hope that someone else will test the model, but what is everybody's business is nobody's business. Indeed, some models are not testable with currently available data. Second, even when a model is actually tested, it is often tested only against the null hypothesis, and this does not tell us whether the inclusion of some other variable in the model would, or would not, substantially change its fit or some of the coefficients.

How well various models fit the data is not always sufficient evidence. Often there is little difference between the goodness of fit of various models, with such differences possibly being idiosyncratic to the particular data sets used. Moreover, differences in the fit may just reflect differences in the quality of the data. If a money demand function that uses wealth does not give as good a fit as one that uses income, does this mean that the demand for money depends on income rather than on wealth, or just that we have better estimates of income than of wealth?

Testing instead by the realism of a model's assumptions has its own problems. First, there is much dispute about whether this is a valid procedure, unless the assumptions can be restated as implications (see for instance Boland, 1979; Friedman, 1953; Gibbard and Varian, 1978; Mäki, 1986; and Mayer, forthcoming). Second, as Allan Gibbard and Hal Varian (1978) have pointed out, many models are not intended to describe the actual world, but to emphasize some particular feature.

Gibbard and Varian (1978, pp. 665 and 673) call them caricature models that emphasize – 'even to the point of distorting – certain selected aspects of the economic situation. ... Often the assumptions of a model are chosen not to approximate reality, but to exaggerate or isolate some feature of reality.' The value of such a model is that it brings out an important feature of the economy that was previously not given enough attention, and that it is robust with respect to the exaggerated assumptions. But it is often not easy to evaluate rival models by these characteristics.

This raises the question of how models are to be appraised. Which of the numerous models of, say, exchange rate equilibrium should one accept? Without some guidance on this the massive modelling effort of recent years has not been very useful. Those who want to understand how our economy functions are not helped much if they are given thirty different models and told: 'Here are thirty answers, some of which differ substantially.'

The large role that formal models play in graduate education is also not without its costs. The more time students spend learning the models, the less time they spend on the underlying theory of which the model is a particular specification. This reduces their mental flexibility. A student who understands a theory can judge alternative models that will subsequently be derived from it. By contrast, someone who knows the current models, but has only a weak grasp of the underlying theory, often cannot distinguish between useful and less useful models. If students can pass exams simply by remembering particular equations of models they tend to lose sight of economics as a broad-based engine of analysis. I suspect that many graduate students, particularly those outside the top departments, find it difficult to discuss some quite simple actual problems. But those who hire economists for research jobs want answers to questions regardless of whether there is a ready-made model that can deal with their questions. Doing problem sets is good training for working with the model of the textbook, but not necessarily for dealing with actual problems. Teachers of undergraduate courses, too, need to know more than can be encompassed in models if they are to make economics come alive to their students. This does not mean, of course, that modelling should not be taught, or that it should not be a major part of graduate work, but merely that the ultimate target, understanding the economy, and not just various models of the economy, should not be lost sight of in graduate training. Means should not become ends.

SOME EXAMPLES

Many of the examples I have cited in previous chapters in connection with the principle of the strongest link and with new classical theory illustrate various problems with formal modelling. Here are some additional examples.

Some monetarists have claimed that fiscal policy is ineffective; that complete crowding-out occurs. In a classic paper Blinder and Solow (1973) use a model based on the government budget constraint to reject this claim. They show that in their model the conditions that lead to complete crowding-out imply that the economy is subject to explosive instability. Since we know that our economy is not unstable, we can infer that complete crowding-out does not occur. But their model makes an assumption (which is critical for its conclusion) that taxes are set just equal to government expenditures on goods and services plus transfer payments other than interest payments. There is nothing wrong with studying a model in which the government behaves that way. But something is wrong in simply assuming, without bothering with any empirical evidence, that *any* government has actually behaved this way, so that the economy being stable can be used in conjunction with the model to show that complete crowding-out cannot occur (see Mayer, 1990). It is likely that Blinder and Solow would have noticed this gap in their argument had they devoted some of the time that they spent on formal modelling on reconsidering instead what it was that they were actually doing.

Even when modellers undertake empirical tests their model can lead them astray. Several economists have fitted production functions with real balances as one of the inputs. Obtaining significant coefficients for the real-balances variable, they conclude that real balances belong in the production function. But as Richard Startz (1984) points out, it is easy to see that there is something wrong here. If one follows the standard procedure of Dennisonian growth rate accounting, and multiplies real balances by a measure of their marginal productivity, i.e. the interest rate, the contribution of real balances to output turns out to be absolutely trivial. Startz suggests that the non-trivial coefficient for real balances in the production function could well be a statistical artifact due to reverse causation – increases in real balances raise aggregate demand, and output might increase for that reason. In this case it was not a lack of empirical tests, but an uncritical interpretation of regression results that was at fault.

The policy conclusions that are drawn from a model are sometimes inappropriate because the model intentionally excludes something that is an irrelevant institutional detail as far as the underlying theory is concerned. But this 'detail' can be important for the model's policy implications. Thus Eugene Fama (1983) presents a model showing that with currency and deposits not being perfect substitutes, the government can control the price level merely by controlling the supply of currency, and does not have to control the volume of deposits. (Fama argues that the demand for currency is as stable, if not more stable, than the demand for M-1.) The advantage of just controlling currency and not controlling deposits is that this avoids the dead-weight burden of the implicit tax on deposits that a binding legal reserve requirement imposes.[3] Early in his paper Fama states his assumption that banks are not required to redeem deposits in currency. However, he does not discuss whether the inconvenience of not being able to redeem deposits in currency would outweigh the efficiency loss from controlling deposits through a reserve requirement. But if banks have to redeem deposits in currency, it is not at all clear that the government could readily control currency. What would happen if the public tried to redeem more deposits than the volume of currency that the banking system had available? Would the banks be able to purchase enough currency back from the public, or would the government have to provide the banks with additional currency to prevent bank failures, even when it does not want the currency stock to increase?[4] And what would happen if the government wanted to increase the public's currency holdings? How would it induce the public to demand this additional currency?[5]

Another example of how the focus on formal modelling can distort economic analysis is Lucas's attempt to measure the cost of output fluctuations. He first estimates the standard deviation of consumption during business cycles, and then measures the cost of this deviation of consumption by using the coefficient of risk aversion. From this calculation he concludes that the social costs of business fluctuations are much less than is often claimed, being 'about $8.50 per person. I want to propose taking these numbers seriously as giving the order-of-magnitude of the potential social product of additional advances in business-cycle theory – or more accurately, as a loose upper bound ...' (Lucas, 1987, p. 27). Lucas then takes up what he considers the 'two most important qualifications or elaborations of this cost estimate' (p. 28). One is that unemployment was higher before World War II than in the postwar period to which his estimate relates, and the second is that variations

> in total consumption do not affect all households equiproportionally, so that the variability of total consumption does not capture anything like all of the consumption risk faced by the typical household. Perhaps correcting for this effect would lead to another tripling of the relevant standard deviation, and hence another multiplication by nine in the cost estimate. ... But as a measure of the possible gains from improvements in aggregative policy, this last ... is way too high. ... Aggregate income variability is but one source of individual income risk, and reduction of aggregate variability – which is all that stabilization policy can accomplish – cannot be expected to eliminate more than a small part of the uninsurable risk borne at the individual level. ... [T]he postwar business cycle is just not a very important problem in terms of individual welfare. The gains from removing *all* existing variability from aggregate consumption ... are surely well below 1 percent of national income (Lucas, 1987, pp. 29, 105).

This is a strange conclusion. The prominence with which unemployment shows up in surveys that ask people to rank current national problems, as well as the role that unemployment plays in regressions that predict election results, both suggest that unemployment is a much more serious problem than Lucas's model implies. Are such considerations to be disregarded as mere 'coffee-break conversation', unfit to enter the list against implications derived from a formal model, or could it be that the formal model disregards important factors that are brought out by the informal considerations?

In a world of perfect foresight and hence of perfect capital markets, cyclical unemployment would indeed be as minor a problem as Lucas's model implies. Knowing that they would be re-employed at a certain date, and being able to borrow in a perfect capital market, the unemployed would suffer neither the fear of running out of assets and out of borrowing capacity, nor the feeling of uselessness and reduced self-esteem that often accompany unemployment. But in a world without perfect foresight unemployment looks very different. Lucas is, of course, aware that our actual world with imperfect foresight, and hence imperfect capital markets, is different from one with perfect foresight. Presumably it is the impossibility of effectively modelling the costs of unemployment in a world with imperfect foresight, joined with his belief that modelling is the royal road to truth, that has led him to present a model of the costs of unemployment which ignores what is probably a great part of the true costs. The model, which in empirical science economics should be merely a means for understanding the economy, appears to have become an end in itself.

Here is a model that its originator does not take all that seriously. Buffet-style restaurants charge a fixed price regardless of how much the customer eats. Using standard modelling techniques it is easy to show that such restaurants cannot exist. Let there be potential customers c_a ... c_n who respectively impose marginal costs p_a....p_n on the restaurant, where p_a ... p_n is a monotonically increasing series. Suppose further that there is perfect competition among restaurants, so that they all charge marginal costs. Consider a customer c_x, where $c_a > c_x < c_n$. If a restaurant charges a price p_x, where $p_a < p_x > p_n$, all customers in the range c_a ... c_x will go elsewhere. The restaurant will cover its marginal costs on customer c_x, but make a loss on all its customers in the range c_{x+1} ... c_n, and hence be unwilling to serve them. Mutually profitable trade between the restaurant and its customers is therefore possible only for a single customer, c_n. But since economies of scale make it unprofitable to serve just a single customer, buffet-style restaurants cannot exist, even though I developed this model while sitting in one. Suppose that such restaurants did not exist. Is it not likely that a journal would then accept a paper presenting a fancier version of this model to explain why we do not observe such restaurants?

CONCLUSION

Explicit modelling is a powerful and extremely useful tool. But it is not the sine qua non of empirical science economics; models have their drawbacks as well as their advantages.

Imagine that academic economic research was not a public good, but was sold in the market place. Would modelling then proceed as it does now, or would competitive pressures lead to a superior product? Many models now consist of statements of assumptions, various logical steps, and a conclusion that is intended to elucidate a particular aspect of the economy. Such models would appeal to those who enjoy the aesthetic pleasure of reading a tightly organized argument, and hence might find a commercial market.

But another segment of the market for economic research would demand a quite different product. Those who want to understand how the economy functions would force suppliers of models to compete in terms of how well the model explains the observed characteristics of the economy. Each modeller would then try to show that his or her model is superior to its rivals. In so far as models can be tested econometrically, modellers would thus be forced to test their models, not just against the null hypothesis, but also against other models. If econometric tests are not feasible, or perhaps to supplement them, modellers would have to provide other evidence, such as showing that the implications of the models are supported by qualitative evidence. To hold down the price of the model they would presumably cut down on the logical rigour of certain steps by not adhering to the principle of the strongest link.

NOTES

1. As a former president of the Econometric Society put it: in ordinary discourse, where we are not blindly manipulating but know all the time what we are doing and what the words mean, we can keep 'at the back of our heads' the necessary reserves and qualifications and adjustments which we shall have to make later on, in a way in which we cannot keep complicated partial differentials 'at the back' of several pages of algebra ... (Keynes, 1936, p. 297).
2. To be sure, using more casual reasoning than formal modelling would not solve the problem either, but it would let the researcher make some allowance for the less tractable factors. It would also avoid the spurious claim to precision and conclusiveness that may result from formal modelling.
3. Another possibility would be to pay a market rate of interest on required reserves.
4. The government, instead of the banks, could provide facilities for obtaining currency. But that would loosen its control over the currency supply.
5. The government could adjust interest rates so that a lower deposit rate would induce the public to hold more currency. But this would interfere with market processes, and the very purpose of the Fama scheme is to reduce government interference.

10. Empirical Testing: Driving a Mercedes down a Cow-track

> The computer revolution has, I believe, induced economists to carry reliance on mathematics and econometrics beyond the point of vanishing returns – something that is perhaps inevitable in the first flush of any revolution (Milton Friedman, 1991, p. 36).

> [T]o my knowledge no economic theory was ever abandoned because it was rejected by some empirical econometric test ... (Aris Spanos, 1986, p. 660).

> There is a growing cynicism among economists towards empirical work. Regression equations are regarded by many as mere stylistic devices, not unlike footnotes referencing obscure scholarly papers (Edward Leamer, 1978, p. 13).

This chapter serves two functions. One is to document my previous assertion that we often do not test our hypotheses adequately, and thus do not achieve the high degree of rigour and precision that we claim for our results. The second is to show that several of the problems that beset empirical testing can be remedied with additional effort, so that we should shift some of our effort away from polishing the strongest link of the argument towards improving empirical testing. I do not offer a catalogue of all the problems that beset applied econometrics, but discuss just a few, particularly those that are avoidable. The reader is probably familiar with much of the material covered, but not with its cumulative import. A natural response to this catalogue of horrors is: 'Everyone does it, so it must be all right.' But just as there is no collective guilt, there is no collective innocence.[1]

This chapter is not however an anti-econometrics tract. Econometrics is a powerful tool, and those who eschew its use grievously weaken their effectiveness. Thus I am not criticizing the use of econometrics to estimate coefficients or to generate forecasts; that is what Hoover (1989) has called the econometrics of measurement. Nor am I criticizing theoretical econometrics; it is not the fault of theoretical econometricians that others misuse their tools. Instead I ask whether the typical paper that tests economic hypotheses generates credible results. Hence my argument is not refuted by the existence of techniques that can overcome some of the problems. If they are not used, they might as well not exist.

SOFT TESTS AND HARD TESTS

Suppose you test a highly confirmed hypothesis, for example, that the price elasticity of demand is negative. What would you do if the computer were to spew out a positive coefficient? Surely you would not claim to have overthrown the law of demand by finding that mythical creature, a Giffen good, but instead would check your data. Suppose that you cannot find an error. Unless you have the self-confidence of the foolhardy you would still not proclaim to have disconfirmed the law of demand. Instead, you would rerun many variants of your regression until the recalcitrant computer finally acknowledged the sovereignty of your theory, or until you tired of this exercise and went on to another task. Thus Cooley and LeRoy (1981, p. 828), in discussing the sign of the interest rate coefficient in demand functions for money, write: 'Our results suggest that researchers who report successful empirical testing of the restrictions implied by the theory do so primarily by building in their conclusions, and that in fact the data do not provide confirmation for the theory.'

Only the naive are shocked by such soft and gentle testing. Staying with a well confirmed theory for quite some time, even though some data disconfirm it, is a standard practice in science. A dogmatic falsificationism, which insists that a hypothesis be dropped as soon as one finds any empirical evidence that contradicts it, is no longer a respected philosophy of science. As Lakatos (1978, p. 30) pointed out: 'Eighty-five years elapsed between the acceptance of the perihelion of Mercury as an anomaly and its acceptance as a falsification of Newton's theory.'

Thus, when dealing with highly confirmed hypotheses, such soft testing that is protective of a theory is a legitimate, though rather useless, activity. And when using such a hypothesis to estimate coefficients or to forecast, data mining (that is trying various data sets and selecting the one that gives the best fit) is legitimate. One can take the truth of the hypothesis as given, and use it to establish what data set is the appropriate one to use in forecasting with that hypothesis. Hence, one reason why soft testing is so popular in economics may well be that estimating coefficients and forecasting account for a substantial proportion of econometric work. If one often mines the data legitimately in forecasting and in measuring elasticities, it is easy to slip into the habit of doing so when testing hypotheses.

Easy it is. But also wrong, when the purpose of the exercise is not to use a hypothesis, but to determine its validity. That requires hard testing. And, as discussed below, then reporting only the best results is inappropriate.

SIGNIFICANCE TESTS, RIGHT WAY ROUND?

As we all know, and as many of us have often taught to undergraduates, failure to disconfirm a hypothesis is not the same as confirming it. If at the 5 per cent level we cannot reject the hypothesis that two means come from the same population, we are not entitled to say that we have shown that there is a high probability that they *do* come from the same population. Similarly, if at the 5 per cent level we cannot reject the hypothesis that the true value of a regression coefficient is zero, we should not claim to have shown that this particular variable has no effect on the dependent variable. Suppose that a regression coefficient has a t value of 0.7 on a two-tailed test with 60 degrees of freedom. Since its t value is well below the t value of 2 that is required for significance at the 5 per cent level, we would usually say that the coefficient is not significant. But actually, the probability of getting a t value of 0.7 on such a test due to sampling error is less than 50 per cent. Hence, despite the regression coefficient not being significant, there is a greater probability of being wrong in saying that the regressor has no effect on the dependent variable than in saying that it does.

This simple point, that one has to worry about both Type I and Type II errors, is sometimes ignored, presumably due to a failure to be aware of what our null hypothesis is. In testing the maintained hypothesis that a certain coefficient is positive against the null hypothesis that it is zero, we rightly give the benefit of the doubt to the null hypothesis. Unless we can show that there is a less than 5 per cent probability that a sampling error accounts for the positive value of the coefficient, we say that the null hypothesis has won.[2] Hence in the above case where the t value is only 0.7, we say that our hypothesis is not confirmed. But now consider the opposite case where our maintained hypothesis is that the coefficient is actually zero or negative. Now if we have a coefficient that is positive at, say, only the 60 per cent level, we should not claim, as is so often done, that our hypothesis is confirmed because the coefficient is not significant at the 95 per cent level. The probability that the true value of the coefficient is positive, and hence that our hypothesis is wrong, is greater than 50 per cent.[3]

The simple distinction between a test failing to show convincingly that a coefficient differs from zero, and its having shown that it is highly probable that this coefficient is actually zero, is relevant not just for those papers that claim that a certain variable does not matter. It also applies to procedures frequently used in other econometric work. I shall discuss several such procedures: the dropping of insignificant variables; the use of cross-equation restrictions; and the pre-testing for serial correlation or stationarity, as well as a more general and much more disturbing misuse of significance tests.

One often reported (and probably even more widely practised) procedure is to eliminate all the regressors with insignificant coefficients. But since collinearity is frequent, dropping seemingly insignificant variables can cause serious error. Suppose that what is critical for a hypothesis is that a certain coefficient is positive. Suppose further that, due to collinearity, it becomes positive only if one eliminates a certain variable that is not significant, that has, say, a t value of 1.3, which corresponds to a probability level of 20 per cent on a two-tailed test with 50 degrees of freedom. Correctly interpreted this tells us that the probability that this variable is actually relevant, and thus should not be dropped, is 80 per cent. Hence if the hypothesis is confirmed only when this variable is dropped, and is disconfirmed if it is kept in the regression, the hypothesis should be treated as more likely to be wrong than right. Yet under the standard procedure of dropping insignificant variables, it would be considered confirmed.

The idea that it is dangerous to drop insignificant variables runs counter to the general-to-specific modelling strategy expounded by David Hendry, often called LSE econometrics. This strategy has its comparative advantage if one is looking for an explanation (i.e. a theory) of what generated a particular data set. Hendry's method is to seek a combination of regressors that can explain the data set in a parsimonious way. If it turns out that the data can be accounted for by regressors $x_1 \ldots x_5$, with regressor x_6 being insignificant (and if an F test shows that the probability that the truncated hypothesis is inferior is no greater than 95 per cent), then x_6 should be excluded. Excluding all insignificant regressors takes care of the problem that, in principle, 'everything depends on everything else.' To be sure, such a rule uses its significance test, the F test, the wrong way round. But if the regressors $x_1....x_5$ provide a good enough explanation of the data, and if adding x_6 would add little to the fit, then even if x_6 does have *some* effect on y, we can say that regressors $x_1....x_5$ provide a theory that satisfactorily explains y in this data set. And it is the explanation of a particular data set that is the focus of LSE econometrics. Thus Spanos (1986, pp. 670–71) writes: 'Econometric modelling is viewed not as the estimation of theoretical relationships nor as procedures for establishing the "trueness" of economic theories, but as an endeavor to understand observable economic phenomena of interest using observed data in conjunction with some underlying theory in the context of a statistical framework.'

By contrast, imagine that we start out, not to explain a particular data set, but to use this data set to test a hypothesis. Suppose that it implies that x_6 is one of the determinants of y. Surely we would not want to say that the hypothesis is disconfirmed because in this data set there is 'only' a, say, 85 per cent probability that x_6 is a determinant of y. Such cases in which we want to test a theory, rather than to explain a data set, are common. While economic historians are interested in what explains British price movements in the nineteenth century, macroeconomists are interested in whether these movements provide evidence for, or against, the quantity theory. Such a conflict about whether a theory should be evaluated by seeing whether it can readily be dispensed with when one describes what generated a particular data set, or whether it should be evaluated by seeing if it contributes to our understanding of this data set, and is thus (at least weakly) confirmed by it, underlies the recent debate between Friedman and Schwartz (1991) and Hendry and Ericsson (1991), a debate that illustrates several of the issues discussed in this chapter.[4]

Another example of the wrong-way-round use of significance tests is the way cross-equation restrictions are often used. Some economists formulate their hypotheses so that they imply that the coefficients of certain regressors in two equations are equal. They then claim success if one cannot reject the hypothesis that the two coefficients are equal. But instead of treating their hypothesis as the maintained hypothesis that has to prove its worth at the 5 per cent level, they treat it as though it were the null hypothesis, and hence should be accepted unless there is strong evidence against it. Suppose, for example, that the difference between the two coefficients has a t value of 1.4 (which corresponds to a probability level of 20 per cent on a two-tailed test with 8 degrees of freedom). They would say that since the difference between the two coefficients is not significant, the implication of their hypothesis, that the two coefficients have the same value, is confirmed. But the probability that the two coefficients differ because they come from different universes is 80 per cent, so that the hypothesis, far from being confirmed, is substantially weakened.

A further example is provided by pre-tests for econometric processing, such as tests for serial correlation, stationarity, or normalcy. To have shown that one cannot be 95 per cent certain that a series is *not* stationary should hardly make one feel confident that it actually is stationary, and hence willing to use a technique for which stationarity is a precondition. Hence, at the very least, one should warn the reader by stating the probability level at which invalidating conditions, such as non-stationarity, can be rejected, rather than referring to a misinterpreted 5 per cent level. Moreover, one should, if possible, avoid any tests for which a departure from weakly tested conditions, such as stationarity, is likely to make a critical difference.

A much more general case of the misuse of significance tests occurs in papers in which the author shows that his or her hypothesis is not rejected by the data, and claims that this amounts to a confirmation of the hypothesis. It is, of course, correct to say that every time a hypothesis survives a test that could have disconfirmed it, its credibility is increased. But suppose the test tells us that, while we cannot reject the hypothesis at the 5 per cent level, there is only a, say, 20 per cent probability that the discrepancy between the data and the prediction of the hypothesis can be explained by sampling error. Surely that should not increase our belief in the hypothesis. Yet, as the reader can readily verify, we are often asked to do so.

It is puzzling why such misuses of significance tests proliferate. Perhaps it is just an example of a general gap between what we think is correct and what we do. Edward Leamer (1978, p. vi) thus speaks of the amazing 'transmogrification of particular individuals who wantonly sinned in the basement [where econometric modelling was done] and metamorphized into the highest of high priests as they ascended to the third floor' where econometric theory was taught. Another possible explanation is that without this erroneous procedure it would be much harder to confirm hypotheses, and thus to claim to have made a discovery. Moreover, there is a temptation to tolerate such helpful errors. Few referees want to cast the first stone and criticize a procedure they use themselves. And once an error becomes commonplace it is hard to object to it. A referee may well feel uneasy about rejecting a paper for doing something that many highly regarded papers also do. Alexander Pope (Bartlett, 1980, p. 337) summarized it well:

> Vice is a monster of such frightful mien
> As to be hated needs but to be seen
> Yet seen too oft, familiar with the face
> We first endure, then pity, then embrace.

A further possible explanation is that the results claimed for empirical tests are not intended to be taken literally, that when someone writes that his or her hypothesis is confirmed, that merely means that it is not strongly disconfirmed.

RIGHT WAY ROUND HELPS, BUT IS NOT ENOUGH

Another problem in using significance tests is the frequent confusion between statistical and substantive e.g. economic significance. This, too, is an obvious point, and something we warn or should warn undergraduates about. A significance test only guards against treating as a genuine difference something that may well be due to sampling error. It tells us nothing about the substantive significance of empirical results.[5] As McCloskey (1985) points out, we do not expect theories to be exactly right; if purchasing power parity holds within, say, 0.01 per cent, surely we would not reject the theory of purchasing power parity, even if this 0.01 per cent were statistically significant because our sample is extremely large. Similarly, suppose we ask whether by the year 1600 there was an integrated world market for wheat. Knowing whether the ratio of wheat prices in Warsaw and in Venice varied by no more than, say, 10 per cent does not resolve the issue: 'From the bare lone number one can infer nothing, because no standard is provided for saying whether the number is large or small' (McCloskey, 1985, p. 143). Leamer (1991, p. 219) is surely right in arguing that a 'defect of most "tests" of economic hypotheses is that no consideration is given to defining the sense in which the hypothesis is approximately correct. This is not merely an oversight, since it is far from easy in most circumstances to select a suitable measure of accuracy of an approximation.' In place of such a measure significance tests are often used, but this is not a valid procedure. It is not our PCs, but we ourselves who must decide whether a theory is accurate enough to be called 'correct'. As McCloskey (1985) points out, in deciding what significance levels to use we should consult our loss function to decide what Type I and Type II errors to risk.

Ignoring the distinction between statistical and substantive significance often makes for an inappropriate test. There is no problem if the hypothesis merely implies that x has *some* effect on y, but most hypotheses imply much more. Thus a hypothesis may imply that x is a major cause of y. To test such a hypothesis one must look, not only at the t value, but also at the β coefficients or partial correlation coefficients, neither of which is usually reported.[6] Or the hypothesis may imply that, even though x does not dominate y, its effect on y is more than trivial. For example, the hypothesis that industrial concentration raises profits is not supported as a meaningful result if a very high concentration ratio raises profits by only 0.001 per cent, even if this coefficient is significant at the 1 per cent level.

The confusion of statistical and substantive significance is hardly unusual, even in a top journal. McCloskey used a small sample of papers published during 1981–83 in the *American Economic Review* to see how often this simple point was ignored. Of the ten papers in his sample, seven

> let statistical significance do the work of substantive significance. ... In four of the seven papers with significant errors in the use of significance, there is some discussion of how large a coefficient would need to be to be large, but even these let statistical significance do most of the work. And even in the three papers that recognize the distinction and apply it consistently, there is flirtation with intellectual disaster. ... Even the best economists, in short, overuse the statistical test of significance (McCloskey, 1985, pp. 171–2).

Significance tests are also often misused in testing compound hypotheses. Some hypotheses are tested in several steps. Thus, someone might first test whether expectations are rational, and upon finding that rationality cannot be rejected at the 97 per cent level, impose the rationality restriction in a second equation. Suppose that in the second equation the strategic coefficient is significantly positive at the 96 per cent level, and that its being positive is a necessary condition for a third and final equation, in which the coefficient that is critical for the hypothesis is confirmed at the 95 per cent level. The hypothesis is then supported by these three tests, not at the 95 per cent level which under current practice would generally be claimed for it, but only at the 88 per cent level.[7]

A further problem is the familiar one that standard significance tests are not appropriate in the presence of pre-testing. And pre-testing is so pervasive that, in many cases, probably neither the author nor the reader is aware of it. For example, there is pre-testing whenever we use Almon lags or some other procedure that asks the computer to calculate lags on the criterion of maximizing R^2, and then report only the regression that has the highest R^2. Peter Kennedy (1979, pp. 51–2) presents the following justification for not worrying about pre-test bias:

> Most econometricians ignore the pre-test bias: in fact few even admit to its existence. The main counter-argument to pre-test bias is that without pre-testing we must rely on an *assumption* concerning what variables are included in the set of independent variables. ... Pretesting is simply a means of providing additional evidence to aid the econometrician in selecting the appropriate set of independent variables. So long as the econometrician views this as evidence to be evaluated sensibly in light of other considerations (such as economic theory) ... pre-test bias should not be a problem.

In the context of testing hypotheses, rather than of estimating coefficients, this is a remarkable argument. Essentially it says that since we need to pre-test, pre-testing does not create a serious problem. The rather optimistic assumption that underlies this argument is that the world is so arranged that whatever is necessary to do econometrics cannot create a serious problem. Leibnitz has remarked that God is a mathematician. Perhaps econometricians believe that He is an econometrician, or at least that He has a special love for econometricians.

REPORTING THE RESULTS: SCIENTISTS OR ADVERTISERS?

In principle, few would disagree that in hard testing a scientist should not run, say, thirty different but equally reliable experiments and then report only the one that confirms the hypothesis, while keeping silent about those that disconfirm it. Thus Richard Feynman, a Nobel Laureate in physics, in contrasting genuine science with pseudo-science, wrote:

> But there is *one* feature ... that is generally missing in ... [pseudo-science.] It's a kind of scientific integrity, a principle of scientific thought that corresponds to a kind of utter honesty – a kind of leaning over backwards. For example, if you are doing an experiment, you should report everything that you think might make it invalid – not only what you think is right about it; ... (Feynman, 1985, p. 311; italics in original).

There is no way of finding out how frequently economists report only the best of many results, but such a practice is reputed to be common. As Michael Lovell (1983, p. 1) points out, papers sometimes contain statements such as: 'Because of space limitations, only the best of a variety of models can be presented here,' or '[w]e let the data specify the model. ...' It is therefore not surprising that Edward Leamer (1983, pp. 36–7) has argued that:

> The econometric art ... involves fitting many, perhaps thousands, of statistical models. One or several that the researcher finds pleasing are selected for reporting purposes. ... The concepts of unbiasedness, consistency, efficiency, maximum-likelihood estimation, in fact all the concepts of traditional theory, utterly lose their meaning by the time an applied researcher pulls from the bramble of computer output the one thorn of a model he likes best, the one he has chosen to portray as a rose. The consuming public is hardly fooled by this chicanery.

Similarly, Cooley and LeRoy (1981, pp. 825–6) have noted: 'particularly in macroeconomics, therefore, we often have what is very nearly a zero-communication information equilibrium. The researcher has the motive and opportunity to present his results selectively, and the reader, knowing this, imputes a low or zero signal-to-noise ratio to the reported results.' This appears to be something of an overstatement. In a questionnaire I sent to a sample of economists asking about their concern over selective reporting of econometric results, less than a third responded that the danger of selective reporting made them 'quite skeptical' or made them 'distrust most, or all, econometric tests', while more than a half responded that it made them 'somewhat, but no more than somewhat, sceptical' (Mayer, 1992).

In any case, reacting to selective reporting with outrage is simplistic. It is only human that what is perceived to be common practice tends to be treated as appropriate practice; if others give their hypotheses a head start by reporting only the best results, why should I handicap my hypothesis by not doing the same? In addition, what is meant by suppressing an unfavourable result is sometimes unclear. Out of curiosity one sometimes runs some regressions whose results are less meaningful than others. Should these be reported too?

What is perhaps just as or more troubling than selective reporting is that due to the publication filter, biased reporting occurs even if no individual researcher acts in a biased manner (Denton, 1988). Positive results are much more likely to reach print than are negatives ones, i.e. 'failures'. Assume that all economists eschew data mining, but many economists independently formulate and test a certain hypothesis, using different regressors. If only their positive results achieve publication, the outcome is a communal data mining that may cause an invalid hypothesis to be accepted.

All in all, the situation is troubling. The market for economic research resembles the market for used cars: the lemon effect plays a large role. Reliable work does not receive the credence it deserves because it cannot be distinguished from the output of the data mine.

ROBUSTNESS TESTS: GOING OUT OF ONE'S WAY TO LOOK FOR TROUBLE

Suppose a researcher who runs only a single one of several equally justifiable regressions obtains a result that favours the hypothesis and reports that. Such a researcher cannot be accused of explicitly hiding disconfirming results, but cannot claim to have adequately validated the hypothesis. Hitting in the first try on a regression that happens to support one's hypothesis may just be due to luck (see Bronfenbrenner, 1972). Stopping when one is ahead is a good rule in gambling, but not in science.

Ideally a researcher testing an economic hypothesis would run all plausible regressions that fairly represent the economic hypothesis.[8] This is often not possible, but he or she could run a fairly large number.[9] Leamer (1983) gives a telling example of how important robustness tests are. He shows that in testing the hypothesis that capital punishment deters murder, one can get all sorts of results, depending on what regressors one includes. Similarly, Salwa Khoury (1987, 1990) demonstrates that the results of monetary policy reaction functions are highly sensitive to more or less arbitrary decisions about the set of variables that are included in the regression.

Using structural econometric models to estimate the effect of monetary and fiscal policies provides another example of how lack of robustness can weaken the results. In the simulations of these policies in a set of models, the outcome varies substantially from model to model (see Fisher et al., 1989; Frankel and Rockett, 1988; and Mayer, 1990, Ch. 5).

Leamer's extreme-bounds analysis provides a systematic way of organizing robustness tests, but one does not have to accept Leamer's Bayesian approach to advocate more robustness testing than currently takes place. Suppose an agronomist, who adheres to classical procedures, investigates whether a certain fertilizer raises yields. He or she will spread this fertilizer, not just on a single plot, but on many plots with different soil conditions, to avoid crediting the fertilizer with a crop yield that could be due to that particular plot having an unusually fertile soil (see Ronald Fisher, 1932, Ch. 8).

Robustness tests should comprise not only tests for omitted variables and for various lags, but also tests for alternative functional forms, such as levels versus first differences, or natural numbers versus logs. To some extent econometric considerations constrain the economist's choice, but often still leave several alternatives. And the choice among them can have important consequences. Thus, for a simple money demand function, Paul Zarembka (1968) shows that the t values of some coefficients depend strongly on the particular functional form that is used. Bronfenbrenner (1972) cites other examples. Hence, to avoid reporting what Leamer calls 'whimsical' results, researchers should test for the appropriate functional form and report the results of such tests (see Los, 1986; Beggs, 1988).

Whenever possible robustness tests should also be used to see how the hypothesis performs on different data sets. Often only one data set is available. But not always. In many cases researchers could use data sets for several countries. Working with foreign data may be laborious, since it may require learning about foreign sources and definitions, as well as watching for special conditions peculiar to each country. But laboriousness is not considered a barrier to demands for a formally spelled-out model, so why should it be a barrier to the use of foreign data?

Moreover, in some cases multiple data sets are available for the same country. Several price indexes exist, and it is often not clear which one should be used. It may then be worth trying more than one since, as Michael Evans (1967) demonstrates, the use of different deflators can have a substantial effect. Another example comes from measures of the US savings rate. As Paul Taubman (1968) pointed out more than thirty years ago, the generally used National Income Accounts data are not the only data that measure the savings rate. He showed that when one tests various savings functions with these different data sets – which all purport to measure the same concept of saving – one can get quite different results. More recently Fred Block (1990) has shown, that while the savings ratio as calculated in the National Income Accounts data fell sharply in the 1980s, the savings ratio calculated from the Fed's flow-of-funds data rose. It is by no means clear that the National Income Accounts data are superior. Numerous discussions about the falling savings ratio have therefore treated as a fact what may well be a non-fact. Similarly, one might ask what would have happened in the extensive tests of the Ricardian equivalence proposition had the flow-of-funds data been used. There is no reason to think that the results of this literature, however elegant its econometrics, are any more reliable than is its underlying assumption that the National Income Accounts data set is the correct one.

It is also important to test whether the hypothesis is robust with respect to the sample period, because there is considerable evidence that, perhaps due to pre-test bias, the results for one sample period are not a reliable guide to what happens in another period. Already in the 1950s Robert Ferber (1953, 1956) showed that the consumption function that predicts best during the sample period frequently does not do so in a post-sample period. Similarly, Martin Schupak (1962), in studying the demand for certain consumer expenditures, found that there is only a weak relation between the relative accuracy with which various regressions fit the data in the sample period and in the post-sample period. Comparing five different regressions, it turned out that in less than a quarter of the cases did the regression that gave the best fit in the sample period also give the best post-sample fit. I extended this analysis by looking at a variety of cases in which a researcher had compared the goodness of fit of two or more hypotheses, and someone had repeated the test for a later sample period. In these cases, which included a wide variety of econometric studies, goodness of fit during the sample period was not a reliable guide to post-sample performance. Even with as few as three competing hypotheses, there is a less than two-thirds probability that the model that performed best during the sample period also performed best in the post-sample period. And when there are four competing hypotheses the probability drops to about one-third (Mayer, 1975).[10]

The importance of testing for changes in the sample period is brought out by looking at what can happen when the sample period is changed slightly by dropping just a single year. When Howrey and Hymans (1978) eliminated a single year from a consumption function that had been fitted to estimate the interest elasticity of saving, the t value of the coefficient of the interest rate fell from -3.24 to -1.62. In examining Peter Temin's (1976) analysis of consumption during the Great Depression, I found that the omission from the period of fit of a single year, 1919 (in which the post-World War I demobilization was not yet completed), changed the results drastically (Mayer, 1978).

How serious a problem is it if the result depends on a single observation, or on just a few observations? An advantage of regression analysis over a mere anecdote – that regression analysis encompasses information from many observations – is not lost entirely when the regression results depend primarily on a single observation, since the other observations still have some effect. All the same, a result that is determined by a single observation is suspect. The dominant observation could be due to an extraneous event, such as a strike. Moreover, the variable may be significant only because it took on an extreme value in that particular year; more normal changes in it may have no meaningful effect on the dependent variable. Hence, saying that this variable is significant tells only part of the story. Put another way, if a regression is dominated by one particular observation, the true sample size for that regression is closer to 2 than to the number of observations that the computer uses in calculating the regression diagnostics. Techniques for dealing with outliers and dominant observations are available (Belsley, Kuh and Welsch, 1980; Beggs, 1988), but even highly effective techniques do not improve the quality of research if they are not used.

THE FREQUENCY OF ROBUSTNESS TESTS

Economists now report the results of robustness tests more often than they used to. Even so, much remains to be done. Many papers do not provide any robustness tests at all, and those that do usually cite only a few. And we are not told whether the authors tried any others that yielded disconcerting results. (Here is an illustration of how unusual it is to discuss unreported regressions: once when I mentioned in a footnote that I had not run any unreported regressions, a referee asked that this footnote be eliminated.)

What ameliorates the problem to some extent is the occasional, though rather infrequent, publication of critical 'Comments'. In a 25 per cent random sample of papers published during 1965–89 in the *American Economic Review*, the *Journal of Political Economy* and the *Review of Economics and Statistics*, Raymond Hubbard and Daniel Vetter (forthcoming) found no pure and simple replications. However, 5.4 per cent of the papers were what they called a 'replication with extension', that is papers that did not try mechanically to reproduce a previously published result, but modified some of the variables used in the previous paper.[11] Such replications, which are actually robustness tests, are surely undertaken much more frequently than this 5.4 per cent figure indicates, because replications that do not change the results are not likely to be published. All the same, it suggests that relatively few papers are subjected to robustness tests once they are published.

One reason replications are relatively scarce is that such work is not highly regarded. It is considered something which anyone can do, and in the ethos of our profession what is easy is not worth doing. As Kane (1984, p. 3) remarked, to economists: 'Uninventive verifying of some-one else's empirical research is not a completely respectable use of one's time. Choosing such a task is widely regarded as *prima facie* evidence of intellectual mediocrity, revealing a lack of creativity and perhaps a bullying spirit.' Another reason is that replication is difficult and often indeed impossible because authors do not cooperate, or because they have not kept their data and adequate records. Dewald, Thursby and Anderson (1986, p. 591) report that when they requested their programmes and data from authors who had previously published papers in the *Journal of Money, Credit and Banking*: 'Approximately one third of the authors (20) never replied to our repeated requests, and an additional one third (20) replied that they could not furnish their programs or data. ... Fourteen [of the latter group] wrote that they had lost or discarded their data.'[12] My own experience in request-ing data from authors was similarly disconcerting.[13] In recent years some journals have tried to persuade authors to be more forthcoming with their data, so the situation may have improved (see Feigenbaum and Levy, forthcoming).

Evidently, economists do not attribute as much importance to replication as natural scientists do. A survey of natural scientists found that 62 per cent called 'replicability of research techniques' 'essential', while a further 18 per cent considered it to be 'very important but not essential'. Neither originality, logical rigour, or any of the other criteria listed in the survey were ranked as 'essential' by so many respondents as was replicability (Chase, 1970).

DAMN THE TORPEDOES, FULL SPEED AHEAD

Another problem with econometric work is that economists place so little emphasis on that most mundane and unglamorous of tasks, getting the arithmetic right.[14] It seems likely that many, if not most, economists and their research assistants do not bother to check the key punching of their data, their computations and the copying from the computer output to their tables. Relying on the accuracy of commercial data bases is also dangerous. Without especially looking for them, I have found errors in both the data bases I have used. As a result, many published results may be invalid. As Dewald, Thursby and Anderson (1986, p. 600) note, due to 'collinearity of data and high correlations among coefficient estimators ... even slight differences in data values or in the numerical precision of computer programs may produce sharply different parameter estimates.'[15]

Beyond the purely mechanical task of checking that the arithmetic is correct, one also has to worry about using the correct arithmetic procedure. As Thomas Gittings (1991) has demonstrated when dealing with index numbers, rounding errors can substantially affect the calculated monthly growth rates, while Boris Pesek (1961) has shown that calculating growth rates is a more complex problem than is usually assumed.

A further problem is that our econometric techniques may not be up to the tasks we set for them presumably, in part, because they are applied to data that do not meet the required conditions. Los (1986, p. 7) reminds us that: 'Many studies have shown that to regress a variable on two or three other variables with only ten or fifteen data points does not provide very robust results.' This is surely no surprise to theoretical econometricians, but there is a substantial gap between what we know and what we do. As Los (1986, p. 7) goes on to point out: 'Although the phenomenon of collinearity is discussed in many econometric textbooks, it is virtually ignored in the daily empirical research.'

Lovell (1983) undertook a test of a then standard econometric procedure – with disturbing results. He set out a consumption function and used Monte Carlo techniques to test whether the diagnostics of various regression equations that someone might fit to these data would allow him or her to select the function that actually generated the data. They did not. Since, as was standard at the time but is no longer, Lovell did not test for unit roots, perhaps his results are no indictment of current state-of-the-art work. But 'perhaps' is not the same as 'surely'. Hence, one might be sceptical even about modern applied econometric work, until someone shows that Lovell's results are not relevant to it.

SO WHERE ARE WE?

In this chapter I have described the rough, unfinished back of the high-tech scenery that the audience sees as it watches the drama (or comedy?) called econometric testing. That gives a biased impression. Econometric tests are far from useless. They are worth doing, and their results do tell us something. If one asks no more of them than that, fine and good.[16]

But many economists insist that economics can deliver more, much more, than merely, more or less, plausible knowledge, that it can reach its results with compelling demonstrations. By such a standard how should one describe our usual way of testing hypotheses? One possibility is to interpret it, as Blaug (1980, p. 256) does, as 'playing tennis with the net down.' Another is to treat it as intentionally soft testing, in Gilbert's (1986, p. 284) apt wording as using econometrics merely to 'illustrate' theories, i.e. as showing that our theory *might* be right. Alternatively one can view it, not so much as a serious investigation of how the economy functions, but more as taking a technique for a walk, similar to a textbook's illustration of how one might apply a technique if one had the right kind of data. A sharper verdict would be to call it institutionally sanctioned pretence. But since most readers are knowledgeable enough to treat the results sceptically, it should probably not be treated as an attempt to deceive. Perhaps it is best viewed, at least in some cases, as a ceremonial activity, as 'the done thing'. Summers (1991, p. 132) calls the influence of econometric results on economic theory 'negligible', and contrasts that state of affairs with the way theoretical physicists treat experimental results.

Such an interpretation of econometric testing as lacking seriousness is supported by the way challenges to the prevailing procedure are often treated.[17] Thus Zarembka's demonstration of the importance for money demand functions of the choice of a functional form should have had much effect on subsequent work. It did not. Taubman's paper, a note published in a leading journal, the *Review of Economics and Statistics*, should have induced economists to test their savings hypotheses with all three set of data. It did not. And Lovell's paper (also published in the *Review of Economics and Statistics*) has been frequently cited for its criticism of biased reporting, but his more dramatic findings about the unreliability of regression diagnostics do not appear to have had much effect. Has any paper mentioned it as a qualification of its results? The validity of certain specific techniques, such as Granger causality or VARs, is debated extensively. Rejecting the use of these techniques is painless for those who have not used them and do not intend to do so. But the problems that affect applied econometrics more generally are not much discussed.

Perhaps my charge that econometric testing lacks seriousness of purpose is wrong; as in so many other discussions of motives there is no way of verifying one's surmise. But regardless of the cause, it should be clear that most econometric testing is not rigorous. Combining such tests with formalized theoretical analysis or elaborate techniques is another instance of the principle of the strongest link. The car is sleek and elegant; too bad the wheels keep falling off.

NOTES

1. An extreme Kuhnian might reply that whatever practitioners do should be treated as good science. But if one accepts that rule one would have to eliminate the barriers against any pseudo-science in which the practitioners share a common methodology. Besides, as discussed in Chapter 2, economists have a self-interest in believing certain things.
2. Frank Denton (1988) mentions an interpretation of significance tests that has nothing to do with sampling error. In that interpretation the t value just measures whether the coefficient is close enough to the predicted value that we can say that our hypothesis is sufficiently accurate. I will ignore this interpretation since it is not the standard one. Its faults are discussed by McCloskey (1985, Ch. 9).
3. How then can we, as we so often want to, go beyond making the negative statement that we have no convincing evidence that a variable *does* matter, to the statement that we have convincing evidence that it *does not* matter? It might be

possible to run many different tests and to combine their results. If in a large
enough sample of tests the coefficient is insignificantly different from zero
enough times, we can reject the hypothesis that its true value is positive.

4. Hendry and Ericsson argue that a Friedman and Schwartz equation for money
demand should be rejected because a Hendry and Ericsson equation encompassed
it by having a smaller variance. Friedman and Schwartz respond that obtaining
the best fit to a particular data set is not the only goal of economic analysis.
Instead one can: 'examine a wide variety of evidence, quantitative as well as
nonquantitative, ... [and] test results from one body of evidence on other bodies
using econometric techniques as one tool in this process, and build up a collection
of simple hypotheses that may or may not be readily viewed as components of a
broader all-embracing hypothesis. ... (Friedman and Schwartz, 1991, p. 39).

In addition, Friedman and Schwartz argue that Hendry and Ericsson's emphasis on techniques is more appropriate to teaching new techniques than to obtaining substantive results; they also object to Hendry and Ericsson's de-emphasis of
the quality and meaning of the data. These criticisms are congruent with the
argument of this chapter.

5. Nor can the substantive significance be read off the value of R^2, except in simple
regressions.

6. The size of the regression coefficient tells us the effect on the dependent variable
of a one-unit change in the regressor, but the importance of the regressor also
depends upon how much it varied during the sample period. The β coefficient is
the regression coefficient multiplied by the ratio of the standard deviation of the
regressor to the standard deviation of the dependent variable. It measures the
relative importance of various regressors.

7. This assumes that the error terms of the three regressions are orthogonal.
Pyramiding not only distorts significance tests, but may also make the point
estimates of the final regression fragile. Suppose that in the first equation the
coefficient that is to be used in the second equation is 0.5 ± 0.2. It would then be
worth seeing whether the second equation yields the same result, if instead of
just using the 0.5 point estimate from the first equation one were to use also
values of 0.3 and 0.7. And similarly for the third equation. But I cannot recall a
case where this was done.

8. A related problem is that in grid searches the best fitting coefficient is often
selected without any discussion of whether its fit is significantly better than that
of another coefficient that might have a quite different implication for the hypothesis being tested. Cartwright (1991) points out that robustness tests are not
as useful as independent tests of the hypothesis that do not share auxiliary
assumptions with the original test. That is so, but independent tests are often not
feasible, and robustness tests are better than no additional tests at all. Moreover,
they guard against the effects of data mining.

9. If one is interested only in the validity of a specific model, then it is not
necessary to test alternatives. But often one wants to know about the truth of a
broader theory, and not just about the truth of a model that is a particular
specification of the theory. Whenever one tests a hypothesis one also tests other,
auxiliary hypotheses along with it. (This is known as the Duhem–Quine problem.) By testing many different versions of the hypothesis one reduces the
probability that the results obtained are due to the particular auxiliary assumptions.

10. My sample may be slightly biased since disconfirming results are more likely to
be published than confirming ones. However, most of the sources I used were not
disconfirming notes dealing with a particular paper, but more comprehensive
surveys.

11. This is similar to the way replication is usually done in natural sciences. See Mulkay and Gilbert (1986).
12. For papers that were accepted and awaiting publication, and for papers still in the refereeing process, the data were more frequently available.
13. In one case I could not tell from a table what units the coefficients were in; none of the usual units seemed to make sense. When I wrote to the author he replied, 'I *think* they are in $100 millions' (italics added).
14. Summers (1991, p. 137n) cites a paper that won the Frisch medal as the best paper in *Econometrica*, 'even after it was recognized that it contained major data errors, which affected the substantive conclusions ... .'
15. Dewald, Thursby and Anderson (1986) cited an error in a paper by Harold Nathan and myself. A single number was recorded incorrectly and the results in the tables changed substantially. This error was small enough so that one would not notice it just by looking at the data.
16. The cynical claim that with sufficient effort one can always get any variable to be significant with the right sign is not correct. To illustrate, I once ran some regressions for a campus committee to explain departmental budgets. Try as I might, I could not get a variable that I felt sure was relevant to become significant. The budget office then told me that it ignored that variable.
17. On the other hand, the *American Economic Review* did publish the Dewald, Thursby and Anderson paper.

11. Good Dentists or Bad Physicists?

If economists could manage to get themselves thought of as humble, competent people, on a level with dentists, that would be splendid (J. M. Keynes, 1972, p. 332).

As just discussed, our econometric tests suffer from serious problems, some of which are currently unavoidable. Hence, at least for now, empirical science economics can only be an inexact science. Not only is it inexact with respect to its empirical base, but also, if researchers allocate their efforts efficiently and avoid the principle of the strongest link, it will often not show great theoretical rigour either.

What I have just said conflicts with a long tradition in economics, which claims that economists can attain empirically relevant results without sacrificing rigour. Introspection allows us to select premises that are indisputably valid. And correct reasoning from valid premises must result in correct conclusions, so that empirical tests and their inevitable inexactitude can be avoided.

This tradition, whose leading proponent was John Stuart Mill, is open to at least three objections. First, to argue from introspection requires that practically everyone's introspection yields the same result. This is so in certain cases, and some simple results can be derived from generally agreed-upon propositions. But not all the results we want. To obtain results that are not trivial we have at times to extend our introspection on to more controversial ground. Thus, many important propositions require the assumption that agents act strictly to maximize their individual welfare. But that assumption cannot be derived merely from introspection. Surely many people believe that the welfare of others plays some role in their own utility function. Second, premises derived from introspection are used jointly with the premise of rational behaviour. But there is much evidence that behaviour is not entirely rational (see Kahneman, Slovic and Tversky, 1982; Thaler, 1990). This does not mean that reasoning that assumes self-interested, rational behaviour should be rejected. But it does mean that hypotheses derived from these premises have to be tested by seeing whether their implications are confirmed. Third, we encounter numerous anomalies (see LeRoy, 1989; Levis, 1989; and Thaler, various dates). If in these cases deductive arguments from generally agreed-upon premises lead us astray, how can we know – except by empirical testing – that we are not led astray in other cases too? This inability to achieve entirely firm conclusions in empirical science economics should shape our research strategy, our publication practices and the training we provide to graduate students.

RESEARCH IN EMPIRICAL SCIENCE ECONOMICS

If I am right, the adherence to the principle of the strongest link has substantially inhibited the development of empirical science economics. But as long as those engaged in empirical science economics consider themselves the poor relations of formalist economists, the temptation to claim great rigour and precision by directing attention to the strongest link will be hard to resist. Hence, those working on empirical science economics must keep in mind that they should worship their own gods, and not those of the formalists. They need not admire papers which use sophisticated techniques merely to translate familiar points into elegant models that add little to our understanding of the economy. As William Baumol (1991, p. 2) warns us: 'The trouble is that if ... only those whose writings are pockmarked by algebraic symbols receive kudos, one can expect a misallocation of resources like that which always results from a distortion of relative prices.' That applies, not just to the kudos received from others, but also the kudos one awards oneself.

If we are to focus on understanding how the economy functions, rather than on how economic models function, economics will have to become less self-referential and more client-oriented. This does not mean that we should address only problems the public is interested in, or that we have to write, as did most economists of yore, in ways that any educated person can understand. Economics is too complex for that. But we should cease to treat incomprehensibility as a virtue, and not admire a paper just because it is so technical that few can understand it. At present, as Blaug (1990, p. 213) has remarked: 'to be intelligible is to be suspect'. This is childish. A theory of value that has the value of a product determined by the technical sophistication of the producers is not good economics. The fewer the people who find a product useful, the *less* valuable it is. A mathematician, E.C. Zeeman (1979, p. vii) tells us: 'As a general rule, whenever mathematics is applied to science the minimum possible mathematics should be used, and it should play a subservient role to the matter being modelled.'

Along the same lines, we economists are rightly proud of possessing a more coherent and developed body of theory than do other social scientists. But we should keep in mind the old proverb 'Beggars mounted, ride their steeds to death'. By all means let us use our theory when it helps to elucidate a problem. But no economist should feel obliged to use theory when it merely clogs up pages and makes a simple point appear complex. Always discussing a problem in the most abstract and theoretical terms possible bears witness to pomposity rather than to superior intellect.

The time saved by eschewing decorative mathematics and ritualistic invocations of 'theory' should be spent on improving empirical testing. As discussed in the previous chapter, there is much to be done, particularly in testing for robustness, using significance tests appropriately, and in showing greater concern about the quality of the data.

Who should undertake the additional robustness testing, the proposer of the hypothesis, or someone else? Cooley and LeRoy (1981, p. 826) argue that natural scientists use the advocacy principle: the proponent of a hypothesis makes the strongest case he or she reasonably can, and relies on others to point out its limitations. But they provide no supporting evidence, and one may well doubt that natural scientists are as neglectful of testing the robustness of their hypotheses as economists are.[1] Feynman's discussion of scientific honesty, cited in the previous chapter, does not support Cooley and LeRoy's contention.

Having others do the robustness tests has the advantage that their testing is likely to be less forgiving. They may also bring to the task insights that the original researchers lacked. But there are also advantages to having the original researchers do their own robustness testing. Since they have the data at hand and are familiar with them, they can do the work faster. Furthermore, in those cases in which robustness tests destroy the hypothesis, it saves journal space and readers' time if the original researchers discover this, and hence do not publish invalid results. Moreover, if robustness tests are done by others, they will appear only with a substantial lag.

But regardless of whether in an ideal world it would be better to have someone else test for robustness, as a practical matter much of it has to be done by the original researcher. The rewards for showing that someone else's results are fragile are hardly great, and anyone planning to test someone else's results has to take into account that the results may turn out to be robust after all, so that the robustness test is unpublishable.[2]

Apart from requiring much more robustness testing, reliable empirical testing also demands that significance tests be used correctly. This can be painful. It forces us in many cases to admit that our results are only weakly confirmed. This is disconcerting, not only when testing the main hypothesis, but also when using a significance test to legitimize some econometric procedure. It is also disconcerting to admit that success on a significance test protects one's results only against the danger of sampling error, and that it does not ensure that the results are economically meaningful. And deciding whether a coefficient is large enough to have economic significance can be an iffy thing, open to dispute. It is not nearly as comforting as looking up the significance level in a table of t values. Moreover, once one makes allowance for pre-test bias, for compound hypotheses, and for the possibility that coefficients vary from time to time, results that previously looked strong may now appear open to dispute.

But why go on pretending to 'have shown at the 5 per cent level?' Most readers know that they should not take such claims seriously. An obvious response is to say: 'This is all very well, but if I admit that my results are confirmed only at a, say, 20 per cent level, how can I get my paper published?' A valid, though somewhat sanctimonious reply is that being truthful is more important than being published – at least once one has tenure. Another reply is that editors and referees should not set standards which the authors, editors and readers all know to be just a facade. Curbing unrealistic claims would not reduce significantly the number of papers that are published, since the number and the size of journals are determined by library budgets and the number of individual subscribers. Individual authors do, of course, have an incentive to exaggerate the validity of their results, but referees and editors are there to police that. Along the same lines, editors and referees should, as discussed in Chapter 6, be more open to papers with circumstantial evidence.

Editors should also enforce greater concern about the quality of the data. One can reply to Leontief's (1983) complaint about using hand-me-down data, by saying that gathering one's own data is generally too expensive. But what is much harder to justify is that we academic economists hardly ever talk to those who gather the data and, I suspect, often do not read available descriptions of how the data are compiled. Empirical papers should be required to have at least a sentence or two, and often a section or an appendix, discussing whether the data are reliable enough for the purpose at hand. For example, I recently refereed a paper that dealt with the Fed's reaction to misses of its monetary targets. The authors seemed unaware that the estimates of the monetary growth rates that the Fed had available when making its decisions differed sharply from the revised data they were using in their paper. Requirements for an appendix on data quality would reduce such errors. It is care about data, rather than use of set theory and linear algebra, that characterizes good empirical science.

The weaknesses of our econometric procedures also suggest that we should pay more attention to other evidence. One possibility is to put greater weight on theoretical reasoning, and to disbelieve disconfirming econometric evidence. By and large, we probably do this already to a sufficient, or more than sufficient, extent. Another possibility is to use empirical evidence that requires relatively little econometric processing. As discussed in Chapter 6, Summers (1991) argues persuasively that the evidence that economists find convincing is not the product of sophisticated econometrics, but of less formal empirical work.

Evidence from surveys can also be useful. The poor reputation that survey evidence has is not entirely unwarranted, because many surveys have been done badly. But sociologists have garnered much expertise in constructing questionnaires, and for certain purposes questionnaires can be used with some confidence.[3] Moreover, as a number of prominent participants in a recent symposium on the future of economics have advocated, we should probably pay more attention to experimental results and to interdisciplinary work (see Fishburn, 1991; Plott, 1991; Schmalensee, 1991; Morishima, 1991; Stiglitz, 1991; Wiseman, 1991).

PUBLICATIONS

The foregoing implies that editors and referees should not induce authors to paste in unneeded mathematics or theory. As Summers (1991, p. 146) remarks, 'all too often researchers, referees and editors ... ask the same questions that jugglers' audiences ask – Have virtuosity and skill been demonstrated? Was something difficult done?' Instead, editors should require authors to pay sufficient attention to the meaning and quality of the data, and to the robustness of their results. Moreover, they should favour papers with results that are significant at, say, the 75 per cent level on a valid significance test, over those that are significant at the 99 per cent level on an invalid test. And they should be more hospitable to tests based on questionnaires and other less mainstream sources.

We also need reports on post-sample tests of time-series papers. Readers of such papers may well wonder whether subsequent data will support the hypothesis as well as do the data the paper uses. Hence journals should encourage (or require?) authors to report after, say, five years, how well their hypotheses performed on subsequent data. If authors are reluctant to do this, the journals could encourage graduate students to do so in their stead. In econometrics courses students are sometimes required to do such follow-up exercises, and some of their results should be published, perhaps as one- or two-paragraph notes. Indeed, if one thinks of applied econometrics as a serious attempt to explain how the economy functions, it is puzzling why such notes have not been published all along.

In addition, editors should apply economic analysis to their choice of papers. The cost of improving the reader's stock of knowledge consists of the cost of the underlying research, the cost of printing it, and the cost of the reader's time in absorbing it. The last of these, which is far from trivial, suggests that the pedagogically simple papers should, ceteris paribus, be given preference over more technically demanding ones.

Moreover, editors should evaluate the importance of a paper by more utilitarian and less self-referential criteria than they sometimes use now. There is a tendency to treat any topic on which several papers have recently appeared in major journals as ipso facto important because it is 'at the cutting edge'. That can result in a rational bubble, as researchers take their cue from what they see published. Referees may well think that the paper they are refereeing deals with a minor topic that does not deserve yet another paper. But they may be reluctant to impose their own tastes by recommending rejection of a state-of-the-art paper on a much-discussed topic, merely because they themselves find it boring.[4] And so another paper joins the pile, and adds to the seeming importance of an actually unimportant issue. Editors could perhaps ask a small sample of subscribers if they want to read yet another paper on this topic. Authors would feel unfairly treated if their papers were rejected merely because they dealt with a topic on which too much had already been published. But a journal's first function is not to reward authors for their hard work, but to advance the field.

Beyond this, journals should function as a means of communication, and not only as archives that enshrine substantial scientific results. They should therefore provide a channel for brief, informal notes that merely make suggestions which others may find useful in their own work. Many of us have ideas that we do not develop because we lack the time or the expertise. The journals could provide a better channel for communicating such ideas than personal contacts do. Students in search of a dissertation topic would find such informal notes helpful. Informal reports could also be useful in policing full-scale papers, because readers who discover an error in a paper may be willing to write a brief note on it, but not a fully worked out 'Comment'.

At one time the *Western Economic Journal* (now called *Economic Inquiry*) had a special section for brief informal communications, but it no longer does. Currently *Economics Letters* partly fills this gap, but its reports are generally much more finished and polished papers than the ones I am suggesting. Perhaps the need could be met by newsletters in specialized fields, such as the informal papers section of *Methodus* and the *Newsletter* of the Cliometrics Society.

We also need more syntheses of previously reported work than the *Journal of Economic Literature* and the *Journal of Economic Surveys* can provide. On many topics there is a plethora of empirical studies that reach divergent conclusions, so that the reader does not know what to believe. Hence, despite the extensive effort that has gone into the empirical testing of hypotheses, readers are often no better off than they would be in the absence of this testing.

To find the genuine message in the noise, what we need are not just summaries of the literature, such as those found in the introductory chapters of dissertations and in most literature reviews, but also *critical evaluations*. When empirical tests reach results that seem irreconcilable, a critical survey could tell us which ones to disregard. Or it might show that the seemingly conflicting results can be reconciled by another hypothesis.[5] And even if it is not possible to weed out all the invalid evidence and to reconcile all the rest, it should be possible to reduce the dissonance to a substantial extent. Meta-analysis reduces the effort required for such a critical survey and makes its results more specific.[6]

GRADUATE TRAINING

Institutionalists and other 'outsiders' have long complained about the content of graduate programmes in economics. They are no longer alone. In 1988 the American Economic Association set up a commission on graduate education in response 'to what seemed like a growing chorus of complaints about the nature of economic research and training in economics departments at most universities' (Krueger, 1991, p. 1035). It found a 'fairly deep dissatisfaction' (p. 1038) of non-academic employers with the education of new Ph.D.s, and a tendency of applied schools, such as schools of public policy, to train and hire their own Ph.D.s. The Commission's major concern, however, was:

> the extent to which graduate education in economics may have become too removed from real economic problems. ... One simple way to state our concern is that the screening process poses substantial barriers for students who find elementary topology difficult but few barriers for students who cannot handle elementary undergraduate applied exercises in economics .... The Commission's fear is that graduate programs may be turning out a generation with too many *idiots savants*, skilled in technique but innocent of real economic issues (pp. 1039, 1042, 1044–5).

In a survey undertaken by the Commission, about 80 per cent of the responding faculty members called for a reduced emphasis on theory and techniques and more emphasis on applications and policy. 'Faculty members believed that mathematical skills should be much less important than they are and creative skills much more important, and that communication skills should be much more important and computation skills less important. Graduate students had quite similar views' (Hansen, 1991, p. 1070). Alan Blinder, a member of the Commission, in commenting on its report, wrote:

> Both students and faculty find economics obsessed with technique over substance. ... The impression I carried away from the many macro and micro theory exams the Commission examined is that they tested mathematical puzzle-solving ability, not substantive knowledge about economics. ... Only 14 percent of the students report that their core courses put substantial emphasis on 'applying economic theory to real-world problems.' This strikes me as a devastating critique (Blinder, 1990 p. 445).

As already discussed in Chapter 1, Klamer and Colander found much dissatisfaction among graduate students, who:

do not like the preoccupation with techniques in graduate school and in the literature. They want more ideas, more policy relevance, more discussion of the fundamental assumptions, and more serious consideration of alternative approaches. ... Many of these students entered graduate school with lofty ideals, and it is sad to see those crushed. And it is sad to sense the student's disillusionment with the discipline (Klamer and Colander, 1990, pp. 170, 184).

That discontent with the formalistic focus of graduate training is so prevalent does not necessarily mean that it is justified. Thus someone might defend the stress on formalism in graduate programmes by urging that mathematical economics is more difficult to learn on one's own than is less formal economics, so that it makes sense for graduate programmes to train students primarily in mathematical economics, and to rely on their learning informal economics on their own. But it is by no means obvious that informal economics is easier to learn by oneself than formal economics. On the contrary, one might well argue that informal economics requires much tacit knowledge. And such knowledge cannot be readily obtained by reading, but must be acquired either from a teacher or else by long, painful experience.

Another possible defence of formalist teaching is to say that formalist techniques can be taught better than intuition (cf. Solow, 1990, p. 449). But that statement too is open to challenge. Where is the empirical evidence?

Even so, suppose that the defenders of formalist training are correct in saying that formalist techniques can be taught better and are harder to acquire on one's own than less formal economics. That could justify giving formalism a larger role in economics training than it has in the everyday work of most economists. But could it justify the prevailing great emphasis on formalism in graduate training? Skill at formalistic analysis beyond a fairly basic level is useful almost only for those who plan to publish papers in certain journals, or to teach certain graduate courses. These are primarily the graduates of top schools, and even many of these take jobs in government or industry, or teach primarily undergraduates. David Colander (1992) and Joanna Woos (1992) argue cogently that teachers of undergraduates would be served much better by a broader training that pays more attention to historical and institutional factors and less attention to narrow and formal theory.

Hence, it would be sensible, at least for the weaker schools, to place less emphasis on formalism. Krueger et al. (1991) rightly complain about a lack of diversity in graduate economics programmes. But the faculty of weaker schools may enhance its own feeling of self-esteem by copying what is done in the most prestigious schools. And given the limited role that the outside market plays in economics, inefficient training may prevail if it serves the interests of the teachers. If engineering graduates did not have to meet criteria set by employers, engineering schools might well teach their students much quantum mechanics but little about such pedestrian topics as the strength of materials. Our bridges would frequently collapse, but the teachers would feel happier.

Moreover, the demand for training in formalism is a derived demand that originates in the demand for formalist research. And, as discussed previously, the high demand for formalistic research is, in part, due to a confusion of formalist theory with empirical science theory. To be sure, formalist economics is a perfectly legitimate field, and courses in it should be offered to those who want them. But there is no more reason to require all students to have substantial facility at formalist theory than to require them all to take a field in labour economics, since it is not formalist theory but empirical science theory that guides teaching and research in the 'fields'.

Furthermore, training in formalist theory often comes at the expense of training in the less formal, more intuitive theory, the type of theory that develops what in German is called a 'Fingerspitzengefühlz', literally 'fingertip-feeling' for economics. The University of Chicago was at one time the leading practitioner of this 'fingertip economics', and its graduates were able to apply economic theory to 'every nook and cranny' of economic life (Miller, 1962). To formalists the ability to deploy that type of theory seems unimportant because it relies on what they consider casual reasoning.

Hence, as the older Chicago methodology became less influential, this useful ability was de-emphasized. The problem does not arise so much with respect to first-rate students: they learn fingertip economics on their own. But I doubt that many other students do. Some of them may know the latest techniques without being able to solve simple problems. They are like someone who can manipulate matrices, but who, if told that John is 40 and twice as old as Bill, cannot tell you how old Bill is.[7] Physics students learn not only quantum mechanics, but also how a pendulum works. But in economics we treat what is simple as not worth knowing. I teach a course for advanced graduate students on the nitty-gritty of research. In this course I ask students to find certain, usually fairly obvious, mistakes in specific sections of certain papers. They have great difficulty with this exercise. But surely this is something that professional economists should be able to do. Of course, my class is only a small and probably not a representative sample, but I suspect that a more reliable sample would show the same result.

The standard response, 'Oh, well, students should obtain a thorough grasp of basic theory as undergraduates', is too facile. They should, but most don't. If we want our Ph.D.'s to be competent professionals we must ensure that they know the basic material well, and never mind where they learn it. If the graduates of a school of pharmacy make elementary mistakes that kill patients, the school can hardly say, 'Oh, well, that is not our fault, they should have learned in their pre-pharmacy chemistry courses how to distinguish these poisons from harmless substances.'

In addition to teaching more empirical-science theory in place of more 'advanced' theory and, as discussed in Chapter 9, more of the underlying theory in place of models, we should also teach students to read more critically and to spot simple mistakes.

We should also teach students about the reliability of their data. In a science that takes its empirical work seriously, students are taught to gauge the accuracy of measurements. But I suspect that some graduate students complete their macro courses without finding out that the GDP data are subject to substantial revisions. Similarly, it is likely that the majority of students who pass their monetary economics exams do not know that the M-1 data are substantially revised for several years after they are released. Furthermore, in statistics and econometrics courses students are not taught to check their key punching, presumably because dealing with such trivia is beneath the dignity of their teachers.[8]

It would also be useful to teach students that bad writing is not the hallmark of a superior intellect or of great scientific dedication. Krueger et al. (1991) rightly recommend that our graduate programmes pay more attention to writing skills. Students should be required to read books on effective writing, such as McCloskey (1987) and Becker (1986).

It may be useful to acquaint students with a broader range of tools, such as observing decision-making processes and using polling data. The important role that some economists see for experimental economics, for interdisciplinary work and for analysing irrational behaviour suggests that we should broaden the range of tools that we teach.

Merely adding such topics to the required curriculum would, however, lengthen the already too long period of graduate study.[9] Perhaps the solution is to have different tracks, with some students learning these tools and less formalist theory than they learn now, while others stay with the present curriculum. Obviously, these tracks should be treated as equally worthy. Such a two-track system would also help to meet the concern (see Bronfenbrenner, 1991; Krueger et al., 1991; Kasper et al., 1991) that the prevailing mathematical emphasis is excluding good students who are more oriented towards the humanities and economic policy.

CONCLUSION

Like many other critics of current practices I have presented an extensive catalogue of current crimes and misdemeanours, followed by a much briefer discussion of the path to salvation. This leaves one task; to issue a portentous warning of the dire fate that will befall the world unless my warnings are heeded. So here goes.

Suppose that the mathematical arms race continues, and papers become more and more abstract and elegant, and less and less concerned with explaining actual economic behaviour. The market, like nature, abhors a vacuum. Hence, the need for empirical science economics will be filled, one way or the other, perhaps by establishing departments of applied economics in business schools, departments which will capture much of the enrolments and funding.[10]

Such a split-up of economics would be bad. Formalist theory can contribute to the development of empirical science economics, both by broadening the horizon of applied economists, and by counteracting the applied theorist's tendency to be somewhat too quick and much too dirty. At the same time, day-to-day contact with empirical science economists can suggest interesting research problems to formalists. Hence it is better for both types of economists to cohabit in the same department. Besides, some economists would have a foot in both departments, and that would create administrative complexities.

It is therefore better that we stay together. And we can do so, if we are willing to exercise a civilized sense of tolerance towards each other, and not evaluate the very different work that others do by the yardstick that is appropriate to our own work. Naturally, in our hearts we know that our own work is the more praiseworthy, but in our heads we know that we might, just possibly, be slightly biased.

NOTES

1. Moreover, as they point out, relying on others to do the robustness testing works less well in economics than in the natural sciences, because in economics there is greater scope for selective reporting.
2. The *Journal of Political Economy* and the *Quarterly Review of Business and Economics* are hospitable to papers that provide replications; others are not.
3. Usually, questionnaires should avoid asking about motivation, or 'what-if' questions. When I recently sent out a questionnaire to academic economists I got a response rate of about two-thirds. This suggests that economists are not as blindly set against survey techniques as is sometimes stated.
4. At least once I have recommended publication of a paper I found boring because I did not know if others would feel the same way.
5. For an attempt to do this see Mayer (1972).
6. Meta-analysis treats the difference in the results reached by various studies as the dependent variable to be explained by particular characteristics of each of the studies (see Stanley and Jarrell, 1989; Wachter, 1988).
7. Krueger et al. (1991, p. 1044) cite several examples. One of my students writing a dissertation in applied econometrics did not know how to rebase an index number. Perhaps questions on such topics should be on the econometrics prelim.
8. Here is a reliable way to check data entry with TSP: Enter the data in a second time, or preferably, have someone else enter them. (If entering them yourself, wait at least a day.) Then, letting x be the first entry and y the second, generate $v=x<>y$ and $z=(v=1)$*na. This generates zeros for z whenever the two entries agree, and 'NA' whenever they differ.
9. It is, of course possible that if students were to acquire these additional tools they would not have to spend so much time searching for a dissertation topic. That may happen, but then it may not.
10. John Pencavel (1991, p. 85) suggests that specialization will increase so substantially that 'distinct departments of economics will exist, all housed in an overarching School of Economics.' The American Economic Association Commission (Hansen, 1991, p. 1061) suggests that the more prestigious business schools might produce Ph.D.'s that compete for positions in economics departments, though it believes that (for the time being?) the high demand for business school faculty makes this unlikely. Harberger (1992, p. 1) suggests that 'old-fashioned economics' might move into schools of public policy.

References

Adler, Moshe (1989) private communication.

Akerlof, George and Yellen, Janet (1985) 'A Near Rational Model of the Business Cycle with Wage and Price Inertia,' *Quarterly Journal of Economics*, vol. 100, August, pp. 823–38.

Allais, Maurice (1990) 'My Conception of Economic Science,' *Methodus*, vol. 2, June, pp. 5–7.

Angier, Natalie (1990) 'Cultures in Conflict: M.D.'s and Ph.D.'s,' *New York Times*, 24 April, pp. B5 and B10.

Aristotle (1941) *The Basic Works of Aristotle*, New York, Random House.

Attfield, C.L.F., Demery, D. and Duck, N. (1991) *Rational Expectations in Macroeconomics: An Introduction to Evidence and Theory*, Oxford, Basil Blackwell.

Ault, David, Rutman, Gilbert and Stevenson, Thomas (1982) 'Some Factors Affecting Mobility in the Labor Market for Academic Economists,' *Economic Inquiry*, vol. 20, January, pp. 104–33.

Ausubel, Lawrence (1991) 'The Failure of Competition in the Credit Card Market,' *American Economic Review*, vol. 81, March, pp. 50–81.

Baba, Yoshihisa, Hendry, David and Starr, Ross (1992) 'The Demand for M1 in the USA, 1960–1988,' *Review of Economic Studies*, vol. 59, January, pp. 25–60.

Backhouse, Roger (1991) 'The Constructivist Critique of Economic Methodology,' University of Birmingham, Department of Economics Discussion Paper, No. 9–12.

Balzer, W. (1982) 'A Logical Reconstruction of Pure Exchange Economics,' *Journal of Unified Sciences*, vol. 17, January, pp. 23–46.

Barrett, Paul (1988) 'To Read this Story in Full, Don't Forget to See the Footnotes,' *Wall Street Journal*, vol. 120, 10 May, pp. 1 and 22.

Bartlett, John (1980) *Familiar Quotations*, Boston, Little Brown.

Baumol, William (1952) 'The Transactions Demand for Cash: An Inventory-theoretic Approach,' *Quarterly Journal of Economics*, vol. 66, November, pp. 545–56.

Baumol, William (1991) 'Towards a Newer Economics: The Future Lies Ahead,' *Economic Journal*, vol. 101, January, pp. 1–8.

Becker, Howard (1986) *Writing for Social Scientists*, Chicago, University of Chicago Press.

Beggs, John (1988) 'Diagnostic Testing in Applied Economics,' *Economic Record*, vol. 64, June, pp. 81–101.

Beller, Steven (1989) *Vienna and the Jews*, Cambridge, Cambridge University Press.

Belsley, David, Kuh, Edwin and Welsch, Roy (1980) *Regression Diagnostics: Identifying Influential Data and Sources of Collinearity*, New York, John Wiley.

Birner, J. (1988) 'Discussion,' in Neil de Marchi (ed.) *The Popperian Legacy in Economics*, Cambridge, Cambridge University Press.

Blackburn, Keith and Christensen, Michael (1989) 'Monetary Policy and Policy Credibility: Theories and Evidence,' *Journal of Economic Literature*, vol. 27, March, pp. 1–45.

Blanchard, Olivier (1984) 'The Lucas Critique and the Volcker Deflation,' *American Economic Review*, vol. 74, May, pp. 211–15.

Blanchard, Olivier (1990) 'Why Does Money Affect Output? A Survey,' in B. Friedman and F. Hahn, *Handbook of Monetary Economics*, Amsterdam, Elsevier.

Blaug, Mark (1980) *The Methodology of Economics*, New York, Cambridge University Press.

Blaug, Mark (1990) *Economic Theories, True or False?*, Aldershot, England, Gower.

Blaug, Mark (1991) 'Afterword' in Neil de Marchi and Mark Blaug (eds) *Appraising Economic Theories*, Aldershot, England, Edward Elgar.

Blinder, Alan (1987) 'Keynes, Lucas and Scientific Progress,' *American Economic Review*, vol. 77, May, pp. 130–36.

Blinder, Alan (1988a) 'The Challenge of High Unemployment,' *American Economic Review*, vol. 78, May, pp. 1–15.

Blinder, Alan (1988b) 'The Fall and Rise of Keynesian Economics,' *Economic Record*, vol. 64, December, pp. 278–87.

Blinder, Alan (1990) 'Discussion,' *American Economic Review*, vol. 80, May, pp. 445–7.

Blinder, Alan (1991) 'Why are Prices Sticky?' *American Economic Review*, vol. 81, May, pp. 89–96.

Blinder, Alan and Solow, Robert (1973) 'Does Fiscal Policy Matter?' *Journal of Public Economics*, vol. 2, November, pp. 119–37.

Block, Fred (1990) 'Bad Data Drive Out Good: The Decline of Personal Savings Reexamined,' *Journal of Post Keynesian Economics*, vol. 13, Fall, pp. 3–19.

Bloor, David (1981) 'The Strength of the Strong Programme,' *Philosophy of the Social Sciences*, vol. 11, pp. 199–213.

Boland, Lawrence (1979) 'A Critique of Friedman's Critics,' *Journal of Economic Literature*, vol. 17, June, pp. 503–22.

Boland, Lawrence (1982) *The Foundations of Economic Method*, London, George Allen and Unwin.

Bonnen, James (1975) 'Improving Information on Agriculture and Rural Life,' *American Journal of Agricultural Economics*, vol. 57, December, pp. 753–63.

Brenner, Reuven (1983) *History – the Human Gamble*, Chicago, University of Chicago Press.

Bronfenbrenner, Martin (1972) 'Sensitivity Analysis for Econometricians,' *Nebraska Journal of Economics*, vol. 2, Autumn, pp. 57–66.

Bronfenbrenner, Martin (1991) 'Economics as Dentistry,' *Southern Economic Journal*, vol. 57, January, pp. 599–605.

Brunner, Karl and Meltzer, Alan (1967) 'Economies of Scale in Cash Balances Reconsidered,' *Quarterly Journal of Economics*, vol. 81, May, pp. 422–36.

Buckle, Robert, Assendelft, Eric and Jackson, Frazer (1990) 'Manufacturers' Expectations of Prices and Quantities: New Zealand Experience, 1964–87,' *Applied Economics*, vol. 22, pp. 579–98.

Buiter, Willem (1989) *Macroeconomic Theory and Stabilization Policy*, Manchester, Manchester University Press.

Cagan, Phillip and Fellner, William (1983) 'Tentative Lessons from the Recent Disinflationary Effort,' *Brookings Papers on Economic Activity*, 2, pp. 603–608.

Caldwell, Bruce (1984) 'Methodological Diversity in Economics,' *Research in the History of Economic Thought and Methodology*, Greenwich, Conn., vol. 5, pp. 207–40.

Caldwell, Bruce (1987) *Beyond Positivism*, London, George Allen and Unwin.

Caldwell, Bruce (1988) 'The Case for Pluralism' in Neil de Marchi (ed.) *The Popperian Legacy in Economics*, Cambridge, Cambridge University Press.

Caldwell, Bruce (1988) 'Does Methodology Matter? How Should it be Practiced?' *Finnish Economic Papers*, vol. 3, Spring, pp. 64–71.

Caldwell, Bruce (1991a) 'Clarifying Popper,' *Journal of Economic Literature*, vol. 29, March, pp. 1–33.

Caldwell, Bruce (1991b) 'Has Formalization Gone too Far?' *Methodus*, vol. 3, June, pp. 27–9.

Carlton, Dennis (1989) 'The Theory and the Facts of How Markets Clear,' in R. Schmalensee and R.D. Willing (eds) *Handbook of Industrial Organization*, Amsterdam, Elsevier.

Cartwright, Nancy (1991) 'Replicability, Reproducibility and Robustness: Comments on Harry Collins,' *History of Political Economy*, vol. 23, Spring, pp. 143–55.

Cetina, Karin Knorr (1991) 'Epistemic Cultures: Forms of Reason in Science,' *History of Political Economy*, vol. 23, Spring, pp. 105–21.

Chase, Janet (1970) 'Normative Criteria for Scientific Publication,' *American Sociologist*, vol. 5, August, pp. 262–4.

Christano, Lawrence and Eichenbaum, Martin (1990) 'Unit Roots in Real GNP: Do we Know, Do we Care?' *Carnegie-Rochester Conference Series on Public Policy*, Spring, vol. 37, pp. 2–62.

Christensen, Michael (1987a) 'Disinflation, Credibility and Price Inertia, A Danish Exposition,' *Applied Economics*, vol. 19, October, pp. 1353–66.

Christensen, Michael (1987b) 'On Interest Rate Determination, Testing for Policy Credibility and the Relevance of the Lucas Critique,' *European Journal of Political Economy*, vol. 3, no. 3, pp. 369–88.

Christensen, Michael (1990) 'Policy Credibility and the Lucas Critique: Some New Tests with an Application to Denmark,' in P. Artus and Y. Baroux, *Monetary Policy*, Dordrecht, Kluwer, pp. 78–104.

Coates, A.W. (1988) 'Economic Rhetoric: The Social and Historical Context,' in Arjo Klamer, Donald McCloskey and Robert Solow, *The Consequences of Economic Rhetoric*, Cambridge, Cambridge University Press.

Coddington, Alan (1975) 'The Rationale of General Equilibrium Theory,' *Economic Inquiry*, vol. 13, December, pp. 539–58.

Cohen, Eliot and Gooch, John (1991) *Military Misfortunes*, New York, Vintage Books.

Colander, David (1989) 'The Invisible Hand of Truth,' in David Colander and A.W. Coats, *The Spread of Economic Ideas*, New York, Cambridge University Press.

Colander, David (1991) *Why Aren't Economists as Important as Garbagemen?* Armonk, New York, M.E. Sharp.

Colander, David (1992) 'Reform of Undergraduate Economics Education,' in David Colander and Reuven Brenner (eds) *Educating Economists*, Ann Arbor, Michigan, University of Michigan Press.

Cooley, Thomas and LeRoy, Stephen (1981) 'Identification and Estimation of Money Demand,' *American Economic Review*, vol. 71, December, pp. 825–43.

Crick, Francis (1988) *What Mad Pursuits*, New York, Basic Books.

Dasgupta, A.K. (1968) *Methodology of Economic Research*, Bombay, Asia Publishing House.

Davis, Phillip and Hersh, Reuben (1986) *Decartes' Dream*, Boston, Harcourt Brace, Jovanovich.

Deane, Phyllis (1990) *Frontiers of Economic Research*, London, Macmillan.

Debreu, Gerard (1991) 'The Mathematization of Economic Theory,' *American Economic Review*, vol. 81, March, pp. 1–7.

Denton, Frank (1988) 'The Significance of Significance: Rhetorical Aspects of Statistical Hypothesis Testing in Economics,' in Arjo Klamer, Donald McCloskey and Robert Solow (eds) *The Consequences of Economic Rhetoric*, Cambridge, Cambridge University Press.

Dewald, William, Thursby, Jerry and Anderson, Richard (1986) 'Replication in Economics: The *Journal of Money, Credit and Banking* Project,' *American Economic Review*, vol. 76, September, pp. 587–603.

Diamond, Arthur (1988) 'The Empirical Progressiveness of the General Equilibrium Research Program,' *History of Political Economy*, vol. 20, pp. 119–35.

Dore, Mohammed, Chakravarty, Sukhamoy and Goodwin, Richard (1989) *John von Neumann and Modern Economics*, Oxford, Clarendon Press.

Dornbusch, Rudiger and Fisher, Stanley (1990) *Macroeconomics*, New York, McGraw-Hill.

Dow, Sheila (1985) *Macroeconomic Thought*, Oxford, Basil Blackwell.

Earl, Peter (1983) 'A Behavioral Theory of Economists' Behavior,' in Alfred Eichner, *Why Economics is Not Yet a Science*, Armonk, New York.

Englander, Steven and Los, Cornelis (1983) 'The Stability of the Phillips Curve and its Implications for the 1980s,' Federal Reserve Bank of New York, Research Paper no. 8303.

Engle, Robert and Hendry, David (1989) 'Testing Superexogeneity and Invariance,' unpublished ms.

Evans, Michael (1967) 'The Importance of Wealth in the Consumption Function,' *Journal of Political Economy*, vol. 75, August, Part 1, pp. 335–51.

Executive Office of the President (1979) *Economic Report of the President*, Government Printing Office, Washington, DC.

Fama, Eugene (1983) 'Financial Intermediation and Price Level Control,' *Journal of Monetary Economics*, vol. 12, July, pp. 7–28.

Favero, Carlo, and Hendry, David (forthcoming) 'Testing the Lucas Critique,' *Econometric Review*.

Feigenbaum, Susan and Levy, David (forthcoming) 'The Market for (Ir)reproducible Econometrics,' *Social Epistemology*.

Ferber, Robert (1953) *A Study of Aggregate Savings Functions*, NBER Technical Paper no. 8, New York, National Bureau of Economic Research.

Ferber, Robert (1956) 'Are Correlations any Guide to Predictive Value?' *Applied Statistics*, vol. 5, June, pp. 113–21.

Feyerabend, Paul (1975) *Against Method*, London, NLB.

Feyerabend, Paul (1989) 'How to be a Good Empiricist – A Plea for Tolerance in Matters Epistemological,' in Brody, Barch and Grandy, Richard, *Readings in the Philosophy of Science*, Englewood Cliffs, N.J., Prentice Hall.

Feynman, Richard (1985) *Surely You're Joking, Mr. Feynman!*, Toronto, Bantam Books.

Fischer, Andreas (1989) 'Policy Regime Changes and Monetary Expectations: Testing for Super Exogeneity,' *Journal of Monetary Economics*, vol. 24, November, pp. 423–36.

Fischer, Stanley (1988a) 'Monetary Policy and Performance in the U.S., Japan and Europe, 1973–86,' in Yoshio Suzuki and Hiroshi Yomo (eds) *Towards a World of Economic Stability: Optimal Monetary Framework and Policy*, Tokyo, University of Tokyo Press.

Fischer, Stanley (1988b) 'Recent Developments in Macroeconomics,' *Economic Journal*, vol. 98, June, pp. 294–339.

Fischer, Stanley (1990) 'Rules vs. Discretion in Monetary Policy,' in Benjamin Friedman and Frank Hahn (eds) *Handbook of Monetary Economics*, Amsterdam, North Holland.

Fishburn, Peter (1991) 'Decision Theory: The Next Hundred Years?' *Economic Journal*, vol. 101, January, pp. 27–32.

Fisher, Franklin (1989) 'Games Economists Play: A Noncooperative View,' *Rand Journal of Economics*, vol. 20, Spring, pp. 113–24.

Fisher, P.G., Tanna, S.K., Turner, D.S., Wallis, F.K., Whitley, J.D. (1989) 'Comparative Properties of Models of the U.K. Economy,' *National Institute Economic Review*, no. 129, August, pp. 69–87.

Fisher, Ronald (1932) *Statistical Methods for Research Workers*, London, Oliver Boyd.

Frank, Robert (1985) *Choosing the Right Pond*, Oxford, Oxford University Press.

Frankel, Jeffrey and Rockett, Katherine (1988) 'International Monetary Policy Coordination When Policymakers do not Agree on the True Model,' *American Economic Review*, vol. 78, June, pp. 318–40.

Friedman, Benjamin (n.d.) 'Discussion,' in Federal Reserve Bank of Boston, *After the Phillips Curve*, Boston, Mass.

Friedman, Milton (1953) *Essays in Positive Economics*, Chicago, University of Chicago Press.

Friedman, Milton (1957) *A Theory of the Consumption Function*, Princeton, Princeton University Press.

Friedman, Milton (1991) 'Old Wine in New Bottles,' *Economic Journal*, vol. 101, January, pp. 33–40.

Friedman, Milton and Schwartz, Anna (1991) 'Alternative Approaches to Analyzing Economic Data,' *American Economic Review*, vol. 81, March, pp. 39–49.

Gavin, William and Karamouzis, Nicholas (1984) 'Monetary Policy and Real Interest Rates: New Evidence from Money Stock Announcements,' Federal Reserve Bank of Cleveland, Working paper 8406.

Gerber, James, Singh, Harinder and Frantz, Roger (1990) 'Macrofoundations for Microanalysis?' *Methodus*, vol. 2, December, 46–9.

Geweke, John (1985) 'Macroeconomic Modeling and the Theory of the Representative Agent,' *American Economic Review*, vol. 75, May, pp. 206–10.

Ghiselin, Michael (1989) *Intellectual Compromise: The Bottom Line*, New York, Paragon Press.

Gibbard, Allan and Varian, Hal (1978) 'Economic Models,' *Journal of Philosophy*, vol. 75, November, pp. 665–7.

Gilbert, Christopher (1986) 'Professor Hendry's Econometric Methodology,' *Oxford Bulletin of Economics and Statistics*, vol. 48, no. 3, pp. 283–307.

Gittings, Thomas (1991) 'Rounding Errors and Index Numbers,' Federal Reserve Bank of Chicago, *Economic Perspectives*, vol. 15, May/June, pp. 2–10.

Goldberg, Victor and Erickson, John (1987) 'Quantity and Price Adjustments in Long-Term Contracts: A Case Study of Petroleum Coke,' *Journal of Law and Economics*, vol. 30, October, pp. 369–98.

Goldfeld, Stephen (1982) 'Rules, Discretion and Reality,' *American Economic Review*, vol. 72, May, pp. 361–6.

Goodwin, Craufurd (1988) 'The Heterogeneity of the Economist's Discourse: Philosopher, Priest and Hired Gun,' in Arjo Klamer, Donald McCloskey and Robert Solow, *The Consequences of Economic Rhetoric*, Cambridge, Cambridge University Press.

Goodwin, Neva (1991) *Social Economics*, London, Macmillan.

Gordon, Robert (1990a) 'The Phillips Curve Now and Then,' NBER Working paper, no. 3393.

Gordon, Robert (1990b) 'What is New-Keynesian Economics?' *Journal of Economic Literature*, vol. 28, September, pp. 1115–71.

Greenwald, Bruce and Stiglitz, Joseph (1989) 'Towards a Theory of Rigidity,' NBER Working paper no. 2938.

Griliches, Zvi (1986) 'Economic Data Issues,' in Zvi Griliches and Michael Intriligator, *Handbook of Econometrics*, Amsterdam, North Holland, vol. 3.

Grübel, Herbert and Boland, Lawrence (1986) 'On the Efficient Use of Mathematics in Economic Theory, Facts and Results of an Opinion Survey,' *Kyklos*, vol. 39, no. 3, pp. 419–42.

Hacking, Ian (1983) *Representing and Intervening*, New York, Cambridge University Press.

Hahn, Frank (1970) 'Some Adjustment Problems,' *Econometrica*, vol. 38, January, pp. 1–17.

Hahn, Frank (1971) 'Professor Friedman's Views on Money,' *Economica*, N.S. vol. 38, February, pp. 61–80.

Hahn, Frank (1983) *Money and Inflation*, Oxford, Basil Blackwell.

Hahn, Frank (1985) *Money, Growth and Stability*, Oxford, Blackwell.

Hahn, Frank (1990) 'John Hicks the Theorist,' *Economic Journal*, vol. 100, June, pp. 539–49.

Hahn, Frank (1991) 'The Next Hundred Years,' *Economic Journal*, vol. 101, January, pp. 47–50.

Hahn, Frank and Matthews, Robbin (1964) 'The Theory of Economic Growth: A Survey,' *Economic Journal*, vol. 74, December, pp. 779–902.

Hall, Robert and Taylor, John (1991) *Macroeconomics*, New York, W.W. Norton.

Haltiwanger, John and Waldman, Michael (1989) 'Limited Rationality and Strategic Complements: The Implications for Macroeconomics,' *Quarterly Journal of Economics*, vol. 104, August, pp. 463–83.

Hands, D. Wade (1984) 'What Economics is Not: An Economist's Response to Rosenberg,' *Philosophy of Science*, vol. 51, pp. 495–503.

Hands, D. Wade (1985) 'Second Thoughts on Lakatos,' *History of Political Economy*, vol. 17, Spring, pp. 1–16.

Hands, D. Wade (1988) 'Ad Hocness in Economics and the Popperian Tradition,' in Neil de Marchi (ed.) *The Popperian Legacy in Economics*, Cambridge, Cambridge University Press, pp. 121–38.

Hands, D. Wade (1990) 'Thirteen Theses on Progress in Economic Methodology,' *Finnish Economic Papers*, vol. 3, Spring, pp. 72–6.

Hansen, W. Lee (1991) 'The Education and Training of Economics Doctorates: Major Findings of the American Economic Association's Commission on Graduate Training in Economics,' *Journal of Economic Literature*, vol. 29, September, pp. 1054–88.

Harberger, Arnold, et al. (1992) 'Interface between Economic Techniques and Economic Policy,' *Contemporary Policy Issues*, vol. 10, July, pp. 1–16.

Hartley, James (1991) 'New Classical Representative Agent Models: A Critique,' unpublished ms.

Hausman, Daniel (1988) 'Economic Methodology and Philosophy of Science,' in Gordon Winston and Richard Teichgraeber III, *The Boundaries of Economics*, Cambridge, Cambridge University Press.

Hawking, Stephen (1988) *A Brief History of Time*, New York, Bantam Books.

Hayek, Friedrich von (1989) 'The Pretence of Knowledge,' *American Economic Review*, vol. 79, December, pp. 3–7.

Haynes, Stephen and Stone, Joe (1990) 'Political Models of the Business Cycle Should be Revived,' *Economic Inquiry*, vol. 28, July, pp. 442–65.

Heller, Walter and Starr, Ross (1979) 'Capital Market Imperfections, the Consumption Function, and the Effectiveness of Fiscal Policy,' *Quarterly Journal of Economics*, vol. 93, August, pp. 454–63.

Hendry, David and Ericsson, Neil (1990) 'Modelling the Demand for Narrow Money in the United Kingdom and the United States,' Board of Governors, Federal Reserve System, International Finance Discussion Paper no. 383.

Hendry, David and Ericsson, Neil (1991) 'An Econometric Analysis of U.K. Money Demand in *Monetary Trends in the United States and the United Kingdom* by Milton Friedman and Anna J. Schwartz,' *American Economic Review*, vol. 81, March, pp. 8–39.

Hicks, John R. (1979) *Causality in Economics*, Oxford, Blackwell.

Hirsch, Abraham and de Marchi, Neil (1990) *Milton Friedman: Economics in Practice*, Hempel Hempstead, Harvester Wheatsheaf.

Holden, K., Peel, D. and Thompson, J. (1985) *Expectations: Theory and Evidence*, London, Macmillan.

Hoover, Kevin (1984) 'Comment on Frazer and Boland -II,' *American Economic Review*, vol. 74, September, 789–94.

Hoover, Kevin (1988) *The New Classical Macroeconomics*, Oxford, Blackwell.

Hoover, Kevin (1989) 'Econometrics as Measurement,' unpublished manuscript.

Hoover, Kevin (1990) 'Scientific Research Program or Tribe? A Joint Appraisal of Lakatos and the New Classical Macroeconomics,' University of California, Davis, Working paper no. 69.

Hoover, Kevin (1991a) 'Calibration and the Econometrics of the Macroeconomy,' unpublished manuscript.

Hoover, Kevin (1991b) Private communication.

Howrey, E. Phillip and Hymans, Saul (1978) 'The Measurement and Determination of Loanable Funds Savings,' *Brookings Papers on Economic Activity*, no. 3, pp. 655–85.

Hubbard, Raymond and Vetter, Daniel (forthcoming) 'The Publication Incidence of Replications and Critical Commentary in Economics,' *American Economist*.

Huizinga, John and Mishkin, Frederic (1986) 'Monetary Policy Regime Shifts and the Unusual Behavior of Real Interest Rates,' *Carnegie-Rochester Conference Series on Public Policy*, vol. 24, Spring, pp. 231–74.

Hutchison, Terence (1972) *Knowledge and Ignorance in Economics*, Chicago, University of Chicago Press.

Hutchison, Terence (1988) 'The Case for Falsification,' in Neil de Marchi (ed.) *The Popperian Legacy for Economics*, New York, Cambridge University Press.

Jaffe, Dwight (1989) *Money, Banking and Credit*, New York, Worth.

Johnson, Harry (1971) 'The Keynesian Revolution and the Monetarist Counter-Revolution,' *American Economic Review*, vol. 61, May, pp. 1–14.

Kahneman, Daniel, Slovic, Payl and Tversky, Amos (1982) *Judgment under Uncertainty*, New York, Cambridge University Press.

Kamarck, Andrew (1983) *Economics and the Real World*, Oxford, Blackwell.

Kane, Edward (1984) 'Why Journal Editors Should Encourage the Replication of Applied Economic Research,' *Quarterly Review of Business and Economics*, vol. 23, Winter, pp. 3–8.

Kasper, Hirshel et al. (1991) 'The Education of Economists: From Undergraduate to Graduate Study,' *Journal of Economic Literature*, vol. 29, September, pp. 1088–109.

Katzner, Donald (1991) 'In Defence of Formalization in Economics,' *Methodus*, June, pp. 17–24.

Kennedy, Peter (1979) *A Guide to Econometrics*, Cambridge, Mass, MIT Press.

Keynes, John Maynard (1936) *The General Theory of Employment, Interest and Money*, New York, Harcourt Brace.

Keynes, John Maynard (1972) *Collected Writings*, London, Macmillan, vol. 9.

Khoury, Salwa (1987) 'The Federal Reserve Reaction Function: a Specification Search,' Ph.D. dissertation, University of California, Davis.

Khoury, Salwa (1990) 'The Federal Reserve Reaction Function,' in Thomas Mayer (ed.) *The Political Economy of American Monetary Policy*, New York, Cambridge University Press.

King, Robert and Plosser, Charles (1984) 'Money, Credit, and Prices in a Real Business Cycle,' *American Economic Review*, vol. 74, June, pp. 363–80.

Klamer, Arjo (1984) *Conversations with Economists*, Totowa, N.J., Rowman and Allanheld.

Klamer, Arjo and Colander, David (1990) *The Making of an Economist*, Boulder, Colorado, Westview Press.

Klamer, Arjo and McCloskey, Donald (1988) 'Economics in the Human Conversation,' in Arjo Klamer, Donald McCloskey and Robert Solow (eds) *The Consequences of Economic Rhetoric*, Cambridge, Cambridge University Press.

Kline, Morris (1980) *Mathematics: The Loss of Certainty*, New York, Oxford University Press.

Krueger, Anne et al. (1991) 'Report on the Commission on Graduate Education in Economics,' *Journal of Economic Literature*, vol. 29, September, pp. 1035–53.

Kuhn, Thomas (1970) *The Structure of Scientific Revolutions*, Chicago, University of Chicago Press.

Kuhn, Thomas (1977), *The Essential Tension*, Chicago, University of Chicago Press.

Kydland, Finn and Prescott, Edward (1991) 'The Econometrics of the General Equilibrium Approach to Business Cycles,' *Scandinavian Journal of Economics*, vol. 93, May, pp. 161–78.

Laidler, David (1984) 'Misconceptions about the Real Bills Doctrine: A Comment on Sargent and Wallace,' *Journal of Political Economy*, vol. 92, February, pp. 149–55.

Lakatos, Imre (1978) *The Methodology of Scientific Research Programmes*, Cambridge, Cambridge University Press.

Landon, Stuart (1987) 'Unanticipated Policy Shocks, Regime Changes and Unemployment in Canada, 1967–83,' *Applied Economics*, vol. 19, August, pp. 1065–81.

Langlois, Richard and Koppl, Roger (1991) 'Fritz Machlup and Marginalism,' *Methodus*, vol. 3. December, pp. 86–102.

Leamer, Edward (1978) *Specification Searches: Ad Hoc Inferences with Nonexperimental Data*, New York, John Wiley.

Leamer, Edward (1983) 'Let's Take the Con out of Econometrics,' *American Economic Review*, vol. 73, March, pp. 31–43.

Leamer, Edward (1991) 'The Interplay of Theory and Data in the Study of International Trade,' in Marc Nerlove (ed.) *Issues in Contemporary Economics*, London, Macmillan/IEA, vol. 2.

Leontief, Wassily (1971) 'Theoretical Assumptions and Nonobservable Facts,' *American Economic Review*, vol. 61, March, pp. 1–7.

Leontief, Wassily (1983) 'Foreword,' in Alfred Eichner *Why Economics is Not Yet a Science*, Armonk, New York, M. E. Sharp.

LeRoy, Stephen (1989) 'Efficient Capital Markets and Martingales,' *Journal of Economic Literature*, vol. 27, December, 1583–1621.

LeRoy, Stephen (1991) 'On Policy Regimes,' unpublished ms.

Levis, Mario (1989) 'Stock Market Anomalies: A Re-assessment Based on UK Evidence,' *Journal of Banking and Finance*, vol. 13, September, pp. 675–96.

Loasby, Brian (1976) *Choice, Complexity and Ignorance*, Cambridge, Cambridge University Press.

Los, Cornelis (1986) 'Quality Control of Empirical Econometrics: A Status Report,' Federal Reserve Bank of New York, Research Paper no. 8606.

Lovell, Michael (1983) 'Data Mining,' *Review of Economics and Statistics*, vol. 55, February, pp. 1–12.

Lovell, Michael (1984) 'Inventories and Rational(?) Expectations,' *Proceedings of the Third International Symposium on Inventories*, Budapest, Hungary.

Lovell, Michael (1986) 'Tests of the Rational Expectations Hypothesis,' *American Economic Review*, vol. 76, March, pp. 110–24.

Lucas, Robert (1980) 'Methods and Problems in Business Cycle Theory,' *Journal of Money, Credit and Banking*, vol. 12, part 2, November, pp. 696–715.

Lucas, Robert (1987) *Models of Business Cycles*, Oxford, Blackwell.

Lucas, Robert and Sargent, Thomas (n.d.) 'After Keynesian Macroeconomics,' in Federal Reserve Bank of Boston, *After the Phillips Curve*, Boston, Mass.

Luoma, Jon (1991) 'Taxonomy, Lacking in Prestige, May be Nearing a Renaissance,' *New York Times*, 10 December, p. B7.

McCallum, Bennett (1989) 'New Classical Macroeconomics: A Sympathetic Account,' *Scandinavia Journal of Economics*, vol. 91, May, pp. 223–52.

McCloskey, Donald (1985) *The Rhetoric of Economics*, Madison, University of Wisconsin Press.

McCloskey, Donald (1987) *The Writing of Economics*, New York, Macmillan.

McCloskey, Donald (1988) 'Thick and Thin Methodologies in the History of Economic Thought,' in Neil de Marchi (ed.) *The Popperian Legacy in Economics*, Cambridge, Cambridge University Press.

McCloskey, Donald (1990) *If You're So Smart*, Chicago, University of Chicago Press.

McCloskey, Donald (1991) 'Economic Science: A Search through the Hyperspace of Assumptions,' *Methodus*, vol. 3, June, pp. 6–16.

McCloskey, Donald (1992) 'The Art of Forecasting, from Ancient to Modern Times,' *Cato Journal*, vol. 11, forthcoming.

McLaughlin, Kenneth (1990) 'Rigid Wages?' University of Rochester, Center for Economic Research, Working paper no. 229.

McNees, Stephen (1990) 'Man vs. Model: The Role of Judgment in Forecasting,' Federal Reserve Bank of New England, *New England Economic Review*, July/August, pp. 41–52.

Mäki, Uskali (1986) 'Rhetoric at the Expense of Coherence: A Reinterpretation of Milton Friedman's Methodology,' in *Research in the History of Economic Thought and Methodology*, vol. 4, pp. 127–43.

Mankiw, Gregory (1985) 'Small Menu Costs and Large Business Cycles: A Macroeconomic Model of Monopoly,' *Quarterly Journal of Economics*, vol. 100, May, pp. 529–38.

Mankiw, Gregory, Miron, Jeffrey and Weil, David (1987) 'The Adjustment of Expectations to a Changing Regime: A Study in the Founding of the Federal Reserve,' *American Economic Review*, vol. 77, June, pp. 358–74.

Mayer, Thomas (1972) *Permanent Income, Wealth and Consumption*, Berkeley, University of California Press.

Mayer, Thomas (1975) 'Selecting Economic Hypotheses by Goodness of Fit,' *Economic Journal*, vol. 85, December, pp. 877–83.

Mayer, Thomas (1978) 'Consumption in the Great Depression,' *Journal of Political Economy*, vol. 86, February, pp. 139–45.

Mayer, Thomas (1980) 'Economics as a Hard Science: Realistic Goal or Wishful Thinking?' *Economic Inquiry*, vol. 18, April, pp. 165–78.

Mayer, Thomas (1990) *Monetarism and Macroeconomic Policy*, Aldershot, England, Edward Elgar.

Mayer, Thomas (1991) 'The Monetarist Debate and the New Methodology,' in Thomas Mayer and Franco Spinelli (eds.), *Macroeconomics and Macroeconomic Policy Issues*, Aldershot, England, Avebury.

Mayer, Thomas (1992) 'What Economists Think of their Econometrics,' University of California, Davis, Working paper no. 406.

Mayer, Thomas (forthcoming) 'Friedman's "Methodology of Positive Economics": A Soft Reading,' *Economic Inquiry*, forthcoming.

Merton, Robert (1957) *Social Theory and Social Structure*, Glenco, Illinois, Free Press.

Miller, Henry (1962) 'On the Chicago School of Economics,' *Journal of Political Economy*, vol. 70, February, pp. 64–9.

Miller, Merton and Orr, Daniel (1966) 'A Model of Demand for Money by Firms,' *Quarterly Journal of Economics*, vol. 80, August, pp. 413–35.

Miller, Preston and Roberds, William (1987) 'The Quantitative Significance of the Lucas Critique,' Federal Reserve Bank of Minneapolis, Staff Report, no. 109.

Minford, Patrick (1991) 'Comments on Tom Mayer's Paper,' in Thomas Mayer and Franco Spinelli (eds) *Studies in Macroeconomics and Macroeconomic Policy Issues*, Aldershot, England, Avebury.

Mirowski, Phillip (1986) *The Reconstruction of Economic Theory*, Amsterdam, Kluwer-Nijhoff.

Mirowski, Philip (1989) *More Heat than Light*, New York, Cambridge University Press.

Morgenstern, Oskar (1963) *On the Accuracy of Economic Observations*, Princeton, Princeton University Press.

Morgenstern, Oskar (1972) 'Descriptive, Predictive and Normative Theory,' *Kyklos*, vol. 25, no. 4, pp. 699–713.

Morishima, Michio (1984) 'The Good and Bad Uses of Mathematics,' in Peter Wiles and Guy Routh (eds) *Economics in Disarray*, Oxford, Blackwell, pp. 51–73.

Morishima, Michio (1991) 'General Equilibrium Theory in the Twentieth Century,' *Economic Journal*, vol. 101, January, pp. 69–74.

Mulkay, Michael and Gilbert, Nigel (1986) 'Replication and Mere Replication,' *Philosophy of Social Science*, vol. 16, March, pp. 21–37.

Nagatani, Keizo (1978) *Monetary Theory*, New York, North Holland.

Nelson, Alan (1984) 'Some Issues Surrounding the Reduction of Macroeconomics to Microeconomics,' *Philosophy of Science*, vol. 51, December, pp. 573–94.

Nelson, Alan (1992) 'Human Molecules,' in Neil de Marchi (ed.) *Economic Methodology*, Dordrecht, Kluwer.

Niehans, Jurg (1987) 'Classical Monetary Theory, New and Old,' *Journal of Money, Credit and Banking*, vol. 19, November, pp. 409–24.

Nordhaus, William (1989) 'Alternative Approaches to the Political Business Cycles,' *Brookings Papers on Economic Activity*, no. 2, pp. 1–49.

O'Connell, Robert (1989) *Of Arms and Men*, New York, Oxford University Press.

Okun, Arthur (1981) *Prices and Quantities: A Macroeconomic Analysis*, Washington, DC., Brookings Institution.

Papell, David (1989) 'Monetary Policy in the United States under Flexible Exchange Rates,' *American Economic Review*, vol. 79, December, pp. 1106–16.

Pencavel, John (1991) 'Prospects for Economics,' *Economic Journal*, vol. 101, January, pp. 81–7.

Perry, George (1983) 'What have we Learned about Disinflation?', *Brookings Papers on Economic Activity*, no. 2, pp. 587–602.

Pesaran, M. Hashem (1987) *The Limits to Rational Expectations*, Oxford, Basil Blackwell.

Pesek, Boris (1961) 'Economic Growth and its Measurement,' *Economic Development and Cultural Change*, vol. 9, April, pp. 295–315.

Phelps-Brown, E.H. (1972) 'The Underdevelopment of Economics,' *Economic Journal*, vol. 82, March, pp. 1–10.

Plott, Charles (1991) 'Economics in 2090: The Views of an Experimentalist,' *Economic Journal*, vol. 101, January, pp. 88–93.

Pool, Robert (1989) 'Strange Bedfellows,' *Science*, vol. 254, 18 August, pp. 700–3.

Poole, William (1970) 'Optimal Choice of Monetary Policy Instruments in a Simple Stochastic Macro Model,' *Quarterly Journal of Economics*, vol. 84, May, pp. 197–216.

Popper, Karl (1961) *The Logic of Scientific Discovery*, New York, Basic Books.

Popper, Karl (1962) *The Open Society and its Enemies*, London, Routledge & Kegan Paul.

Popper, Karl (1983) *Realism and the Aim of Science*, Totowa, New Jersey, Rowman and Littlefield.

Prescott, Edward (1986) 'Theory Ahead of Business Cycle Measurement,' Federal Reserve Bank of Minneapolis, *Quarterly Review*, vol. 10, Fall, pp. 9–22.

Price, Derek de Solla (1986) *Little Science, Big Science and Beyond*, New York, Columbia University Press.

Putnam, Hilary (1990) 'The Idea of Science,' *Midwest Studies in the Philosophy of Science*, Notre Dame, Indiana, University of Notre Dame Press, pp. 57–64.

Rivlin, Alice (1975) 'Income Distribution – Can Economists Help?' *American Economic Review*, vol. 65, May, pp. 1–15.

Romer, David (1991) 'Openness and Inflation: Theory and Evidence,' unpublished ms.

Rosenberg, Alexander (1983) 'If Economics Isn't Science, What is it?' *Philosophical Forum*, vol. 14, Spring-Summer, pp. 296–314.

Rotemberg, Julio (1982) 'Sticky Prices in the United States,' *Journal of Political Economy*, vol. 90, December, pp. 1187–1211.

Samuelson, Paul (1958) 'An Exact Consumption-Loan Model of Interest with and without the Social Contrivance of Money,' *Journal of Political Economy*, vol. 66, December, pp. 467–82.

Sargent, Thomas (1976) 'A Classical Macroeconomic Model for the United States,' *Journal of Political Economy*, vol. 84, April, pp. 207–38.

Sargent, Thomas and Wallace, Neil (1976) '"Rational Expectations" and the Theory of Economic Policy,' *Journal of Monetary Economics*, vol. 2, April, pp. 169–83.

Sargent, Thomas and Wallace, Neil (1982) 'The Real Bills Doctrine vs. the Quantity Theory: A Reconsideration,' *Journal of Political Economy*, vol. 90, December, pp. 1212–36.

Schmalensee, Richard (1991) 'Continuity and Change in the Economics Industry,' *Economic Journal*, vol. 101, January, pp. 115–21.

Schön, Donald (1983) *The Reflective Practitioner*, New York, Basic Books.

Schumpeter, Joseph (1954) *History of Economic Analysis*, New York, Oxford University Press.

Schupak, Martin (1962) 'The Predictive Accuracy of Empirical Demand Analyses,' *Economic Journal*, vol. 72, pp. 550–75.

Schwert, G. William (1986) 'The Time Series Behavior of Real Interest Rates: A Comment,' *Carnegie-Rochester Conference Series on Public Policy*, vol. 24, Spring, pp. 275–88.

Shapiro, Matthew (1987) 'Are Cyclical Fluctuations in Productivity Due More to Supply Shocks or Demand Shocks?,' *American Economic Review*, vol. 77, May, pp. 118–24.

Shaw, George Bernard (1971) 'Caesar and Cleopatra,' in *Collected Plays with their Prefaces*, London, Bodley Head, vol. 2.

Sheffrin, Steven (1983) *Rational Expectations*, Cambridge, Cambridge University Press.

Shubik, Martin (1988) 'What is an Application and When is a Theory a Waste of Time?' Cowles Foundation Paper no. 695.

Siebrand, J.C. (1988) 'Macroeconomic Modelling for Economic Policy,' in W. Driehuis, M.M. Fase and H. Den Hartog (eds.) *Challenges for Macroeconomic Modelling*, Amsterdam, North Holland.

Siegfried, John (1991) 'Review of A. Klamer and D. Colander "The Making of an Economist",' *Journal of Economic Education*, vol. 22, Fall, pp. 387–91.

Sims, Christopher (1982) 'Policy Analysis with Econometric Models,' *Brookings Papers on Economic Activity*, no. 1, pp. 107–52.

Sims, Christopher (1989) 'Models and their Uses,' *American Journal of Agricultural Economics*, vol. 71, May, pp. 489–94.

Smith, Vernon (1989) 'Theory, Experiment and Economics,' *Journal of Economic Perspectives*, vol. 3, Winter, pp. 151–70.

Solow, Robert (1985) 'Economic History and Economics,' *American Economic Review*, vol. 75, May, pp. 328–31.

Solow, Robert (1986) 'What is a Nice Girl Like You Doing in a Place Like This? Macroeconomics after Fifty Years,' *Eastern Economic Journal*, vol. 12, July–September, pp. 191–8.

Solow, Robert (1990) 'Discussion,' *American Economic Review*, vol. 80, May, pp. 448–50.

Sombart, Werner (1916) *Der Moderne Kapitalismus*, Munich, Duncker & Humblot.

Spanos, Aris (1986) *Statistical Foundations of Econometric Modelling*, New York, Cambridge University Press.

Stanley, T. D. and Jarrell, Stephen (1989) 'Meta-Regression Analysis: A Quantitative Method of Literature Surveys,' *Journal of Economic Surveys*, vol. 3, pp. 159–70.

Startz, Richard (1984) 'Can Money Matter?' *Journal of Monetary Economics*, vol. 13, May, pp. 381–5.

Stigler, George (1982) *The Economist as Preacher*, Chicago, University of Chicago Press.

Stigler, George (1988) *Memoirs of an Unregulated Economist*, New York, Basic Books.

Stiglitz, Joseph (1991) 'Another Century of Economic Science,' *Economic Journal*, vol. 101, January, pp. 134–41.

Streeten, Paul (1972) *The Frontiers of Development Studies*, New York, Macmillan.

Summers, Lawrence (1986) 'Some Skeptical Observations on Real Business Cycle Theory,' Federal Reserve Bank of Minneapolis, *Quarterly Review*, vol. 10, Fall, pp. 23–31.

Summers, Lawrence (1991) 'The Scientific Illusion in Empirical Macroeconomics,' *Scandinavian Journal of Economics*, vol. 93, March, pp. 129–48.

Taubman, Paul (1968) 'Personal Saving: A Time Series Analysis of Three Measures of the Same Conceptual Series,' *Review of Economics and Statistics*, vol. 50, February, pp. 125–9.

Taylor, John (1984) 'Recent Changes in Macro Policy and its Effects: Some Time Series Evidence,' *American Economic Review*, vol. 74, May, pp. 206–10.

Temin, Peter (1976) *Did Monetary Forces Cause the Great Depression?* New York, W.W. Norton.

Thaler, Richard (1990) 'Anomalies: Saving, Fungibility and Mental Accounts,' *Journal of Economic Perspectives*, vol. 4, Winter, pp. 193–206.

Thaler, Richard (various dates) 'Anomalies,' *Journal of Economic Perspectives*.

Tobin, James (1956) 'The Interest Elasticity of Transactions Demand for Cash,' *Review of Economics and Statistics*, vol. 38, August, pp. 241–7.

Todd, Richard (1990) 'Vector Autoregression Evidence on Monetarism: Another Look at the Robustness Debate,' Federal Reserve Bank of Minneapolis, *Quarterly Review*, Spring, pp. 19–37.

Tullock, Gordon (1966) *The Organization of Inquiry*, Durham, N.C., Duke University Press.

Veblen, Thorstein (1899) *The Theory of the Leisure Class*, New York, Macmillan.

Vercelli, Alessandro (1991) *Methodological Foundations of Macroeconomics: Keynes and Lucas*, Cambridge, Cambridge University Press.

Vroman, Wayne (1983) *Wage Inflation: Prospects for Deceleration*, Washington, DC., The Urban Institute.

Wachter, Kenneth (1988) 'Disturbed by Meta-Analysis?' *Science*, vol. 24, September, pp. 1407–8.

Wall Street Journal (1991) 'A Sampling of Interest-Rate, Economic and Currency Forecasts,' *Wall Street Journal*, 5 July, p. A2.

Wallace, Neil (1983) 'A Legal Restrictions Theory of the Demand for "Money" and the Role of Monetary Policy,' Federal Reserve Bank of Minneapolis, *Quarterly Review*, vol. 7, Winter, pp. 1–8.

Wallace, Neil (1988) 'A Suggestion for Oversimplifying the Theory of Money,' *Economic Journal*, vol. 98, *Supplement*, pp. 25–36.

Ward, Benjamin (1972) *What's Wrong with Economics?* New York, Basic Books.

Weintraub, E. Roy (1985) *General Equilibrium Analysis*, Cambridge, Cambridge University Press.

Weintraub, E. Roy (1988a) 'Discussion' in Neil de Marchi (ed.) *The Popperian Legacy in Economics*, Cambridge, Cambridge University Press.

Weintraub, E. Roy (1988b) 'The Neo-Walrasian Program is Empirically Progressive,' in Neil de Marchi (ed.) *The Popperian Legacy in Economics*, Cambridge, Cambridge University Press.

White, Lawrence (1987) 'Accounting for Non-interest-bearing Currency: A Critique of the Legal Restrictions Theory,' *Journal of Money, Credit and Banking*, vol. 19, November, pp. 448–56.

Whitley, Richard (1977) 'Changes in the Social and Intellectual Organisation of the Science: Professionalisation and the Arithmetic Ideal,' in Everett Mendelsohn and Peter Weingart (eds.) *The Social Production of Scientific Knowledge*, Dordrecht, D. Reidel.

Whitley, Richard (1986) 'The Structure and Context of Economics as a Scientific Field,' *Research in the History of Economic Thought and Methodology*, Greenwich, Conn, JAI Press.

Wiener, Norbert (1964) *God and Golem*, Cambridge, Mass, MIT Press.

Winter, Sidney (1963) 'Economics, "Natural Selection" and the Theory of the Firm,' *Yale Economic Essays*, vol. 4, Spring, pp. 225–71.

Wiseman, Jack (1991) 'The Black Box,' *Economic Journal*, vol. 101, January, pp. 149–55.

Wolf, Charles (1979) 'A Theory of Market Failure,' *The Public Interest*, vol. 55, Spring, pp. 114–33.

Wolfe, Thomas (1981) *From Bauhaus to Our House*, New York, Farrer, Strauss Giroux.

Woo, Henry (1986) *What's Wrong with Formalization in Economics?* Newark, California, Victoria Press.

Woo, Henry (1990) 'Scientific Reduction, Reductionism and Metaphysical Reduction – A Broad View of Economic Methodology,' *Methodus*, vol. 2, no. 2, pp. 61–8.

Woos, Joanna (1992) 'From Graduate Student to Liberal Arts Professor,' in David Colander and Reuven Brenner (eds.) *Educating Economists*, Ann Arbor, Michigan, University of Michigan Press.

Zarembka, Paul (1968) 'Functional Form in the Demand for Money,' *Journal of the American Statistical Association*, vol. 63, June, pp. 502–11.

Zeeman, E.C. (1979) 'Foreword' in Michael Thompson, *Rubbish Theory*, Oxford, Oxford University Press.

Zellner, Arnold (1987) 'Science, Economics and Public Policy,' Graduate School of Business, University of Chicago, Working paper no. 87–44.

Index

academic research, 10, 12–14, 43,
    46
ad hoc, 88–93, 95, 105
    defined, 90–91
    New Classical attitude towards,
        82, 89–90
    New Classical itself ad hoc, 95–7
Adler, M., 40n
advantages of modelling, 122–3
aesthetic, 32, 85–8, 123, 130
aggregator function, 95
agricultural economists, 70
Akerlof, G., 112
Allais, M., 27
Amazon river, 56
American Economic Association, 2,
    4, 27, 159, 164n
    see also Commission on Graduate
        Education.
American Economic Review, 139,
    151
American tradition in economics, 35
Anderson, P., 29
Anderson, R., 146, 147, 151n
Angier, N., 40n
Aristotle, 56
arithmetic, 69, 147
arms race, 20, 163
Arrow, K., 29, 37–9, 50
Assendelft, E., 107
Attfield, C., 105, 106
Ault, D., 20
Austrian School, 54n
Ausubel, L., 33

Baba, Y., 101
Backhouse, R., x, 9n
Balzer, W., 34
Barrett, P., 21

Baumol, W., 60, 61, 153
Becker, G., 18, 51, 162
Becker, H., 162
Beggs, J., 143, 145
Belsley, D., 145
beta coefficient, 139
bias, 124, 140, 142, 144, 145
Birner, J., 39
Black Sea, 38
Blackburn, K., 64
Blanchard, O., 98, 100, 111
Blaug, M., x, 28, 39, 40, 148, 153
Blinder, A., 80, 93, 111, 112, 127,
    159
Block, F., 114
Bloor, D., 13
Boland, L., 22n, 106, 125
Bonnen, J., 70
Booth, James, 22n
Brahe, T., 51
Brenner, R., 113
Britain, 42, 65, 101, 125
British tradition in economics, 35
Bronfenbrenner, M., 28, 75, 142,
    143, 163
Brunner, K., 25, 26
Buckle, R., 107
buffet, 130
Buiter, W., 86, 96, 113

Caesar and Cleopatra, 26
Cagan, P., 97
Caldwell, B., 6, 9n, 54
calibration, 87, 88, 116
Canada, 73, 99, 119
Cape Cod, 23
capital punishment, 142
Cargill, T., x
caricature models, 126

Carlton, D., 111, 112, 114
Cartwright, 150n
cash-in-advance model, 31
cavalry, 124
central bank, 31, 63–5
    see also Federal Reserve, mon-
        etary policy
Chakravarty, S., 68
Chase, J., 147
chemistry, 47, 93, 162
Chicago, University of, 3, 161
Christano, L., 116
Christensen, M., 64, 99, 100
Christmas cards, 34, 40n
Cliometrics Society, 158
Coddington, A., 37
coexistence of money and securities,
    33
coffee-break conversation, 82, 129
Cohen, E., 75
Colander, D., x, 3, 21, 47, 57, 84,
    122, 159, 160
collinearity, 135, 147, 148
Columbia University, 3
comments, 78, 146, 158
Commission on Graduate Education,
    159, 164n
communication, 77, 78, 158, 159
compensating balances, 61
complexity, 17, 18, 77–8
consumption function, 29, 71, 101,
    107, 144, 145, 148
contracts, 121n
Cooley, T., 133, 141, 154
coordination problems, 96
cost of output fluctuations, 128–30
costs of modelling, 123
creationism, 68
credit cards, 33
credit rationing, 59, 60
Crick, F., 23
critical rationalism, 6
cross equation restrictions, 136–7
crowding out, 127
currency, 119, 128, 131n
    see also legal restrictions theory

Darwin, C., 83

Dasgupta, A., 22n
data, 143, 146, 164n
    attitude towards collecting, 70–71,
        73
    entry, 164
    foreign, 143
    mining, 140–42
    providing, 146
    quality of, 73–4, 154–6
Davis, P., 47
de Marchi, N., 9n, 52, 86
Deane, P., 27
Debreu, G., 27, 34, 37–9
deep parameter, 33, 72, 94, 101n,
    107–8
Demery, D., 105, 106
Denton, F., 142, 149n
Dewald, W., 146, 147, 151n
Diamond, A., 21n
digits, number in calculations, 57, 69
disagreements in economics, 2, 8, 33
Divisia money, 44
Dore, M., 68
Dornbusch, R., 61
Dow, S., 59
Duck, N., 105, 106
Duke University, 20

Earl, P., 21n
econometric models, 94, 98, 122,
    143
Econometric Society, 2, 131n
Economic Report of the President,
    118
Economics Letters, 16, 158
economists, salaries of, 1
editors, 12–13, 23n, 155–7
    see also journals, graduate
        education
efficient markets, 77
Eichenbaum, M., 16, 158
electrons, 26
Englander, S., 99
Engle, R., 101
Erickson, J., 121n
Ericsson, N., 101, 136, 150n
Eschker, E., x
Evans, M., 144

evolution, 68, 83
Executive Office of the President, 118
experimental economics, 156, 162
experiments, 16, 26, 51, 72, 75, 141
extreme bounds analysis, 143

falsificationism, 53, 133
Fama, E., 71, 128, 131n
Favero, C., 101
Federal Reserve, 61–2, 64, 65, 66, 100
  see also central bank, monetary policy
Feigenbaum, S., 21, 146
Fellner, W., 97, 98
Ferber, R., 144
Feyerabend, P., 69, 83
Feynman, R., 141, 154
fiat money, 119
FIFO, 76
fingertip economics, 161
first differences, 74, 79n, 143
fiscal policy, 127, 143
Fishburn, P., 156
Fischer, S., 61, 63, 65, 74, 94, 125
Fisher A., 101
Fisher, F., 63
Fisher, P., 143
Fisher, R., 143
FOMC (Federal Open Market Committee), 67n, 98
Ford Foundation, 22n
forecasts, 17, 101, 105, 132, 133
Frank, R., 113
Frankel, J., 143
Frantz, R., 106
Friedman, B., 94
Friedman, M., 5, 9n, 29–33, 35, 51, 52, 71, 86, 89, 91, 125, 132, 136, 150n
Frisch prize, medal, 151n
functional form, 143, 149

game, good, 3, 41
game theory, 39, 53, 63–5, 75, 113
gas stations, 35, 40n
Gavin, W., 101
general equilibrium, 34, 36–40, 51

general-to-specific modelling, 135
geometry, 16, 24, 25, 40n, 43, 54
Gerber, J., 106
Geweke, J., 95
Ghiselin, M., 16, 28, 42
Gibbard, C., 125, 126
Gilbert, C., 148
Gilbert, N., 151
Gitting, T., 147
God, as mathematician, 140
Goldberg, V., 121n
Goldfeld, S., 60
Gooch, J., 75
Goodwin, C., 22n
Goodwin, N., 124
Goodwin, R., 68
Gordon, R., 95, 99, 111
graduate education, 3, 14, 48, 78, 126, 159
Granger tests, 62
grants, 42–3, 54n
Greenwald, B., 113, 114
grid search, 150
Griliches, Z., 73
growth rates, 147, 156
growth theory, 57
Grübel, H., 22n

Hacking, I., 26, 50, 51
Hahn, F., 2, 30, 31, 35, 37–9, 41, 57, 86, 104, 114
Hall, R., 61
Haltigwanger, J., 108
Hammond, D., x
Hands, D., 21n, 22, 90, 91, 101n
Hansen, L., 72, 73
Hansen, W., 159, 164n
hard tests, 133–4
Harberger, A., 2, 164
Hartley, J., x, 101n
Harvard University, 3, 20
Hausman, D., 6
Hawking, S., 83
Hayek, F., 20
Haynes, S., 120n
Heckman, J., 39
Heller, W., 33
Hendry, D., 101, 135, 136, 150n

Hersh, R., 47
heuristic, 32, 90, 104, 110, 122
Hicks, J., 41
high-brow, 36, 54, 55n
Hirsch, A., x, 9n, 52, 86
history of economic thought, 20, 43, 53
Holden, K., 106, 108
Homeric hero, 10
Hoover, K., x, 1, 83, 85, 89, 92, 96, 103, 109, 116, 117, 119, 132
Howrey, P., 145
Hubbard, R., 146
hubris, 82–4
Huizinga, J., 100
Hutchison, T., 41–4
Hymans, S., 145

illustrating theories, 148
imaginary numbers, 43
incomprehensibility, 153–4
indifference curves, 40n
infant industry, 97
inflationary bias, 64–5
insignificant variables, 135, 136
institutionalists, 5, 41, 114, 159
instrumentalism, 91, 92
interdisciplinary research, 156–62
interest rates, 33, 119, 133, 145
    and Federal Reserve, 62, 100, 119
    and Lucas critique, 100
    and saving, 62, 100, 109
    in Baumol model, 60, 61
    on currency, 119, 131n
interviewing, 112
introspection, 86, 92, 118, 119, 152
inventories, 76, 112
invisible hand, 4, 6, 37, 38, 40

Jackson, F., 107
Jaffe, D., 61
Japan, 125
Jarrell, S., 164n
Johnson, H., 101n
Journal of Economic Literature, 158
Journal of Economic Surveys, 158
Journal of Money, Credit and Banking, 146

Journal of Political Economy, 146, 164n
journals, 4, 49–50, 74, 77, 157–8
    see also editors, referees, *specific journals*
Jowett, B., 83

Kahneman, D., 106, 152
Kamarck, A., 23, 69, 73
Kane, E., 146
Karamouzis, N., 101
Kasper, H., 163
Katzner, D., 43
Kennedy, P., 140
Kepler, J., 51, 73
Keynes, J. M., 131n, 152
Khoury, S., 142
King, R., 121n
Klamer, A., x, 3, 25, 47, 81, 84, 87, 159, 160
Kline, M., 38
Knorr-Cetina, K., 25
Krueger, A., 159, 160, 162–4n
Kuh, E., 145
Kuhn, T., 6, 10, 53, 75, 85
Kydland, F., 88

Laidler, D., 121n
Lakatos, I., 21, 40n, 90, 103, 133
Landon, S., 99
law of demand, 133
Law Reviews, 21
Leamer, E., 132, 137, 138, 141–3
learning and rational expectations, 104, 107
legal restrictions theory, 119–20, 121n
Leibnitz, G., 140
lemon effect, 142
Leontief, W., 2, 73, 155
Lerner, A., 79n
LeRoy, S., 94, 101n, 107, 133, 141, 153, 154
Levis, M., 153
Levy, D., 21n, 146
Loasby, B., 25
Los, C., 73, 99, 143, 147
loss function, 76, 139

Lovell, M., 107, 141, 148, 149
low-brow, 36
LSE econometrics, 135, 136
Lucas critique, 93–5, 100
Lucas, R., 43, 72, 83, 85, 87, 97–
    101, 104, 107, 114, 115
    see also Lucas critique
Luoma, J., 54

McCallum, B., 109
McCloskey, D., x, 3, 6, 9, 24, 25, 51,
    56, 75, 76, 122, 138, 139, 149n,
    162
McLaughlin, K., 114, 121n
McNees, S., 17
Mäki, U., 125
Mankiw, G., 100, 102n, 112
market clearing, 109–16
market failure, 10
Marshallian economics, 35, 36
mathematical economics, 13, 48–9,
    160
mathematics, 1, 17, 24, 25, 55
    and economics, 1, 13, 17, 25, 34,
        41, 54, 132, 154, 156
    and rent seeking, 22n
    and science, 27, 28, 29, 49, 78
    pure, toasted, 55n
    training in, 27, 48
maths phobia, 41
Matthews, R., 57
Mayer, T., 17, 52, 54n, 66n, 92, 125,
    127, 141, 143, 145, 164n
medical research, 40n
Meltzer, A., 61
Merton, R., 55n
Meta-analysis, 158, 164n
methodological individualism, 92
methodologists, 4, 5, 91
Methodology, defence of, 4–5, 9
Methodus, 158
Michelson–Morley experiment, 93
microeconomic foundations, 81, 91
Milberg, W., x
Mill, J. S., 152
Miller, H., 161
Miller, M., 61
Miller, P., 98

Miller–Orr model, 61
Minford, P., 84
Miron, J., 100
Mirowski, P., 15, 16, 21n, 54n
Mishkin, F., 100
MIT, 3, 28, 47
monetarist experiment, 54n
monetary history, 30, 72
monetary policy, 60, 61–6
    see also central bank, Federal
        Reserve
monetary rule, 60, 64
monetary theory, 30, 32, 33, 117,
    119, 121n
money illusion, 72, 96, 114
money market forecasts, 101
monopoly, 112
Morgenstern. O., 51, 73
Morishima, M., 156
Mulkay, M., 151n
music, 9n, 26

Nagatani, K., 32
National Bureau of Economic
    Research, 1
National Income Accounts, 149
Nelson, A., 92, 101n
Nelson, J., x
Neumann, J., 68
New Zealand, 107
Newton, I., 51, 73
Niehans, J., 121n
Nordhaus, W., 108
normal distribution assumed, 137
null hypothesis, 125, 131, 134, 136

O'Connell, R., 10
Okun, A., 111
overlapping generations, 89, 117,
    118, 121n

Papell, D., 63
paradigm shift, 85
partial correlation coefficient, 139
Peel, D., 106, 108
Pencavel, J., 164
perfect market, 32
Perry, G., 98, 99, 102n

Pesaran, M., 105
Pesek, B., x, 147
pharmacists, 162
Phelps-Brown, E. 2
Phillips curve, 97–100, 102
physics, 16, 47, 161
  comparison with economics, 1,
    21, 25, 29, 57, 71
  reductionism in physics, 93
  role of mathematics, 29
Plosser, C., 121n
Plott, C., 156
policy advice, 64, 76, 95
policy invariance proposition, 80,
    81, 110, 113
political business cycle, 108–9, 120n
Pool, R., 29
Poole, W., 61
Pope, A., 138
Popper, K., 6, 25, 26, 28, 68, 69, 86,
    90
positivism, 44, 54n
Post-Keynesians, 5, 41
post-sample fit, 144, 145, 157
prediction coefficient, 69
predictive tests, 88, 89
Prescott, E., 88, 116
presidential addresses, 23, 27, 34
prestige ranking, 46–7, 53–4
pre-testing, 140
Price, D., 14, 21, 50
price indexes, 143–4
prices, flexibility of, 111–14
principal/agent, 43
principle of the strongest link
  see strongest link
prisoners' dilemma, 96
producer sovereignty in economics,
    10
production function, 62, 121n, 127
psychology, 92
public choice theory, 11, 21n
Punch, 124
purchasing power parity, 138
Putnam, H., 8n
pyramiding, 150

quantum mechanics, 93, 161

*Quarterly Review of Business and
  Economics*, 164n
questionnaires, 19, 71, 108, 141,
    156, 164n

ranking of subfields, 53–4
rational bubbles, 157
rational expectations, 96, 104–9
rationality, 33, 41
reading critically, 162
real balances, 127
real bills, doctrine, 118, 121n
real business cycles, 44, 116
realism of assumptions, 82
reductionism, 91–3, 101n
referees, 12–14, 19, 54n, 58, 75,
    138, 146, 155–7
regressors, 134, 135, 136, 142–50n
relative wages, 113
replicability, 147
representative agents, 95–6
residuals, 62, 69, 98
restaurants, 130
Ricardian equivalence, 144
Ricardian Vice, 7
rigour, 18, 23, 29, 33, 48, 58
  and general equilibrium, 36
  and new classicals, 80–82, 85–6
  and strongest link 52, 60
  vs. precision, 60
  vs. relevance, 7, 23
Rivlin, A., 70
Roberds, W., 98
robustness tests, 142–7, 149, 150,
    154, 155, 157, 164n
Rockett, K., 143
Romer, D., 66n
Rosenberg, A., 1, 8, 16, 22n
Rotemberg, J., 111
rounding errors, 147
Royal Economic Society, 2
Rutman G., 20

sample period, 87, 144, 145
Samuelson, P., 13, 121n
Santa Fe conference, 28–9, 50
Sargent, T., 80, 81, 83, 84, 88, 118,
    121n

savings rate, 90, 144
Schmalensee, R., 156
Schön, D., 47
Schumpeter, J., 7, 84
Schupak, M., 144
Schwartz, A., 71, 136, 141–2, 150
Schwert, G., 100
scientific terms as vague, 60
selective reporting, 142, 164n
self-interest, 13–15, 20–22n, 46, 101n, 149
self-referential, economics as, 12, 86, 153, 157
serial correlation, 137
Shapiro, M., 62
Shaw, G. B., 26
sheep, 56
Sheffrin, S., 108
Shubik, M., 44
Siebrand, J., 94
Siegfried, J., 3
significance tests, 134–40, 149n, 150, 154, 155, 157
Sims, C., 63, 94, 95
Singleton, K., 72
Singh, H., 106
Slovic, P., 152
Smith, A., 40, 57
Smith, V., 16
social science, 15, 17, 28
sociology, 15, 16, 110, 156
soft tests, 133–4, 148
Solow, R., 16, 28, 71, 87, 92, 127, 160
Sombart, W., 22
Spanos, A., 132, 136
spurious precision, 68–70, 123
square root rule, 60, 61
Stanley, T., 164n
Starr, R., 33, 40n, 101
Startz, R., 121n, 127
stationarity, 137
Stevenson, T., 20
Stigler, G., 20, 28, 42
Stiglitz, J., 113, 114, 156
Stone, J., 120n
Streeten, P., 10
strongest link, 7, 52, 57–9, 68, 131, 153

and econometrics, 132
as protecting from criticism, 78
and new classical theory, 80, 82, 85
and time inconsistency theory, 64, 65
students, 3, 23, 39, 47–9, 70–71, 126, 159–64n
Summers, L., 33, 51, 71, 72, 116, 148, 151n, 156
suppressing unfavourable result, 140–42

t values,
  see significance tests
targeting, 138–40
Taubman, P., 144, 149
taxonomy, 54n
Taylor, J., 61, 98
technicians, 87
Temin, P., 145
tennis, 148
term structure, 100
textbooks, 61, 121n
Thaler, R., 152, 153
thermodynamics, 50, 93
Thompson, J., 106, 108
Thursby, J., 146, 147, 151
tight rope walker, 49
time inconsistency, 63–6n, 74, 103, 109
Tobin, J., 29, 61
Todd, R., 62, 63
Townsend, R., 81
trades, mutually beneficial, 110
traditionalists, 86–9, 91, 97
transactions demand for money, 60–61
travellers' cheques, 119
TSP (Time Series Processor), 164n
Tullock, G., 50
tunnel vision, 124
Tversky, A., 152
Type I and Type II errors, 76, 134, 139

unemployment, 98–100, 115, 128, 129

universities, 11, 22n, 42, 159
  see also graduate education
university president, 40n
Ussher, J., 68

VAR, 62
Varian, H., 125, 126
Veblen, T., 5, 55n, 113
Vercelli, A., 104
Vetter, D., 146
Volcker, P., 97, 100, 101
voters, 108, 109, 120
Vroman, W., 98

Wachter, K., 164n
wage rigidity, 64, 111, 113–15, 119,
  121n, 125
  see also Phillips curve
wages, 86, 96, 98, 99, 119, 125
  see also wage rigidity
Waldman, M., 108
Wallace, N., 31, 32, 80, 83, 118,
  119, 121n
Walrasian, economics, 35, 36, 39, 40

Ward, B., 53, 54, 76
Weil, D., 100
Weintraub, E., 39, 40
Welsch, R., 145
Western Economic Journal, 158
wheat prices, 138
White, L., 119
Whitley, R., 21n, 47
Wiener, N., 71
Winter, S., 109
Wiseman, J., 156
Wolf, C., 11
Wolfe, T., 10
Woo, H., 6, 57, 77, 92, 101n, 125
Woos, J., 160
writing, teaching of, 162
Wulwick, N., x

Yale University, 3, 20
Yellen, J., 112

Zarembka, P., 143, 149
Zeeman, E., 154
Zellner, A., 17